FUEL FILTER
PUR

Citroën
Diesel
Engine
Owners
Workshop
Manual

A K Legg T Eng MIMI

Models covered
This manual covers the Citroën 1769 cc and 1905 cc
(1.7 and 1.9 litre) Diesel engines used in the Visa
Saloon, Visa C15 Van and BX models (including the
1.7 litre turbocharged engine used in the BX)

(1379-5S2)   ABCDE
FGHIJ
KLMN

Haynes
THE BOOK ®

Haynes Publishing Group
Sparkford Nr Yeovil
Somerset BA22 7JJ England

Haynes Publications, Inc
861 Lawrence Drive
Newbury Park
California 91320 USA

Acknowledgements

Certain illustrations are the copyright of Citroën Cars Limited and are used with their permission. Thanks are due to Duckhams Oils who provided lubrication data, Sykes-Pickavant who supplied some of the workshop tools, and all the staff at Sparkford who helped in the production of this Manual.

© Haynes Publishing Group 1990

A book in the **Haynes Owners Workshop Manual Series**

Printed by J. H. Haynes & Co. Ltd, Sparkford, Nr Yeovil, Somerset BA22 7JJ, England

ISBN 1 85010 695 9

British Library Cataloguing in Publication Data
Legg, A. K. (Andrew K.) *1942–*
    Citroën diesel engine owners workshop manual. 2nd ed.
    1. Cars. Maintenance & repair
    I. Title   II. series
    629.28722
    ISBN 1-85010-695-9

Contents

4

Front three-quarter view of Citroën XUD engine. Timing belt cover has been removed

1 Timing belt
2 Oil filler cap and ventilation hose
3 Injectors
4 Diagnostic socket
5 Temperature sensors
6 Fast idle thermo unit
7 Thermostat cover
8 Injection pump (Roto-Diesel)
9 Coolant hose to oil cooler
10 Drivebelt tension adjusting bolt
11 Flywheel
12 Alternator
13 Oil filler
14 Sump
15 Alternator drivebelt
16 Crankshaft pulley
17 Water pump
18 Timing belt intermediate roller
19 Injection pump sprocket
20 Timing belt tensioner
21 Right-hand engine mounting bracket
22 Camshaft sprocket

About this manual

Its aim

The aim of this manual is to help you get the best value from your vehicle. It can do so in several ways. It can help you decide what work must be done (even should you choose to get it done by a garage), provide information on routine maintenance and servicing, and give a logical course of action and diagnosis when random faults occur. However, it is hoped that you will use the manual by tackling the work yourself. On simpler jobs it may even be quicker than booking the car into a garage and going there twice, to leave and collect it. Perhaps most important, a lot of money can be saved by avoiding the costs a garage must charge to cover its labour and overheads.

The manual has drawings and descriptions to show the function of the various components so that their layout can be understood. Then the tasks are described and photographed in a step-by-step sequence so that even a novice can do the work.

Unlike most Haynes manuals, which cover a particular vehicle in different trim levels and engine sizes, this book covers one engine and its associated equipment as fitted to a range of vehicles. Items which are common to Diesel and petrol models – eg bodywork, transmission and running gear – are not covered in this book.

Its arrangement

The manual is divided into eight Chapters, each covering a logical sub-division of the vehicle. The Chapters are each divided into Sections, numbered with single figures, eg 5; and the Sections into paragraphs (or sub-sections), with decimal numbers following on from the Section they are in, eg 5.1, 5.2, 5.3 etc.

It is freely illustrated, especially in those parts where there is a detailed sequence of operations to be carried out. There are two forms of illustration: figures and photographs. The figures are numbered in sequence with decimal numbers, according to their position in the Chapter – eg Fig. 6.4 is the fourth drawing/illustration in Chapter 6. Photographs carry the same number (either individually or in related groups) as the Section or sub-section to which they relate.

There is an alphabetical index at the back of the manual as well as a contents list at the front. Each Chapter is also preceded by its own individual contents list.

References to the 'left' or 'right' of the vehicle are in the sense of a person in the driver's seat facing forwards. However, in Chapter 1, references to the 'front' of the engine are in respect of the timing belt end with the engine removed from the vehicle.

Unless otherwise stated, nuts and bolts are removed by turning anti-clockwise, and tightened by turning clockwise.

Vehicle manufacturers continually make changes to specifications and recommendations, and these, when notified, are incorporated into our manuals at the earliest opportunity.

Project vehicles

The vehicles used in the preparation of this manual, and which appear in many of the photographs, were a BX Diesel and a Visa Diesel.

The vehicle used in the preparation of the Supplement (Chapter 8) was a BX Turbo Diesel.

Whilst every care is taken to ensure that the information in this manual is correct, no liability can be accepted by the authors or publishers for loss, damage or injury caused by any errors in, or omissions from, the information given.

Introduction to the Citroën 1.7 and 1.9 diesel engines

The Citroën diesel engines covered in this manual were first fitted to BX models in early 1984 and subsequently fitted to Visa models in early 1985.

They are built at the highly automated Citroën factory at Tremery in France and are given the code names of XUD 7 for the 1.7 and XUD 9 for the 1.9.

Compared with petrol engines of similar capacity the diesel version is extremely quiet on the road, only a certain amount of clatter at idle betraying its presence to the driver. Routine maintenance tasks are few and easily carried out, but work on the fuel injection pump will require the use of one or two dial test indicators.

Outside the engine bay the vehicles to which these engines are fitted are much the same as petrol-engined versions. For complete coverage of a particular vehicle, the appropriate manual for petrol engined vehicles will be needed as well.

General dimensions, weights and capacities

Dimensions
Overall length:
  Visa:
    Saloon .... 3.725 m (146.7 in)
    Van .... 3.995 m (157.3 in)
  BX .... 4.230 m (166.5 in)
Overall width:
  Visa:
    Saloon .... 1.526 m (60.1 in)
    Van .... 1.636 m (64.4 in)
  BX .... 1.660 m (65.4 in)
Overall height:
  Visa:
    Saloon .... 1.410 m (55.5 in)
    Van .... 1.801 m (70.9 in)
  BX .... 1.360 m (53.5 in)
Wheelbase:
  Visa .... 2.420 m (95.3 in)
  BX .... 2.66 m (104.7 in)

Weights
Kerb weight:
  Visa:
    Saloon .... 890 kg (1962 lb)
    Van .... 850 kg (1874 lb)
  BX .... 990 kg (2183 lb)
Maximum trailer weight:
  Visa .... 750 kg (1653 lb)
  BX .... 1100 kg (2425 lb)
Maximum roof rack load:
  Visa .... 60 kg (132 lb)
  BX .... 75 kg (165 lb)
Gross train weight:
  Visa .... 2050 kg (4519 lb)
  BX .... 2580 kg (5688 lb)

Capacities (approx)
Engine oil, drain and refill .... 4.5 litres (7.9 pints)
Cooling system:
  Visa .... 7.5 litres (13.2 pints)
  BX .... 7.0 litres (12.3 pints)
Fuel tank:
  Visa .... 43 litres (9.5 gallons)
  BX .... 52 litres (11.4 gallons)
Manual gearbox oil .... 1.8 litres (3.2 pints)
Automatic transmission fluid, drain and refill .... 2.5 litres (4.4 pints)

Jacking (Visa Saloon models)

The jack and spare wheel are located in the luggage compartment at the rear of the car (photos).

Jack and wheelbrace on Visa Saloon models

Spare wheel on Visa Saloon models

Buying spare parts

Only Citroën spare parts should be used if the vehicle (or engine) is still under warranty. The use of other makes of parts may invalidate the warranty if a claim has to be made. In any case, only buy parts of reputable make. 'Pirate' parts, often of unknown origin, may not meet the maker's standards either dimensionally or in material quality.

Large items or sub-assemblies – eg cylinder heads, starter motors,

injection pumps – may be available on an 'exchange' basis. Consult a Citroën dealer for availability and conditions. Dismantled or badly damaged units may not be accepted in exchange.

When buying engine parts, be prepared to quote the engine number. This is stamped on the front of the cylinder block.

General repair procedures

Whenever servicing, repair or overhaul work is carried out on the car or its components, it is necessary to observe the following procedures and instructions. This will assist in carrying out the operation efficiently and to a professional standard of workmanship.

Joint mating faces and gaskets

Where a gasket is used between the mating faces of two components, ensure that it is renewed on reassembly, and fit it dry unless otherwise stated in the repair procedure. Make sure that the mating faces are clean and dry with all traces of old gasket removed. When cleaning a joint face, use a tool which is not likely to score or damage the face, and remove any burrs or nicks with an oilstone or fine file.

Make sure that tapped holes are cleaned with a pipe cleaner, and keep them free of jointing compound if this is being used unless specifically instructed otherwise.

Ensure that all orifices, channels or pipes are clear and blow through them, preferably using compressed air.

Oil seals

Whenever an oil seal is removed from its working location, either individually or as part of an assembly, it should be renewed.

The very fine sealing lip of the seal is easily damaged and will not seal if the surface it contacts is not completely clean and free from scratches, nicks or grooves. If the original sealing surface of the component cannot be restored, the component should be renewed.

Protect the lips of the seal from any surface which may damage them in the course of fitting. Use tape or a conical sleeve where possible. Lubricate the seal lips with oil before fitting and, on dual lipped seals, fill the space between the lips with grease.

Unless otherwise stated, oil seals must be fitted with their sealing lips toward the lubricant to be sealed.

Use a tubular drift or block of wood of the appropriate size to install the seal and, if the seal housing is shouldered, drive the seal down to the shoulder. If the seal housing is unshouldered, the seal should be fitted with its face flush with the housing top face.

Screw threads and fastenings

Always ensure that a blind tapped hole is completely free from oil, grease, water or other fluid before installing the bolt or stud. Failure to do this could cause the housing to crack due to the hydraulic action of the bolt or stud as it is screwed in.

When tightening a castellated nut to accept a split pin, tighten the nut to the specified torque, where applicable, and then tighten further to the next split pin hole. Never slacken the nut to align a split pin hole unless stated in the repair procedure.

When checking or retightening a nut or bolt to a specified torque setting, slacken the nut or bolt by a quarter of a turn, and then retighten to the specified setting.

Locknuts, locktabs and washers

Any fastening which will rotate against a component or housing in the course of tightening should always have a washer between it and the relevant component or housing.

Spring or split washers should always be renewed when they are used to lock a critical component such as a big-end bearing retaining nut or bolt.

Locktabs which are folded over to retain a nut or bolt should always be renewed.

Self-locking nuts can be reused in non-critical areas, providing resistance can be felt when the locking portion passes over the bolt or stud thread.

Split pins must always be replaced with new ones of the correct size for the hole.

Special tools

Some repair procedures in this manual entail the use of special tools such as a press, two or three-legged pullers, spring compressors etc. Wherever possible, suitable readily available alternatives to the manufacturer's special tools are described, and are shown in use. In some instances, where no alternative is possible, it has been necessary to resort to the use of a manufacturer's tool and this has been done for reasons of safety as well as the efficient completion of the repair operation. Unless you are highly skilled and have a thorough understanding of the procedure described, never attempt to bypass the use of any special tool when the procedure described specifies its use. Not only is there a very great risk of personal injury, but expensive damage could be caused to the components involved.

Tools and working facilities

Introduction

A selection of good tools is a fundamental requirement for anyone contemplating the maintenance and repair of a motor vehicle. For the owner who does not possess any, their purchase will prove a considerable expense, offsetting some of the savings made by doing-it-yourself. However, provided that the tools purchased meet the relevant national safety standards and are of good quality, they will last for many years and prove an extremely worthwhile investment.

To help the average owner to decide which tools are needed to carry out the various tasks detailed in this manual, we have compiled three lists of tools under the following headings: *Maintenance and minor repair, Repair and overhaul,* and *Special.* The newcomer to practical mechanics should start off with the *Maintenance and minor repair* tool kit and confine himself to the simpler jobs around the vehicle. Then, as his confidence and experience grow, he can undertake more difficult tasks, buying extra tools as, and when, they are needed. In this way, a *Maintenance and minor repair* tool kit can be built-up into a *Repair and overhaul* tool kit over a considerable period of time without any major cash outlays. The experienced do-it-yourselfer will have a tool kit good enough for most repair and overhaul procedures and will add tools from the *Special* category when he feels the expense is justified by the amount of use to which these tools will be put.

It is obviously not possible to cover the subject of tools fully here. For those who wish to learn more about tools and their use there is a book entitled *How to Choose and Use Car Tools* available from the publishers of this manual.

Maintenance and minor repair tool kit

The tools given in this list should be considered as a minimum requirement if routine maintenance, servicing and minor repair operations are to be undertaken. We recommend the purchase of combination spanners (ring one end, open-ended the other); although more expensive than open-ended ones, they do give the advantages of both types of spanner.

Combination spanners - 10, 11, 12, 13, 14 & 17 mm
Adjustable spanner - 9 inch
Engine sump/gearbox drain plug key
Set of feeler gauges
Brake bleed nipple spanner
Screwdriver - 4 in long x $^1/4$ in dia (flat blade)
Screwdriver - 4 in long x $^1/4$ in dia (cross blade)
Combination pliers - 6 inch
Hacksaw (junior)
Tyre pump
Tyre pressure gauge
Oil can
Fine emery cloth (1 sheet)
Wire brush (small)
Funnel (medium size)
Chain or strap wrench

Repair and overhaul tool kit

These tools are virtually essential for anyone undertaking any major repairs to a motor vehicle, and are additional to those given in the *Maintenance and minor repair* list. Included in this list is a comprehensive set of sockets. Although these are expensive they will be found invaluable as they are so versatile - particularly if various drives are included in the set. We recommend the ½ in square-drive type, as this can be used with most proprietary torque wrenches. If you cannot afford a socket set, even bought piecemeal, then inexpensive tubular box spanners are a useful alternative.

The tools in this list will occasionally need to be supplemented by tools from the *Special* list.

Sockets (or box spanners) to cover range in previous list, plus 27 mm for injectors
Reversible ratchet drive (for use with sockets)
Extension piece, 10 inch (for use with sockets)
Universal joint (for use with sockets)
Torque wrench (for use with sockets)
'Mole' wrench - 8 inch
Ball pein hammer
Soft-faced hammer, plastic or rubber
Screwdriver - 6 in long x $^5/16$ in dia (flat blade)
Screwdriver - 2 in long x $^5/16$ in square (flat blade)
Screwdriver - $1^1/2$ in long x $^1/4$ in dia (cross blade)
Screwdriver - 3 in long x $^1/8$ in dia (electricians)
Pliers - electricians side cutters
Pliers - needle nosed
Pliers - circlip (internal and external)
Cold chisel - $^1/2$ inch
Scriber
Scraper
Centre punch
Pin punch
Hacksaw
Valve grinding tool
Steel rule/straight-edge
Allen keys (inc. splined/Torx type if necessary)
Selection of files
Wire brush (large)
Axle-stands
Jack (strong trolley or hydraulic type)
Two dial test indicators and stands
12 volt light with extension lead

Special tools

The tools in this list are those which are not used regularly, are expensive to buy, or which need to be used in accordance with their manufacturers' instructions. Unless relatively difficult mechanical jobs are undertaken frequently, it will not be economic to buy many of these tools. Where this is the case, you could consider clubbing together with friends (or joining a motorists' club) to make a joint purchase, or borrowing the tools against a deposit from a local garage or tool hire specialist.

The following list contains only those tools and instruments freely available to the public, and not those special tools produced by the vehicle manufacturer specifically for its dealer network. You will find occasional references to these manufacturers' special tools in the text of this manual. Generally, an alternative method of doing the job without the vehicle manufacturers' special tool is given. However, sometimes, there is no alternative to using them. Where this is the case and the relevant tool cannot be bought or borrowed, you will have to entrust the work to a franchised garage.

Valve spring compressor (where applicable)
Piston ring compressor
Balljoint separator
Universal hub/bearing puller
Impact screwdriver
Micrometer and/or vernier gauge
Universal electrical multi-meter
Cylinder compression gauge
Lifting tackle
Trolley jack

Buying tools

For practically all tools, a tool factor is the best source since he will have a very comprehensive range compared with the average garage or accessory shop. Having said that, accessory shops often offer excellent quality tools at discount prices, so it pays to shop around.

There are plenty of good tools around at reasonable prices, but always aim to purchase items which meet the relevant national safety standards. If in doubt, ask the proprietor or manager of the shop for advice before making a purchase.

Care and maintenance of tools

Having purchased a reasonable tool kit, it is necessary to keep the tools in a clean serviceable condition. After use, always wipe off any dirt, grease and metal particles using a clean, dry cloth, before putting the tools away. Never leave them lying around after they have been used. A simple tool rack on the garage or workshop wall, for items such as screwdrivers and pliers is a good idea. Store all normal wrenches and sockets in a metal box. Any measuring instruments, gauges, meters, etc, must be carefully stored where they cannot be damaged or become rusty.

Take a little care when tools are used. Hammer heads inevitably become marked and screwdrivers lose the keen edge on their blades from time to time. A little timely attention with emery cloth or a file will soon restore items like this to a good serviceable finish.

Working facilities

Not to be forgotten when discussing tools, is the workshop itself. If anything more than routine maintenance is to be carried out, some form of suitable working area becomes essential.

It is appreciated that many an owner mechanic is forced by circumstances to remove an engine or similar item, without the benefit of a garage or workshop. Having done this, any repairs should always be done under the cover of a roof.

Wherever possible, any dismantling should be done on a clean, flat workbench or table at a suitable working height.

Any workbench needs a vice: one with a jaw opening of 4 in (100 mm) is suitable for most jobs. As mentioned previously, some clean dry storage space is also required for tools, as well as for lubricants, cleaning fluids, touch-up paints and so on, which become necessary.

Another item which may be required, and which has a much more general usage, is an electric drill with a chuck capacity of at least 5/16 in (8 mm). This, together with a good range of twist drills, is virtually essential for fitting accessories such as mirrors and reversing lights.

Last, but not least, always keep a supply of old newspapers and clean, lint-free rags available, and try to keep any working area as clean as possible.

Spanner jaw gap comparison table

Jaw gap (in)	Spanner size
0.250	1/4 in AF
0.276	7 mm
0.313	5/16 in AF
0.315	8 mm

Jaw gap (in)	Spanner size
0.344	11/32 in AF; 1/8 in Whitworth
0.354	9 mm
0.375	3/8 in AF
0.394	10 mm
0.433	11 mm
0.438	7/16 in AF
0.445	3/16 in Whitworth; 1/4 in BSF
0.472	12 mm
0.500	1/2 in AF
0.512	13 mm
0.525	1/4 in Whitworth; 5/16 in BSF
0.551	14 mm
0.563	9/16 in AF
0.591	15 mm
0.600	5/16 in Whitworth; 3/8 in BSF
0.625	5/8 in AF
0.630	16 mm
0.669	17 mm
0.686	11/16 in AF
0.709	18 mm
0.710	3/8 in Whitworth; 7/16 in BSF
0.748	19 mm
0.750	3/4 in AF
0.813	13/16 in AF
0.820	7/16 in Whitworth; 1/2 in BSF
0.866	22 mm
0.875	7/8 in AF
0.920	1/2 in Whitworth; 9/16 in BSF
0.938	15/16 in AF
0.945	24 mm
1.000	1 in AF
1.010	9/16 in Whitworth; 5/8 in BSF
1.024	26 mm
1.063	1 1/16 in AF; 27 mm
1.100	5/8 in Whitworth; 11/16 in BSF
1.125	1 1/8 in AF
1.181	30 mm
1.200	11/16 in Whitworth; 3/4 in BSF
1.250	1 1/4 in AF
1.260	32 mm
1.300	3/4 in Whitworth; 7/8 in BSF
1.313	1 5/16 in AF
1.390	13/16 in Whitworth; 15/16 in BSF
1.417	36 mm
1.438	1 7/16 in AF
1.480	7/8 in Whitworth; 1 in BSF
1.500	1 1/2 in AF
1.575	40 mm; 15/16 in Whitworth
1.614	41 mm
1.625	1 5/8 in AF
1.670	1 in Whitworth; 1 1/8 in BSF
1.688	1 11/16 in AF
1.811	46 mm
1.813	1 13/16 in AF
1.860	1 1/8 in Whitworth; 1 1/4 in BSF
1.875	1 7/8 in AF
1.969	50 mm
2.000	2 in AF
2.050	1 1/4 in Whitworth; 1 3/8 in BSF
2.165	55 mm
2.362	60 mm

Conversion factors

Length (distance)
Inches (in)	X	25.4	= Millimetres (mm)	X	0.0394	= Inches (in)
Feet (ft)	X	0.305	= Metres (m)	X	3.281	= Feet (ft)
Miles	X	1.609	= Kilometres (km)	X	0.621	= Miles

Volume (capacity)
Cubic inches (cu in; in³)	X	16.387	= Cubic centimetres (cc; cm³)	X	0.061	= Cubic inches (cu in; in³)
Imperial pints (Imp pt)	X	0.568	= Litres (l)	X	1.76	= Imperial pints (Imp pt)
Imperial quarts (Imp qt)	X	1.137	= Litres (l)	X	0.88	= Imperial quarts (Imp qt)
Imperial quarts (Imp qt)	X	1.201	= US quarts (US qt)	X	0.833	= Imperial quarts (Imp qt)
US quarts (US qt)	X	0.946	= Litres (l)	X	1.057	= US quarts (US qt)
Imperial gallons (Imp gal)	X	4.546	= Litres (l)	X	0.22	= Imperial gallons (Imp gal)
Imperial gallons (Imp gal)	X	1.201	= US gallons (US gal)	X	0.833	= Imperial gallons (Imp gal)
US gallons (US gal)	X	3.785	= Litres (l)	X	0.264	= US gallons (US gal)

Mass (weight)
Ounces (oz)	X	28.35	= Grams (g)	X	0.035	= Ounces (oz)
Pounds (lb)	X	0.454	= Kilograms (kg)	X	2.205	= Pounds (lb)

Force
Ounces-force (ozf; oz)	X	0.278	= Newtons (N)	X	3.6	= Ounces-force (ozf; oz)
Pounds-force (lbf; lb)	X	4.448	= Newtons (N)	X	0.225	= Pounds-force (lbf; lb)
Newtons (N)	X	0.1	= Kilograms-force (kgf; kg)	X	9.81	= Newtons (N)

Pressure
Pounds-force per square inch (psi; lbf/in²; lb/in²)	X	0.070	= Kilograms-force per square centimetre (kgf/cm²; kg/cm²)	X	14.223	= Pounds-force per square inch (psi; lbf/in²; lb/in²)
Pounds-force per square inch (psi; lbf/in²; lb/in²)	X	0.068	= Atmospheres (atm)	X	14.696	= Pounds-force per square inch (psi; lbf/in²; lb/in²)
Pounds-force per square inch (psi; lbf/in²; lb/in²)	X	0.069	= Bars	X	14.5	= Pounds-force per square inch (psi; lbf/in²; lb/in²)
Pounds-force per square inch (psi; lbf/in²; lb/in²)	X	6.895	= Kilopascals (kPa)	X	0.145	= Pounds-force per square inch (psi; lbf/in²; lb/in²)
Kilopascals (kPa)	X	0.01	= Kilograms-force per square centimetre (kgf/cm²; kg/cm²)	X	98.1	= Kilopascals (kPa)
Millibar (mbar)	X	100	= Pascals (Pa)	X	0.01	= Millibar (mbar)
Millibar (mbar)	X	0.0145	= Pounds-force per square inch (psi; lbf/in²; lb/in²)	X	68.947	= Millibar (mbar)
Millibar (mbar)	X	0.75	= Millimetres of mercury (mmHg)	X	1.333	= Millibar (mbar)
Millibar (mbar)	X	0.401	= Inches of water (inH₂O)	X	2.491	= Millibar (mbar)
Millimetres of mercury (mmHg)	X	0.535	= Inches of water (inH₂O)	X	1.868	= Millimetres of mercury (mmHg)
Inches of water (inH₂O)	X	0.036	= Pounds-force per square inch (psi; lbf/in²; lb/in²)	X	27.68	= Inches of water (inH₂O)

Torque (moment of force)
Pounds-force inches (lbf in; lb in)	X	1.152	= Kilograms-force centimetre (kgf cm; kg cm)	X	0.868	= Pounds-force inches (lbf in; lb in)
Pounds-force inches (lbf in; lb in)	X	0.113	= Newton metres (Nm)	X	8.85	= Pounds-force inches (lbf in; lb in)
Pounds-force inches (lbf in; lb in)	X	0.083	= Pounds-force feet (lbf ft; lb ft)	X	12	= Pounds-force inches (lbf in; lb in)
Pounds-force feet (lbf ft; lb ft)	X	0.138	= Kilograms-force metres (kgf m; kg m)	X	7.233	= Pounds-force feet (lbf ft; lb ft)
Pounds-force feet (lbf ft; lb ft)	X	1.356	= Newton metres (Nm)	X	0.738	= Pounds-force feet (lbf ft; lb ft)
Newton metres (Nm)	X	0.102	= Kilograms-force metres (kgf m; kg m)	X	9.804	= Newton metres (Nm)

Power
Horsepower (hp)	X	745.7	= Watts (W)	X	0.0013	= Horsepower (hp)

Velocity (speed)
Miles per hour (miles/hr; mph)	X	1.609	= Kilometres per hour (km/hr; kph)	X	0.621	= Miles per hour (miles/hr; mph)

Fuel consumption*
Miles per gallon, Imperial (mpg)	X	0.354	= Kilometres per litre (km/l)	X	2.825	= Miles per gallon, Imperial (mpg)
Miles per gallon, US (mpg)	X	0.425	= Kilometres per litre (km/l)	X	2.352	= Miles per gallon, US (mpg)

Temperature

Degrees Fahrenheit = (°C x 1.8) + 32

Degrees Celsius (Degrees Centigrade; °C) = (°F - 32) x 0.56

*It is common practice to convert from miles per gallon (mpg) to litres/100 kilometres (l/100km),
where mpg (Imperial) x l/100 km = 282 and mpg (US) x l/100 km = 235

Safety first!

Professional motor mechanics are trained in safe working procedures. However enthusiastic you may be about getting on with the job in hand, do take the time to ensure that your safety is not put at risk. A moment's lack of attention can result in an accident, as can failure to observe certain elementary precautions.

There will always be new ways of having accidents, and the following points do not pretend to be a comprehensive list of all dangers; they are intended rather to make you aware of the risks and to encourage a safety-conscious approach to all work you carry out on your vehicle.

Essential DOs and DON'Ts

DON'T rely on a single jack when working underneath the vehicle. Always use reliable additional means of support, such as axle stands, securely placed under a part of the vehicle that you know will not give way.

DON'T attempt to loosen or tighten high-torque nuts (e.g. wheel hub nuts) while the vehicle is on a jack; it may be pulled off.

DON'T start the engine without first ascertaining that the transmission is in neutral and the parking brake applied.

DON'T suddenly remove the filler cap from a hot cooling system – cover it with a cloth and release the pressure gradually first, or you may get scalded by escaping coolant.

DON'T attempt to drain oil until you are sure it has cooled sufficiently to avoid scalding you.

DON'T grasp any part of the engine or exhaust without first ascertaining that it is sufficiently cool to avoid burning you.

DON'T allow brake fluid or antifreeze to contact vehicle paintwork.

DON'T syphon toxic liquids such as fuel, brake fluid or antifreeze by mouth, or allow them to remain on your skin.

DON'T inhale dust – it may be injurious to health (see *Asbestos* below).

DON'T allow any spilt oil or grease to remain on the floor – wipe it up straight away, before someone slips on it.

DON'T use ill-fitting spanners or other tools which may slip and cause injury.

DON'T attempt to lift a heavy component which may be beyond your capability – get assistance.

DON'T rush to finish a job, or take unverified short cuts.

DON'T allow children or animals in or around an unattended vehicle.

DO wear eye protection when using power tools such as drill, sander, bench grinder etc, and when working under the vehicle.

DO use a barrier cream on your hands prior to undertaking dirty jobs – it will protect your skin from infection as well as making the dirt easier to remove afterwards; but make sure your hands aren't left slippery. Note that long-term contact with used engine oil can be a health hazard.

DO keep loose clothing (cuffs, tie etc) and long hair well out of the way of moving mechanical parts.

DO remove rings, wristwatch etc, before working on the vehicle – especially the electrical system.

DO ensure that any lifting tackle used has a safe working load rating adequate for the job.

DO keep your work area tidy – it is only too easy to fall over articles left lying around.

DO get someone to check periodically that all is well, when working alone on the vehicle.

DO carry out work in a logical sequence and check that everything is correctly assembled and tightened afterwards.

DO remember that your vehicle's safety affects that of yourself and others. If in doubt on any point, get specialist advice.

IF, in spite of following these precautions, you are unfortunate enough to injure yourself, seek medical attention as soon as possible.

Asbestos

Certain friction, insulating, sealing, and other products – such as brake linings, clutch linings, gaskets, etc – contain asbestos. *Extreme care must be taken to avoid inhalation of dust from such products since it is hazardous to health*. If in doubt, assume that they *do* contain asbestos.

Fire

Remember at all times that fuel is highly flammable. Never smoke, or have any kind of naked flame around, when working on the vehicle. But the risk does not end there – a spark caused by an electrical short-circuit, by two metal surfaces contacting each other, by careless use of tools, or even by static electricity built up in your body under certain conditions, can ignite fuel vapour, which in a confined space is highly explosive.

Always disconnect the battery earth (ground) terminal before working on any part of the fuel or electrical system, and never risk spilling fuel on to a hot engine or exhaust.

It is recommended that a fire extinguisher of a type suitable for fuel and electrical fires is kept handy in the garage or workplace at all times.

Note: *Any reference to a 'torch' appearing in this manual should always be taken to mean a hand-held battery-operated electric lamp or flashlight. It does NOT mean a welding/gas torch or blowlamp.*

Fumes

Certain fumes are highly toxic and can quickly cause unconsciousness and even death if inhaled to any extent. Fuel vapour comes into this category, as do the vapours from certain solvents such as trichloroethylene. Any draining or pouring of such volatile fluids should be done in a well ventilated area.

When using cleaning fluids and solvents, read the instructions carefully. Never use materials from unmarked containers – they may give off poisonous vapours.

Never run the engine of a motor vehicle in an enclosed space such as a garage. Exhaust fumes contain carbon monoxide which is extremely poisonous; if you need to run the engine, always do so in the open air or at least have the rear of the vehicle outside the workplace.

If you are fortunate enough to have the use of an inspection pit, never drain or pour fuel, and never run the engine, while the vehicle is standing over it; the fumes, being heavier than air, will concentrate in the pit with possibly lethal results.

The battery

Never cause a spark, or allow a naked light, near the vehicle's battery. It will normally be giving off a certain amount of hydrogen gas, which is highly explosive.

Always disconnect the battery earth (ground) terminal before working on the fuel or electrical systems.

If possible, loosen the filler plugs or cover when charging the battery from an external source. Do not charge at an excessive rate or the battery may burst.

Take care when topping up and when carrying the battery. The acid electrolyte, even when diluted, is very corrosive and should not be allowed to contact the eyes or skin.

If you ever need to prepare electrolyte yourself, always add the acid slowly to the water, and never the other way round. Protect against splashes by wearing rubber gloves and goggles.

When jump starting a car using a booster battery, for negative earth (ground) vehicles, connect the jump leads in the following sequence: First connect one jump lead between the positive (+) terminals of the two batteries. Then connect the other jump lead first to the negative (–) terminal of the booster battery, and then to a good earthing (ground) point on the vehicle to be started, at least 18 in (45 cm) from the battery if possible. Ensure that hands and jump leads are clear of any moving parts, and that the two vehicles do not touch. Disconnect the leads in the reverse order.

Mains electricity and electrical equipment

When using an electric power tool, inspection light etc, always ensure that the appliance is correctly connected to its plug and that, where necessary, it is properly earthed (grounded). Do not use such appliances in damp conditions and, again, beware of creating a spark or applying excessive heat in the vicinity of fuel or fuel vapour. Also ensure that the appliances meet the relevant national safety standards.

Diesel fuel

Diesel injection pumps supply fuel at very high pressure, and extreme care must be taken when working on the fuel injectors and fuel pipes. It is advisable to place an absorbent cloth around the union before slackening a fuel pipe, and *never expose the hands or any part of the body to injector spray, as the high working pressure can cause the fuel to penetrate the skin, with possibly fatal results.*

Routine maintenance

For modifications, and information applicable to later models, see Supplement at end of manual

The maintenance schedules below are basically those recommended by the manufacturer. Servicing intervals are determined by mileage or time elapsed – this is because fluids and systems deteriorate with age as well as with use. Follow the time intervals if the appropriate mileage is not covered within the specified period.

Vehicles operating under adverse conditions may need more frequent maintenance. 'Adverse conditions' include climatic extremes, full-time towing or taxi work, driving on unmade roads, and a high proportion of short journeys. The use of inferior fuel (such as may be found in some foreign countries) can cause early degradation of the engine oil. Consult a dealer for full guidance.

Some of the tasks called up will be described in detail in the appropriate manual for petrol-engined vehicles.

Under-bonnet view of a Visa Diesel (air cleaner removed)

1 Coolant filler cap and expansion tank	8 Brake fluid reservoir and filler cap	14 Heater plug relay	21 Starter motor
2 Injectors	9 Washer pump	15 Clutch cable	22 Oil filter
3 Accelerator cable	10 Washer reservoir	16 Reversing light switch	23 Injection pump (Bosch)
4 Brake vacuum pump	11 Front suspension upper mounting	17 Top hose	24 Alternator
5 Fusebox	12 Brake master cylinder	18 Radiator	25 Fuel filter
6 Servo unit	13 Battery	19 Fast idle thermo unit	26 Right-hand engine mounting
7 Speedometer cable		20 Engine oil dipstick and filler cap	

Front under view of a Visa Diesel

1   Subframe
2   Exhaust pipe
3   Right-hand driveshaft support bracket

4   Lower engine mounting
5   Exhaust resonator
6   Engine oil drain plug

7   Gearbox
8   Track control arm

9   Anti-roll bar
10   Track rod
11   Final drive oil drain plug

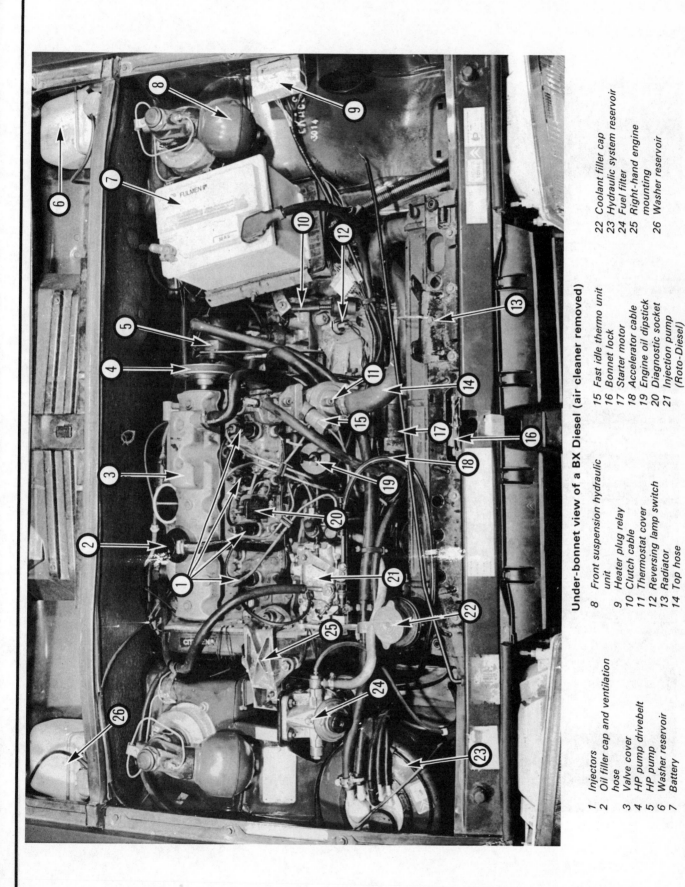

Under-bonnet view of a BX Diesel (air cleaner removed)

1 Injectors
2 Oil filler cap and ventilation hose
3 Valve cover
4 HP pump drivebelt
5 HP pump
6 Washer reservoir
7 Battery

8 Front suspension hydraulic unit
9 Heater plug relay
10 Clutch cable
11 Thermostat cover
12 Reversing lamp switch
13 Radiator
14 Top hose

15 Fast idle thermo unit
16 Bonnet lock
17 Starter motor
18 Accelerator cable
19 Engine oil dipstick
20 Diagnostic socket
21 Injection pump (Roto-Diesel)

22 Coolant filler cap
23 Hydraulic system reservoir
24 Fuel filter
25 Right-hand engine mounting
26 Washer reservoir

Front under view of a BX Diesel

1 Gearchange
2 Exhaust pipe
3 Subframe
4 Track rod

5 Front suspension arm
6 Right-hand driveshaft
  support bracket
7 Lower engine mounting

8 Thermo-switch
9 Radiator
10 Engine oil drain plug

11 Crossmember
12 Gearbox
13 Left-hand driveshaft
14 Final drive oil drain plug

At weekly intervals, or before a long journey

Engine
Check oil level

Cooling system
Check coolant level

Braking system
Check fluid level, investigate any sudden fall

Suspension and steering
Check tyre pressures (including spare)
Examine tyres for wear and damage

Electrical system
Check battery electrolyte level (if applicable)
Check operation of lights, wipers and horn
Check washer fluid level(s)

Every 5000 miles (7500 km) or six months, whichever comes first

Engine
Renew oil and filter
Clean oil filler cap (BX models)

Fuel and exhaust systems
Drain water from fuel filter
Examine exhaust system for corrosion and leakage

Clutch
Check adjustment

Transmission
Check oil/fluid level (when applicable – see Chapter 8)

Hydraulic system (BX models)
Check fluid level in the reservoir
Check hydraulic lines for condition and security

Braking system
Check disc pads for wear
Check brake hydraulic circuit for leaks, damaged pipes etc
Check handbrake adjustment
Check discs for condition

Steering and suspension
Check front wheel alignment
Check security and condition of steering gear and balljoints, and condition of rubber bellows and dust excluders

General
Lubricate all controls, linkages, door locks and hinges

Every 10 000 miles (15 000 km) or twelve months, whichever comes first

In addition to the work specified in the previous schedule

Braking system
Check rear brake shoes for wear (if applicable)

Every 15 000 miles (22 500 km) or 18 months, whichever comes first

In addition to the work specified in previous schedules (where applicable)

Fuel and exhaust systems
Check idling speed
Renew fuel filter (Visa models)

Clutch
Lubricate clutch pedal and cable pivot points with grease

Braking system
Check oil level and security of vacuum pump (Visa models)

Suspension and steering
Check wheel bearings

Bodywork and fittings
Check seat belts and anchorages

General
Check wiper blades
Check drivebelt tension(s)

Every 20 000 miles (30 000 km) or 2 years, whichever comes first

In addition to the work specified in previous schedules (where applicable)

Fuel and exhaust systems
Renew air cleaner element
Renew fuel filter (BX models)

Hydraulic system (BX models)
Clean filter

Every 30 000 miles (45 000 km) or 2 years, whichever comes first

In addition to the work specified in previous schedules (where applicable)

Cooling system
Renew coolant

Transmission
Renew automatic transmission fluid

Braking system (Visa models)
Renew fluid
Check rear brake linings

Every 45 000 miles (67 500 km) or 2 years, whichever comes first

Hydraulic system (BX models)
Renew fluid

Engine
Renew timing belt

Every 65 000 miles (97 500 km) or 3 years, whichever comes first

Transmission
Renew manual gearbox oil

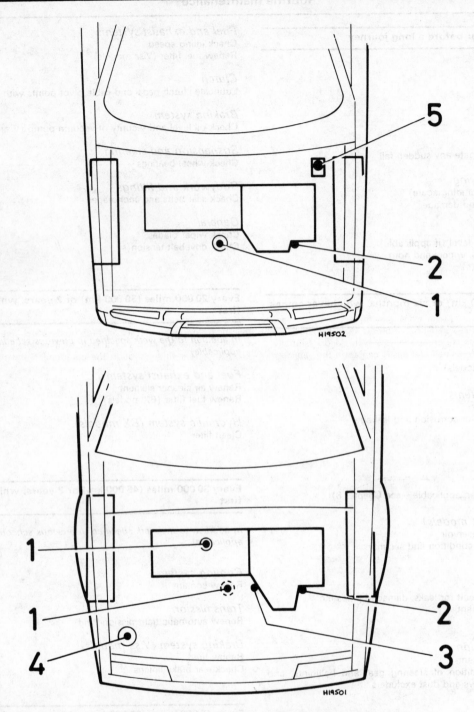

Recommended lubricants and fluids

Component or system	Lubricant type/specification	Duckhams recommendation
1 Engine	Multigrade engine oil, viscosity SAE 15W/40	Duckhams QXR or Hypergrade
2 Manual gearbox	Gear oil, viscosity SAE 75W/80W	Duckhams Hypoid 75W/90S
3 Automatic transmission	Dexron II type ATF	Duckhams D-Matic
4 Hydraulic system (BX models)	Green LHM fluid	Duckhams LHM Fluid
5 Brake hydraulic system (Visa models)	Hydraulic fluid to SAE J1703 C	Duckhams Universal Brake and Clutch Fluid

Fault diagnosis

Introduction

The vehicle owner who does his or her own maintenance according to the recommended schedules should not have to use this section of the manual very often. Modern component reliability is such that, provided those items subject to wear or deterioration are inspected or renewed at the specified intervals, sudden failure is comparatively rare. Faults do not usually just happen as a result of sudden failure, but develop over a period of time. Major mechanical failures in particular are usually preceded by characteristic symptoms over hundreds or even thousands of miles. Those components which do occasionally fail without warning are often small and easily carried in the vehicle.

With any fault finding, the first step is to decide where to begin investigations. Sometimes this is obvious, but on other occasions a little detective work will be necessary. The owner who makes half a dozen haphazard adjustments or replacements may be successful in curing a fault (or its symptoms), but he will be none the wiser if the fault recurs and he may well have spent more time and money than was necessary. A calm and logical approach will be found to be more satisfactory in the long run. Always take into account any warning signs or abnormalities that may have been noticed in the period preceding the fault – power loss, high or low gauge readings, unusual noises or smells, etc – and remember that failure of components such as fuses may only be pointers to some underlying fault.

The pages which follow here are intended to help in cases of failure to start or breakdown on the road. There is also a Fault Diagnosis Section at the end of each Chapter which should be consulted if the preliminary checks prove unfruitful. Whatever the fault, certain basic principles apply. These are as follows:

Verify the fault. This is simply a matter of being sure that you know what the symptoms are before starting work. This is particularly important if you are investigating a fault for someone else who may not have described it very accurately.

Don't overlook the obvious. For example, if the vehicle won't start, is there fuel in the tank? (Don't take anyone else's word on this particular point, and don't trust the fuel gauge either!) If an electrical fault is indicated, look for loose or broken wires before digging out the test gear.

Cure the disease, not the symptom. Substituting a flat battery with a fully charged one will get you off the hard shoulder, but if the underlying cause is not attended to, the new battery will go the same way.

Don't take anything for granted. Particularly, don't forget that a 'new' component may itself be defective (especially if it's been rattling round in the boot for months), and don't leave components out of a fault diagnosis sequence just because they are new or recently fitted. When you do finally diagnose a difficult fault, you'll probably realise that all the evidence was there from the start.

Electrical faults

Electrical faults can be more puzzling than straightforward mechanical failures, but they are no less susceptible to logical analysis if the basic principles of operation are understood. Vehicle electrical wiring exists in extremely unfavourable conditions – heat, vibration and chemical attack – and the first things to look for are loose or corroded connections and broken or chafed wires, especially where the wires pass through holes in the bodywork or are subject to vibration.

All metal-bodied vehicles in current production have one pole of the battery 'earthed', ie connected to the vehicle bodywork, and in nearly all modern vehicles it is the negative (–) terminal. The various electrical components – motors, bulb holders etc – are also connected to earth, either by means of a lead or directly by their mountings. Electric current flows through the component and then back to the battery via the bodywork. If the component mounting is loose or corroded, or if a good path back to the battery is not available, the circuit will be incomplete and malfunction will result. The engine and/or gearbox are also earthed by means of flexible metal straps to the body or subframe; if these straps are loose or missing, starter motor and generator trouble may result.

Assuming the earth return to be satisfactory, electrical faults will be due either to component malfunction or to defects in the current supply. If supply wires are broken or cracked internally this results in an open-circuit, and the easiest way to check for this is to bypass the suspect wire temporarily with a length of wire having a crocodile clip or suitable connector at each end. Alternatively, a 12V test lamp can be used to verify the presence of supply voltage at various points along the wire and the break can be thus isolated.

If a bare portion of a live wire touches the bodywork or other earthed metal part, the electricity will take the low-resistance path thus formed back to the battery: this is known as a short-circuit. Hopefully a short-circuit will blow a fuse, but otherwise it may cause burning of the insulation (and possibly further short-circuits) or even a fire. This is why it is inadvisable to bypass persistently blowing fuses with silver foil or wire.

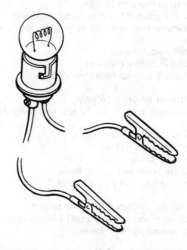

Simple test lamp is useful for tracing electrical faults

Spares and tool kit

Most vehicles are supplied only with sufficient tools for wheel changing; the *Maintenance and minor repair* tool kit detailed in *Tools and working facilities,* with the addition of a hammer, is probably sufficient for those repairs that most motorists would consider attempting at the roadside. In addition a few items which can be fitted without too much trouble in the event of a breakdown should be carried. Experience and available space will modify the list below, but the following may save having to call on professional assistance:

> *Drivebelt(s) – emergency type may suffice*
> *Spare fuses*
> *Set of principal light bulbs*
> *Tin of radiator sealer and hose bandage*
> *Exhaust bandage*
> *Roll of insulating tape*
> *Length of soft iron wire*
> *Length of electrical flex*
> *Torch or inspection lamp (can double as test lamp)*
> *Battery jump leads*
> *Tow-rope*
> *Litre of engine oil*
> *Sealed can of hydraulic fluid*
> *Emergency windscreen*
> *Worm drive clips*

If spare fuel is carried, a can designed for the purpose should be used to minimise risks of leakage and collision damage. A first aid kit and a warning triangle, whilst not at present compulsory in the UK, are obviously sensible items to carry in addition to the above.

When touring abroad it may be advisable to carry additional spares which, even if you cannot fit them yourself, could save having to wait while parts are obtained. The items below may be worth considering:

> *Clutch and throttle cables*
> *Cylinder head gasket*
> *Alternator brushes*
> *Fuel injector(s) and fire-seal washer(s)*
> *Tyre valve core*

One of the motoring organisations will be able to advise on availability of fuel etc in foreign countries.

Engine will not start

Engine fails to turn when starter operated

Flat battery (recharge, use jump leads, or push start)
Battery terminals loose or corroded
Battery earth to body defective
Engine earth strap loose or broken
Starter motor (or solenoid) wiring loose or broken
Automatic transmission selector in wrong position, or inhibitor switch faulty
Ignition/starter switch faulty
Major mechanical failure (seizure)
Starter or solenoid internal fault (see Chapter 7)

Starter motor turns engine slowly

Partially discharged battery (recharge, use jump leads, or push start)
Battery terminals loose or corroded
Battery earth to body defective
Engine earth strap loose
Starter motor (or solenoid) wiring loose
Starter motor internal fault (see Chapter 7)

Starter motor spins without turning engine

Starter motor reduction gears stripped (where applicable)
Starter motor mounting bolts loose

Engine turns normally but fails to start

No fuel in tank
Wax formed in fuel (in very cold weather)

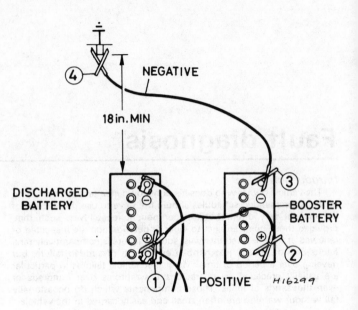

Jump start lead connections for negative earth vehicles – connect leads in order shown

Poor compression (see Chapter 1)
Fuel system or preheater fault (see Chapter 3)
Major mechanical failure

Engine fires but will not run

Preheater fault (see Chapter 3)
Wax formed in fuel (in very cold weather)
Other fuel system fault (see Chapter 3)

Engine cuts out and will not restart

Engine misfires before cutting out – fuel fault

Fuel tank empty
Fuel filter blocked (check for delivery)
Fuel tank filler vent blocked (suction will be evident on releasing cap)
Other fuel system fault (see Chapter 3)

Engine cuts out – other causes

Serious overheating
Major mechanical failure (eg camshaft drive)

Engine overheats

Coolant loss due to internal or external leakage (see Chapter 2)
Thermostat defective
Low oil level
Brakes binding
Radiator clogged externally or internally
Electric cooling fan not operating correctly
Engine waterways clogged

Note: *Do not add cold water to an overheated engine or damage may result*

Low engine oil pressure

Gauge reads low or warning light illuminated with engine running
    Oil level low or incorrect grade
    Defective gauge or sender unit
    Wire to sender unit earthed
    Engine overheating
    Oil filter clogged or bypass valve defective
    Oil pressure relief valve defective
    Oil pick-up strainer clogged
    Oil pump worn or mountings loose
    Worn main or big-end bearings
Note: *Low oil pressure in a high-mileage engine at tickover is not necessarily a cause for concern. Sudden pressure loss at speed is far more significant. In any event, check the gauge or warning light sender before condemning the engine.*

Engine noises

    To inexperienced ears the diesel engine sounds alarming, even when there is nothing wrong with it, so it may be prudent to have an unusual noise expertly diagnosed before making renewals or repairs.

Whistling or wheezing noises
    Leaking vacuum hose
    Leaking manifold gasket
    Blowing head gasket

Tapping or rattling
    Incorrect valve clearances
    Worn valve gear
    Worn oil pump chain
    Broken piston ring (ticking noise)

Knocking or thumping
    Unintentional mechanical contact (eg fan blades)
    Worn drivebelt
    Peripheral component fault (alternator, water pump etc)
    Fuel injector(s) leaking or sticking (see Chapter 3)
    Worn big-end bearings (regular heavy knocking, perhaps less under load)
    Worn main bearings (rumbling and knocking, perhaps worsening under load)
    Piston slap (most noticeable when cold, not to be confused with diesel knock)

Chapter 1 Engine

For modifications, and information applicable to later models, see Supplement at end of manual

Contents

Specifications

General

Type	Four-cylinder, in-line, four-stroke, overhead camshaft, compression-ignition, mounted transversely and inclined 30° to rear. Transmission mounted on left-hand end of engine.

Designation:
Visa and BX17 .... XUD 7 – 161A
BX 19 .... XUD 9 – 162
Number of cylinders 4
Bore and stroke:
1.7 .... 80.0 x 88.0 mm (3.150 x 3.465 in)
1.9 .... 83.0 x 88.0 mm (3.268 x 3.465 in)
Compression ratio:
1.7 .... 23.0 : 1
1.9 .... 23.5 : 1

Compression pressures (engine hot, cranking speed):
Minimum .... 18 bar (261 lbf/in²)
Normal .... 25 to 30 bar (363 to 435 lbf/in²)
Maximum difference between any two cylinders .... 5 bar (73 lbf/in²)
Cubic capacity:
1.7 .... 1769 cc (107.9 cu in)
1.9 .... 1905 cc (116.2 cu in)
Maximum torque (ISO):
1.7 .... 110 Nm (81 lbf ft) at 2200 rpm
1.9 .... 118 Nm (87 lbf ft) at 2000 rpm
Maximum power (ISO):
1.7 .... 43.5 kW at 4600 rpm
1.9 .... 47.0 kW at 4600 rpm
Maximum speed:
No load .... 5100 rpm
Laden .... 4600 rpm
Firing order .... 1-3-4-2 (No 1 at flywheel end)

Cylinder block
Cylinder bore diameter:
1.7 .... 80.000 to 80.018 mm (3.1496 to 3.1503 in)
   or 80.030 to 80.048 mm (3.1508 to 3.1515 in)
1.9 .... 83.000 to 83.018 mm (3.2677 to 3.2684 in)
   or 83.030 to 83.048 mm (3.2689 to 3.2696 in)

Pistons and piston rings
Piston diameter:
1.7 .... 79.93 ± 0.008 mm (3.1468 ± 0.0003 in)
   or 76.96 ± 0.008 mm (3.1480 ± 0.0003 in)
1.9 .... 82.930 ± 0.009 mm (3.2650 ± 0.0004 in)
   or 82.960 ± 0.009 mm (3.2661 ± 0.0004 in)
Piston ring end gaps (fitted):
Top compression .... 0.20 to 0.40 mm (0.008 to 0.016 in)
2nd compression .... 0.15 to 0.35 mm (0.006 to 0.014 in)
Oil scraper .... 0.10 to 0.30 mm (0.004 to 0.012 in)
Connecting rod small-end bush inner diameter .... 25.007 to 25.020 mm (0.9845 to 0.9850 in)
Maximum weight difference between any two pistons ...... 2.5 g (0.09 oz)
Maximum piston protrusion difference between any two pistons ... 0.12 mm (0.0047 in)

Crankshaft
Endfloat .... 0.07 to 0.32 mm (0.003 to 0.013 in)
Main bearing journal diameter:
Standard .... 60.0 +0 −0.019 mm (2.3622 +0 −0.0008 in)
Undersize .... −0.3 mm (0.0118 in)
Crankpin diameter:
Standard .... 50.0 +0 −0.016 mm (1.9685 +0 −0.0006 in)
Undersize .... −0.3 mm (0.0118 in)
Maximum journal/crankpin out-of-round .... 0.007 mm (0.0003 in)

Cylinder head
Warp limit .... 0.07 mm (0.0028 in) subject to camshaft turning freely
Refinishing limit (see text) .... 0.40 mm (0.016 in)
Swirl chamber protrusion .... 0 to 0.03 mm (0 to 0.001 in)

Valves
Seat angle (inclusive):
Inlet .... 120°
Exhaust .... 90°
Valve recess below cylinder head:
Inlet .... 0.50 to 1.00 mm (0.0197 to 0.0394 in)
Exhaust .... 0.90 to 1.40 mm (0.0354 to 0.0551 in)
Valve clearances (cold):
Inlet .... 0.15 ± 0.08 mm (0.006 ± 0.003 in)
Exhaust .... 0.30 ± 0.08 mm (0.012 ± 0.003 in)

Valve timing (at 1.0 mm clearance):
Inlet opens .... 8° BTDC
Inlet closes .... 40° ABDC
Exhaust opens .... 56° BBDC
Exhaust closes .... 12° ATDC

Camshaft
Endfloat .... 0.07 to 0.16 mm (0.003 to 0.006 in)

Lubrication system
Oil type/specification .... Multigrade engine oil, viscosity SAE 15W/40 (Duckhams QXR or Hypergrade)
Oil capacity (drain and refill) .... 4.5 litres (7.9 pints)
Oil pressure (at engine temperature of 80°C/176°F):
Minimum .... 2.0 bar (29.0 lbf/in²) at 800 rpm
Maximum .... 3.5 to 5.0 bar (51 to 73 lbf/in²) at 4000 rpm
Oil pressure switch operating pressures:
On .... 0.58 to 0.44 bar (8.4 to 6.4 lbf/in²)
Off .... 0.8 bar (11.6 lbf/in²) maximum

Oil pump
Type .... Two gear
Pressure relief valve opens .... 4.0 bar (58 lbf/in²)
Gear endfloat .... 0.12 mm (0.005 in)
Clearance between gear lobes and housing .... 0.064 mm (0.0025 in)

Torque wrench settings

	Nm	lbf ft
Camshaft bearing cap	18	13
Big-end bearing cap	50	37
Oil gallery plug	28	21
Main bearing cap	70	52
Front housing	11	8
Oil pump cover	9	7
Oil pump mounting	13	10
Sump	19	14
Flywheel/driveplate	50	37
Cylinder head bolts:		
Stage 1	30	22
Stage 2	60	44
Stage 3 Loosen 1/4 turn then	60	44
Stage 4 (after 10 mins at 3000 rpm). Loosen 1/4 turn then	65	48
Injection pump bracket	20	15
Camshaft sprocket	35	26
Bottom timing cover	12	9
Crankshaft pulley bolt:		
Stage 1	40	30
Stage 2	plus 60° or to 150	plus 60° or to 111
Oil pressure switch	30	22
Valve cover	2	1.5
Pump pulley to camshaft	35	26
Oil cooler	68	50
Sump oil drain bracket	3	2.2
Oil filter	14	10
Left-hand engine mounting:		
Centre nut	35	26
Small nuts	18	13
Centre stud to transmission	50	37
Right-hand lower engine mounting bracket	18	13
Right-hand upper engine mounting bracket:		
To engine	35	26
To mounting rubber	28	21
Lower link mounting	35	26
Timing belt tensioner	18	13
Timing belt intermediate roller	18	13

1 General description

The engine is of four-cylinder overhead camshaft design, mounted transversely and inclined 30° to the rear, with the transmission mounted on the left-hand side. Both the block and the cylinder head are of cast iron.

A toothed timing belt drives the camshaft, injection pump and water pump. Bucket tappets are fitted between the camshaft and valves, and valve clearance adjustment is by means of selective shims.

The camshaft is supported by three bearings machined directly in the cylinder head.

The crankshaft runs in five main bearings of the usual shell type. Endfloat is controlled by thrust washers either side of No 2 main bearing.

The pistons are selected to be of matching weight, and incorporate fully floating gudgeon pins retained by circlips.

The oil pump is chain driven from the front of the crankshaft. An oil cooler is fitted to the 1.9 engine.

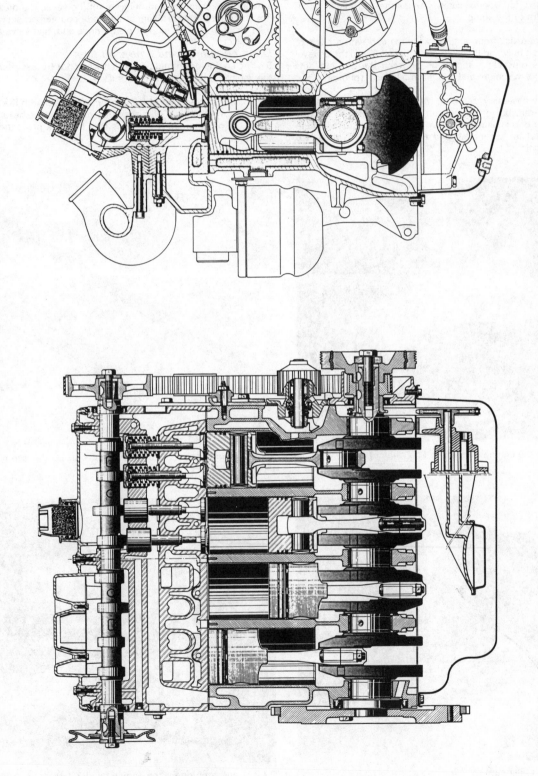

Fig. 1.2 Engine transverse cross-section (Sec 1)

Fig. 1.1 Engine longitudinal cross-section (Sec 1)

2 Routine maintenance

Carry out the following procedures at the intervals given in Routine Maintenance at the beginning of this manual or the corresponding petrol engine manual.

Check engine oil level
1 The vehicle must be parked on level ground and the engine must have been stopped for approximately 10 minutes to allow oil in circulation to return to the sump.

2 Withdraw the dipstick from its tube, wipe the end with a piece of clean rag, re-insert it fully and then withdraw it again. Read the oil level on the end of the dipstick; it should be between the two cut-outs which represent the maximum and minimum oil levels (photos).

3 It is not strictly necessary to top up the engine oil until it reaches the minimum cut-out, but on no account allow the level to fall any lower. The amount of oil needed to top up from minimum to maximum is 1 litre (1.8 pints) for 1.7 models and approximately 1.5 litres (2.6 pints) for 1.9 models.

4 When topping-up is necessary, use clean engine oil of the specified type, preferably of the same make and grade as that already in the engine. Top up by removing the filler cap from the valve cover or the filler tube as applicable (photos). Allow time for the oil to run down to the sump before rechecking the level on the dipstick. Refit the filler cap and dipstick on completion.

5 All engines use some oil, depending on the degree of wear and the pattern of use. Oil which is not being lost through external leaks is entering the cylinders and being burnt, however, the diesel engine is not so prone to this problem as its petrol counterpart since there is no inlet vacuum to suck oil past piston rings and inlet valve stems.

Drain engine oil and renew oil filter
6 The engine oil should be drained when hot (ie just after a run) with the vehicle parked on level ground.

7 Position a drain pan of adequate capacity beneath the sump. Wipe clean around the drain plug then unscrew it using a hexagon key and allow the oil to drain. If the oil is very hot take precautions to avoid scalding.

2.2A Withdrawing the engine oil dipstick (1.7 engine)

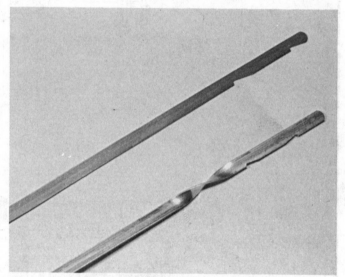

2.2B Minimum and maximum level cut-outs on the two types of dipstick

2.4A Removing the filler cap ...

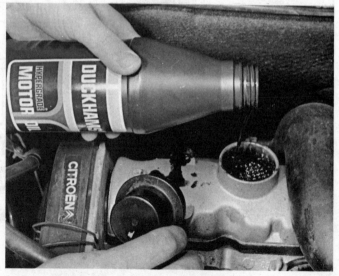

2.4B ... and topping up the engine oil (BX 19)

2.4C Topping-up the engine oil (Visa)

2.10 Unscrewing the oil filter with a strap wrench

2.11 Tighten the oil filter by hand only

8   Remove the oil filler cap and allow the oil to drain for at least 15 minutes.

9   Check and if necessary renew the drain plug washer then wipe the sump, refit the drain plug and tighten it.

10   Position the drain pan beneath the oil filter on the front of the cylinder block. Using a strap wrench, unscrew the filter and remove it (photo). If a strap wrench is not available a screwdriver can be driven through the filter and used as a lever to remove it.

11   Wipe clean the filter seat on the cylinder block or oil cooler (as applicable). Smear a little engine oil on the sealing ring of the new oil filter then screw on the filter until it just touches the seat. Hand tighten the oil filter by a further two-thirds of a turn (photo).

12   Fill the engine with the correct grade and quantity of oil as previously described.

13   Start the engine and allow it to idle. Check that the oil pressure warning light goes out and also check that there is no oil leakage from the oil filter.

14   Switch off the engine and recheck the oil level.

15   Put the old oil into a sealed container and dispose of it safely.

Clean oil filler cap (models with cap on valve cover)
16   Pull the oil filler cap from the top of the valve cover then loosen the clip and disconnect the crankcase ventilation hose.

17   Clean the wire mesh filter in paraffin and allow to dry. If it is blocked with sludge, however, renew the cap complete.

18   Refit the hose to the filler cap and fit the cap to the valve cover.

Renew the timing belt
19   Refer to Section 4.

3   Major operations possible with the engine in the vehicle

The following operations can be carried out without having to remove the engine from the car:

    (a)   *Timing belt – removal and refitting*
    (b)   *Camshaft – removal and refitting*
    (c)   *Cylinder head – removal and refitting*
    (d)   *Camshaft oil seals – renewal*
    (e)   *Crankshaft oil seals – renewal*
    (f)   *Sump – removal and refitting*
    (g)   *Oil pump – removal and refitting*
    (h)   *Pistons and connecting rods – removal and refitting*
    (i)   *Flywheel/driveplate – removal and refitting*

4   Timing belt – inspection, removal, refitting and tensioning

1   The timing belt drives the camshaft, injection pump, and water pump from a toothed sprocket on the front of the crankshaft. If it breaks in service the pistons are likely to hit the valve heads and result in an expensive repair.

2   The timing belt should be renewed at 45 000 mile (67 500 km) intervals, however, if it is contaminated with oil or if it is at all noisy in operation (a 'scraping' noise due to uneven wear) it should be renewed earlier. Where a Bosch injection pump is fitted, excessive play in the front bearing can wear the sides of the timing belt.

3   On Visa models apply the handbrake. On BX models chock the rear wheels and release the handbrake, as the handbrake operates on the front wheels.

4   On manual gearbox models jack up the front right-hand corner of the vehicle until the wheel is just clear of the ground. Support the vehicle on an axle stand and engage 4th or 5th gear. This will enable the engine to be turned easily by turning the right-hand wheel. On automatic transmission models use an open-ended spanner on the crankshaft pulley bolt.

5   Remove the engine splash guard from under the right-hand front wheel arch.

6   Disconnect the battery negative lead.

7   Loosen the alternator pivot and adjustment bolts then unscrew the tension bolt until it is possible to slip the drivebelt from the pulleys.

8   With 4th or 5th gear selected on manual gearbox models have an assistant depress the footbrake pedal, then unscrew the crankshaft pulley bolt. On BX models the handbrake may be applied instead of the footbrake pedal to hold the crankshaft stationary. On automatic transmission models unbolt the transmission cover and lock the starter ring gear. Note that the bolt is extremely tight.

9   Slide the pulley from the front of the crankshaft. Unbolt the bottom timing cover.

10 Support the weight of the engine using a hoist or trolley jack.

11 Unscrew the nuts and remove the right-hand engine mounting bracket (photo).

12 Pull up the front clip (early models), release the spring clips, and withdraw the two timing cover sections (photos). Note that the spring clip is not fitted to later models, which have a modified cover and fastenings.

13 Turn the engine by means of the front right-hand wheel or crankshaft pulley bolt until the three bolt holes in the camshaft and injection pump sprockets are aligned with the corresponding holes in the engine front plate.

14 Insert an 8.0 mm diameter metal dowel rod or drill through the special hole in the left-hand rear flange of the cylinder block by the starter motor, then carefully turn the engine either way until the rod enters the TDC hole in the flywheel (see photo 23.26).

15 Insert three M8 bolts through the holes in the camshaft and injection pump sprockets and screw them into the engine front plate fingertight (Fig. 1.3A).

16 Loosen the timing belt tensioner pivot nut and adjustment bolt, then turn the bracket anti-clockwise to release the tension and retighten the adjustment bolt to hold the tensioner in the released position. If available use a ⅜ inch square drive extension in the hole provided to turn the bracket against the spring tension.

17 Mark the timing belt with an arrow to indicate its normal direction of turning then remove it from the camshaft, injection pump, water pump and crankshaft sprockets.

18 Inspect the belt for cracks, fraying, and damage to the teeth. Pay particular attention to the roots of the teeth. If any damage is evident or if the belt is contaminated with oil it must be renewed and any oil leak rectified.

19 Commence refitting by locating the timing belt on the crankshaft sprocket, making sure that, where applicable, the rotation arrow is facing the correct way.

20 Hold the timing belt engaged with the crankshaft sprocket then feed it over the roller and onto the injection pump, camshaft, and water pump sprockets and over the tensioner roller. To ensure correct engagement, locate only a half width on the injection pump sprocket before feeding the timing belt onto the camshaft sprocket keeping the belt taut and fully engaged with the crankshaft sprocket. Locate the timing belt fully onto the sprockets. (See photos 27.54A, 27.54B and 27.54C later in this Chapter.)

21 With the pivot nut loose, slacken the tensioner adjustment bolt while holding the bracket against the spring tension. Slowly release the bracket until the roller presses against the timing belt. Retighten the adjustment bolt.

22 Remove the bolts from the camshaft and injection pump sprockets. Remove the metal dowel rod from the cylinder block.

23 Rotate the engine two complete turns in its normal direction. Do not rotate the engine backwards as the timing belt must be kept tight between the crankshaft, injection pump and camshaft sprockets.

24 Loosen the tensioner adjustment bolt to allow the tensioner spring to push the roller against the timing belt, then tighten both the adjustment bolt and pivot nut.

25 Recheck the engine timing as described in paragraphs 13 and 14 then remove the metal dowel rod.

26 Refit the three timing cover sections and secure with the special clip and spring clips.

4.11 Right-hand engine mounting bracket

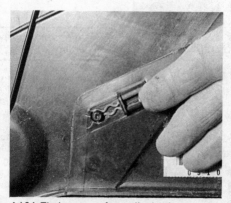
4.12A Timing cover front clip (early models) ...

4.12B ... and spring clips

27 Refit the right-hand engine mounting bracket and tighten the nuts.

28 Remove the trolley jack or hoist.

29 Slide the pulley onto the front of the crankshaft.

30 Apply three drops of locking fluid on the threads of the crankshaft pulley bolt then insert it and tighten to the specified torque while holding the crankshaft stationary using the method described in paragraph 8.

31 Refit the alternator drivebelt and tension it as described in Chapter 7.

32 Reconnect the battery negative lead.

33 Refit the engine splash-guard under the right-hand front wheelarch.

34 Lower the vehicle to the ground.

5 Timing belt tensioner and right-hand engine mounting bracket – removal and refitting

1 On Visa models apply the handbrake. On BX models chock the rear wheels and release the handbrake.

2 On manual gearbox models jack up the front right-hand corner of the vehicle until the wheel is just clear of the ground. Support the vehicle on an axle stand and engage 4th or 5th gear so that the engine may be rotated by turning the right-hand wheel. On automatic transmission models use an open-ended spanner on the crankshaft pulley bolt.

3 Support the weight of the engine using a hoist or trolley jack.

4 Unscrew the nuts and remove the right-hand engine mounting bracket (see photo 4.11).

Visa models
5 Remove the battery and the tray, then unbolt the support bracket (photo).

6 Unscrew the nut from the left-hand engine mounting and remove the rubber mounting.

7 Move the engine and gearbox to the left as far as possible and support it in this position.

All models
8 Pull up the special clip, release the spring clips and withdraw the two timing cover sections (see photos 4.12A and 4.12B).

9 Turn the engine by means of the front right-hand wheel or crankshaft pulley bolt until the three bolt holes in the camshaft and injection pump sprockets are aligned with the corresponding holes in the engine front plate.

10 Insert an 8.0 mm diameter metal dowel rod or drill through the special hole in the left-hand rear flange of the cylinder block by the starter motor, then carefully turn the engine either way until the rod enters the TDC hole in the flywheel (see photo 23.26).

11 Insert three M8 bolts through the holes in the camshaft and injection pump sprockets and screw them into the engine front plate fingertight (Fig. 1.3A).

12 Loosen the timing belt tensioner pivot nut and adjustment bolt, then turn the bracket anti-clockwise until the adjustment bolt is in the middle of the slot and retighten the bolt. If available use a ⅜ inch square drive extension in the hole provided to turn the bracket against the spring tension.

13 A tool must now be obtained in order to hold the tensioner plunger in the mounting bracket. Citroën tool 7009-T1 (Fig. 1.3B) is designed

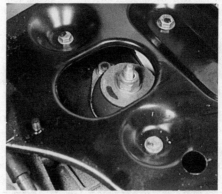

5.5 Battery support bracket, also showing left-hand engine/transmission mounting

to slide in the two lower bolt holes of the mounting bracket, and it should be quite easy to fabricate a similar tool out of sheet metal using long bolts instead of metal dowel rods.

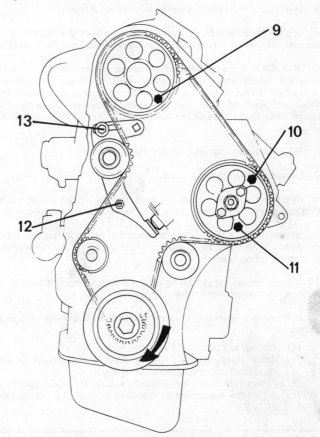

Fig. 1.3A Holding camshaft and injection pump sprockets in position using M8 bolts (Sec 4)

9, 10 and 11   M8 bolts   13 Tensioner adjustment bolt
12 Tensioner pivot nut

Fig. 1.3B Citroën tool 7009-T1 for holding the tensioner plunger (Sec 5)

14 Unscrew the two lower bolts then fit the special tool. Grease the inner surface of the tool to prevent any damage to the end of the tensioner plunger.

15 Unscrew the pivot nut and adjustment bolt and withdraw the tensioner bracket, complete with roller.

16 Unbolt the engine mounting bracket noting that the uppermost bolt is on the inside face of the engine front plate.

17 Compress the tensioner plunger into the mounting bracket, remove the special tool then withdraw the plunger and spring.

18 Refitting is a reversal of removal, but refer to Section 4, paragraphs 21 to 25 for details of the timing belt adjustment procedure.

6 Timing belt intermediate roller – removal and refitting

1 Follow the procedure given in paragraphs 1 to 12 of Section 5.

2 Remove the engine splash guard from under the right-hand front wheel arch.

3 Disconnect the battery negative lead on BX models.

4 Loosen the alternator pivot and adjustment bolts then unscrew the tension bolt until it is possible to slip the drivebelt from the pulleys.

5 With 4th or 5th gear selected on manual gearbox models have an assistant depress the footbrake pedal, then unscrew the crankshaft pulley bolt. On BX models the handbrake may be applied instead of the footbrake pedal to hold the crankshaft stationary. On automatic transmission models unbolt the transmission cover and lock the starter ring gear.

6 Slide the pulley from the front of the crankshaft.

7 Unbolt the lower timing cover.

8 Remove the spacer from the stud for the upper timing cover sections. Note the position of the stud then unscrew and remove it.

9 Unscrew the remaining bolts securing the intermediate roller bracket to the cylinder block noting that the upper bolt also secures the engine mounting bracket.

10 Slightly loosen the remaining engine mounting bracket bolts then slide out the intermediate roller and bracket.

11 Refitting is a reversal of removal, but note the following additional points:

   (a) *Tighten all bolts to the specified torque*
   (b) *Apply three drops of locking fluid to the threads of the crankshaft pulley bolt before inserting it*
   (c) *Tension the alternator drivebelt as described in Chapter 7*
   (d) *Adjust the timing belt as described in Section 4, paragraphs 21 to 25*

7 Camshaft – removal and refitting

1 Follow the procedure given in paragraphs 1 to 12 of Section 5.

2 Remove the timing belt from the camshaft sprocket and tie it to one side without bending it excessively.

3 Unscrew the M8 bolt holding the camshaft sprocket in the timing position.

4 Where applicable, remove the oil filler cap/breather from the valve cover and position it to one side (photo).

5 On BX models disconnect the battery negative lead and also disconnect the air inlet hose from the inlet manifold and air cleaner.

7.4 Oil filler cap/breather (BX 19)

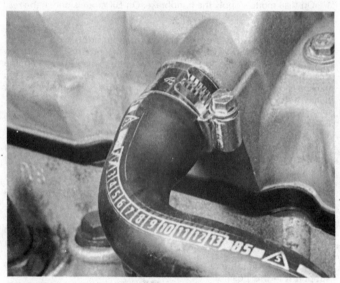

7.7 Crankcase ventilation hose (1.9 engine)

6 Loosen the pivot and adjustment bolts of the hydraulic high pressure pump (BX models), or vacuum pump (Visa models), swivel the unit upwards, and disconnect the drivebelt from the pulleys.

7 On the 1.9 engine, disconnect the crankcase ventilation hose from the valve cover (photo).

8 Unbolt and remove the valve cover. Remove the gasket (photos).

9 Hold the camshaft stationary with a spanner on the special lug between the 3rd and 4th cams or by using a lever in the sprocket holes then unscrew the camshaft sprocket bolt and withdraw the sprocket (photos). Recover the Woodruff key if it is loose. Do not rotate the camshaft otherwise the valves will strike the pistons of Nos 1 and 4 cylinders. If necessary turn the engine one quarter turn to position all the pistons halfway down the cylinders in order to prevent any damage, however, release the timing belt from the injection pump sprocket first.

10 Mark the position of the camshaft bearing caps numbering them from the flywheel end and making the marks on the manifold side.

7.8A Unbolt the valve cover ...

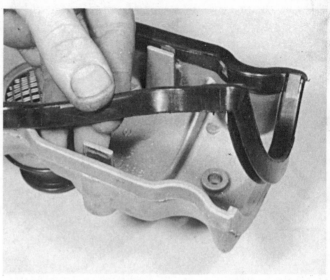

7.8B ... and remove the gasket

7.9A Special lug (arrowed) for holding the camshaft

7.9B Removing the camshaft sprocket

11 Progressively unscrew the nuts then remove the bearing caps.

12 Lift the camshaft and withdraw it through the front engine plate. Remove the oil seal from the timing end of the camshaft.

13 Hold the camshaft stationary with a spanner on the special lug between the 3rd and 4th cams, then unscrew the bolt and remove the pump pulley from the flywheel end of the camshaft. Use a puller if it is tight (photo). Recover the Woodruff key if it is loose.

14 Remove the oil seal from the flywheel end of the camshaft.

15 Clean all the components including the bearing surfaces in the cylinder head. Examine the components carefully for wear and damage, in particular check the surface of the cams for scoring and pitting. Renew components as necessary and obtain new oil seals.

16 Commence reassembly by lubricating the cams and bearing journals with engine oil.

7.13 Using a puller to remove the pump pulley from the camshaft

17 Locate the camshaft on the cylinder head, passing it through the engine front plate and with the tips of cams 4 and 6 facing downwards and resting on the bucket tappets. The cast DIST marking on the camshaft should be at the timing belt end of the cylinder head (photo) and the key slot for the camshaft sprocket should be facing upwards.

18 Fit the centre bearing cap the correct way round as previously noted then screw on the nuts and tighten them two or three turns.

19 Apply sealing compound to the end bearing caps on the areas shown in Fig. 1.4. Fit them in the correct positions and tighten the nuts two or three turns (photo).

20 Tighten all the nuts progressively to the specified torque making sure that cams 4 and 6 remain facing downwards (photo). Check that the camshaft endfloat is as given in the Specifications using feeler blades (photo). The only answer if it is not correct is to renew the cylinder head.

21 If the original camshaft is being refitted and it is known that the valve clearances are correct, proceed to paragraph 22, otherwise check and adjust the valve clearances as described in Section 8. Note that as the timing belt is disconnected at this stage, the crankshaft must be turned one quarter turn either way from the TDC position so that all the pistons are halfway down the cylinders. This will prevent the valves

7.17 The DIST marking must be at the timing belt end

7.19 Fitting a camshaft end bearing cap

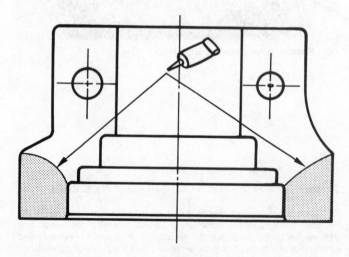

Fig. 1.4 Areas on camshaft end bearing caps to apply sealing compound (Sec 7)

7.20A Tightening the camshaft bearing cap nuts

striking the pistons when the camshaft is rotated. Release the timing belt from the injection pump sprocket while turning the engine as the timing bolts are still in position.

7.20B Checking the camshaft endfloat

7.22 Using a socket and bolt to fit a camshaft oil seal

22 Smear the lips of the oil seals with oil then fit them over each end of the camshaft, open end first, and press them in until flush with the end faces of the end caps. Use an M10 bolt, washers and a suitable socket to press in the oil seals (photo).

23 Fit the Woodruff key and pump pulley to the flywheel end of the camshaft, insert the bolt and tighten it while holding the camshaft stationary.

24 Fit the Woodruff key and camshaft sprocket to the timing end of the camshaft. Apply locking fluid to the threads then insert the bolt and tighten it to the specified torque while holding the camshaft stationary.

25 Refit the valve cover, together with a new gasket, and tighten the bolts.

26 Refit the crankcase ventilation hose.

27 Locate the drivebelt on the camshaft pulley and hydraulic pump (BX models), or vacuum pump (Visa models) pulley. Press the pump downwards until the deflection of the belt midway between the two pulleys is approximately 5.0 mm (0.2 in) under firm thumb pressure. Tighten the adjustment bolt followed by the pivot bolt.

28 On BX models reconnect the battery negative lead and the air inlet hose.

29 Refit the oil filler cap/breather.

30 Align the holes and refit the M8 timing bolt to the camshaft sprocket.

31 If the crankshaft was turned a quarter turn from TDC as in paragraphs 9 and 21, turn the crankshaft back the quarter turn so that pistons 1 and 4 are again at TDC. Do not turn the engine more than a quarter turn otherwise pistons 2 and 3 will pass their TDC positions and will strike valves 4 and 6.

32 Refit the TDC dowel rod to the flywheel.

33 Refit and adjust the timing belt with reference to Section 4, paragraphs 20 to 25. The remaining procedure is a reversal of removal.

8 Valve clearances – checking and adjustment

Checking
1 On Visa models apply the handbrake. On BX models chock the rear wheels and release the handbrake.

2 On manual gearbox models jack up the front right-hand corner of the vehicle until the wheel is just clear of the ground. Support the vehicle on an axle stand and engage 4th or 5th gear so that the engine may be rotated by turning the right-hand wheel. On automatic transmission models use an open-ended spanner on the crankshaft pulley bolt.

3 Disconnect the battery negative lead.

4 Remove the oil filler cap/breather and position it to one side.

5 On BX models disconnect the air inlet hose from the inlet manifold and air cleaner.

6 Disconnect the crankcase ventilation hose from the valve cover.

7 Unbolt and remove the valve cover. Remove the gasket.

8 On a piece of paper draw the outline of the engine with the cylinders numbered from the flywheel end and also showing the position of each valve, together with the specified valve clearance. Above each valve draw two lines for noting (1) the actual clearance and (2) the amount of adjustment required.

9 Turn the engine until the inlet valve of No 1 cylinder (nearest the flywheel) is fully closed and the apex of the cam is facing directly away from the bucket tappet.

10 Using feeler gauges measure the clearance between the base of the cam and the bucket tappet (photo). Record the clearance on line (1).

11 Repeat the measurement for the other seven valves, turning the engine as necessary so that the cam lobe in question is always facing directly away from the particular bucket tappet.

12 Calculate the difference between each measured clearance and the desired value and record it on line (2). Since the clearance is different for inlet and exhaust valves make sure that you are aware which valve you are dealing with. The valve sequence from either end of the engine is:

Inlet – Exhaust – Exhaust – Inlet – Inlet – Exhaust – Exhaust – Inlet

13 If all the clearances are within tolerance, refit the valve cover using a new gasket if necessary. If any clearance measured is outside the specified tolerance, adjustment must be carried out as described below.

8.10 Checking the valve clearances with feeler gauges

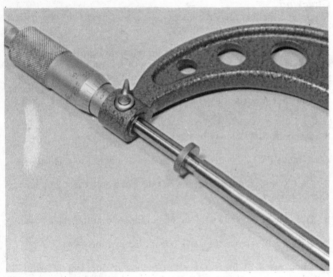

8.15 Checking the shim thickness with a micrometer

Adjustment
14 Remove the camshaft as described in Section 7.

15 Withdraw the first bucket tappet and its shim. Be careful that the shim does not fall out of the tappet. Clean the shim and measure its thickness with a micrometer (photo).

16 Refer to the clearance recorded for the valve concerned. If the clearance was more than the amount required the shim thickness must be increased by the difference recorded (2), if too small the thickness must be decreased.

17 Draw three more lines beneath each valve on the calculation paper as shown in Fig. 1.5. On line (4) note the measured thickness of the shim then add or deduct the difference from line (2) to give the final shim thickness required on line (5).

18 Shims are available in thicknesses between 2.225 mm and 3.025 mm in steps of 0.025 mm, and between 3.100 mm and 3.550 mm in steps of 0.075 mm. Clean new shims before measuring or fitting them.

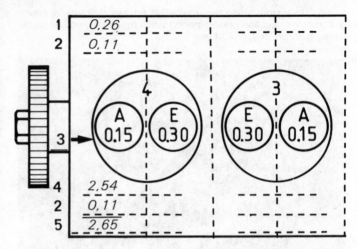

Fig. 1.5 Example of valve shim thickness calculation (Sec 8)

19 Repeat the procedure given in paragraphs 15 to 17 on the remaining valves keeping each tappet identified for position.

20 When reassembling, oil the shim and fit it on the valve stem first with the size marking facing downwards then oil the bucket tappet and lower it onto the shim. Do not raise the tappet after fitting as the shim may become dislodged.

21 When all the tappets are in position with their shims, refit the camshaft with reference to Section 7, but recheck the clearances to make sure they are correct.

9 Cylinder head – removal and refitting

1   On Visa models apply the handbrake. On BX models chock the rear wheels and release the handbrake.

2   On manual gearbox models jack up the front right-hand corner of the vehicle until the wheel is just clear of the ground. Support the vehicle on an axle stand and engage 4th or 5th gear so that the engine may be rotated by turning the right-hand wheel. On automatic transmission models use an open-ended spanner on the crankshaft pulley bolt.

3   Drain the cooling system as described in Chapter 2.

4   Disconnect the battery negative lead.

5   Remove the air cleaner as described in Chapter 3.

6   Support the weight of the engine using a hoist or trolley jack.

7   Unscrew the nuts and remove the right-hand engine mounting bracket.

8   Pull up the special clip, release the spring clips and withdraw the two timing cover sections.

9   Turn the engine by means of the front right-hand wheel or crankshaft pulley bolt until the three bolt holes in the camshaft and injection pump sprockets are aligned with the corresponding holes in the engine front plate.

10 Insert an 8.0 mm diameter metal dowel rod or a drill through the special hole in the left-hand rear flange of the cylinder block by the starter motor, then carefully turn the engine either way until the rod enters the TDC hole in the flywheel (see photo 23.26).

11 Insert three M8 bolts through the holes in the camshaft and injection pump sprockets and screw them into the engine front plate fingertight.

12 Loosen the timing belt tensioner pivot nut and adjustment bolt, then turn the bracket anti-clockwise to release the tension and retighten the pivot nut to hold the tensioner in the released position. If available use a ⅜ inch square drive extension in the hole provided to turn the bracket against the spring tension.

13 Remove the timing belt from the camshaft sprocket and tie it to one side without bending it excessively.

14 Unscrew the M8 bolt holding the camshaft sprocket in the timing position. Also unscrew the tensioner adjustment bolt, and the two upper bolts from the engine mounting bracket.

15 At this stage the right-hand engine mounting bracket may be temporarily refitted and the hoist or trolley jack removed.

16 Disconnect the heater hose from the flywheel end of the cylinder head.

17 Disconnect the two small hoses from the thermostat housing then unbolt the housing from the cylinder head and position it to one side.

18 Remove the oil filler cap/breather and position it to one side.

19 On BX models disconnect the air inlet hose from the inlet manifold.

20 Loosen the pivot and adjustment bolts of the hydraulic high pressure pump (BX models), or vacuum pump (Visa models), swivel the unit upwards, and disconnect the drivebelt from the pulleys.

21 Disconnect the crankcase ventilation hose from the valve cover.

22 Unbolt and remove the valve cover. Remove the gasket.

23 Unscrew the union nuts securing the injection pipes to the injectors and fuel injection pump, and remove the pipes as two assemblies.

24 Unbolt the left-hand engine lifting bracket.

25 Disconnect the wiring from the glow plugs.

26 Disconnect the fuel return pipes from the injection pump.

27 Hold the camshaft stationary with a spanner on the special lug between the 3rd and 4th cams or by using a lever in the sprocket holes, then unscrew the camshaft sprocket bolt and withdraw the sprocket. Recover the Woodruff key if it is loose. Do not rotate the camshaft otherwise the valves will strike the pistons of Nos 1 and 4 cylinders. If necessary release the timing belt from the injection pump sprocket and turn the engine one quarter turn in either direction to position all the pistons halfway down the cylinders in order to prevent any damage.

28 Unscrew the exhaust manifold to downpipe bolts. Recover the springs.

29 Progressively unscrew the cylinder head bolts in the reverse order to that shown in Fig. 1.8. Remove the washers.

30 Release the cylinder head from the cylinder block and location dowel by rocking it. The Citroën tool for doing this consists simply of two metal dowel rods with 90° angled ends (Fig. 1.6).

31 Lift the cylinder head from the block and remove the gasket.

32 Do not dispose of the old gasket until a new one has been obtained. The correct thickness of gasket is determined after measuring the protrusion of the pistons at TDC.

33 Clean the gasket faces of the cylinder head and cylinder block, preferably using a soft blunt instrument to prevent damage to the mating surfaces. Clean the threads of the cylinder head bolts and the corresponding holes in the cylinder block.

34 Check that the timing belt is clear of the injection pump sprocket, then turn the engine until pistons 1 and 4 are at TDC. Position a dial

Fig. 1.6 Removing the cylinder head using angled dowel rods (Sec 9)

9.34 Checking the piston protrusion

test indicator on the cylinder block and zero it on the block face. Transfer the probe to the centre of piston 1 then slowly turn the crankshaft back and forth past TDC noting the highest reading on the indicator (photo). Record this reading.

35 Repeat this measurement procedure on piston 4 then turn the crankshaft half a turn (180°) and repeat the procedure on pistons 2 and 3.

36 If a dial test indicator is not available, piston protrusion may be measured using a straight-edge and feeler blades or vernier calipers, however, these methods are inevitably less accurate and cannot therefore be recommended.

37 Ascertain the greatest piston protrusion measurement and use this to determine the correct cylinder head gasket from the following chart:

Piston protrusion	Gasket identification
0.54 to 0.65 mm (0.021 to 0.026 in)	1 notch or 1 hole
0.65 to 0.77 mm (0.026 to 0.030 in)	2 notches or 2 holes
0.77 to 0.82 mm (0.030 to 0.032 in)	3 notches or 3 holes

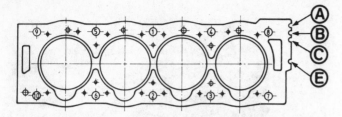

Fig. 1.7 Head gasket thickness identification notches (Sec 9)

A = 1.49 mm (0.059 in)
A + B = 1.61 mm (0.063 in)
A + B + C = 1.73 mm (0.068 in)
E = 1.7 engine identification

9.39 Cylinder head gasket identification notches (arrowed)

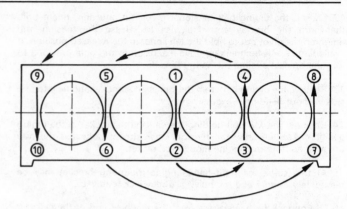

Fig. 1.8 Cylinder head bolt tightening sequence (Sec 9)

Note that the notch on the centre line of the gasket (Fig. 1.7) identifies the gasket for use only on the 1.7 engine (type XUD 7) and has no significance for the gasket thickness.

38 Turn the crankshaft clockwise (viewed from the timing belt end) until pistons 1 and 4 pass bottom dead centre (BDC) and commence to rise, then position them halfway up their bores. Pistons 2 and 3 will also be at their mid-way positions, but descending their bores.

39 Fit the correct gasket the right way round on the cylinder block with the identification notches or holes at the flywheel/driveplate end (photo). Make sure that the location dowel is in place at the timing end of the block.

40 Lower the cylinder head onto the block.

41 Grease the threads and contact faces of the cylinder head bolts, then insert them, together with their washers, and tighten them in the sequence shown in Fig. 1.8 in three stages as given in Specifications.

42 Recheck the valve clearances with reference to Section 8 and adjust them as necessary. Do this even if the clearances have been adjusted with the cylinder head removed, as there may be minor differences.

43 Lubricate the exhaust manifold-to-downpipe contact surfaces with heat resistant grease, then reconnect them and fit the bolts, together with the springs, cups and self-locking nuts. On 1.9 engines the bolts incorporate a shoulder to ensure that the springs are compressed correctly, however, on 1.7 engines, tighten the nuts progressively until approximately four threads are visible and the springs are compressed to 22.0 mm (0.866 in) in length.

44 Check that the Woodruff key is in place on the camshaft then fit the camshaft sprocket and bolt. Tighten the bolt to the specified torque while holding the camshaft stationary with a spanner on the special lug between the 3rd and 4th cams.

45 Turn the camshaft until the tips of cams 4 and 6 (counting from the flywheel end) are facing downwards.

46 Turn the crankshaft a quarter turn clockwise until pistons 1 and 4 are at TDC, and fit the TDC dowel rod to the flywheel. Do not turn the crankshaft anti-clockwise otherwise pistons 2 and 3 will pass their TDC positions and will strike valves 4 and 6.

47 Align the hole and refit the M8 timing bolt to the camshaft sprocket.

48 Refit the valve cover, together with a new gasket.

49 Apply locking fluid to the threads then refit and tighten the two upper bolts to the right-hand engine mounting bracket. Also refit the tensioner adjustment bolt and tighten it. Loosen the tensioner pivot nut.

50 Refit and adjust the timing belt with reference to Section 4, paragraphs 20 to 25.

51 Reconnect the fuel return pipes to the injection pump.

52 Reconnect the glow plug wiring.

53 Refit the left-hand engine lifting bracket.

54 Refit the injection pipes and tighten the union nuts.

55 Reconnect the crankcase ventilation hose to the valve cover.

56 Locate the drivebelt on the camshaft pulley and hydraulic pump (BX models), or vacuum pump (Visa models), pulley. Press the pump downwards until the deflection of the belt midway between the two pulleys is approximately 5.0 mm (0.2 in) under firm thumb pressure. Tighten the adjustment bolt followed by the pivot bolt.

57 On BX models reconnect the air inlet hose to the inlet manifold.

58 Refit the oil filler cap/breather.

59 Clean the thermostat housing mating faces then refit it, together with a new gasket, and tighten the bolts. Refit the two small hoses.

60 Reconnect the heater hose to the cylinder head.

61 Refit the timing cover sections.

62 Refit the right-hand engine mounting bracket and tighten the nuts. Remove the hoist or trolley jack.

63 Refit the air cleaner (Chapter 3).

64 Reconnect the battery negative lead.

65 Refill the cooling system (Chapter 2).

66 Lower the vehicle to the ground.

67 Run the engine at 3000 rpm for 10 minutes then switch off the ignition and let the engine cool for at least $3^1/2$ hours.

68 Remove the filler cap from the cooling system expansion tank to release any remaining pressure, then refit it.

69 Working on each cylinder head bolt in turn in the correct sequence first loosen the bolt 90° then retighten to the final torque given in the Specifications (photo).

9.69 Retightening the cylinder head bolts

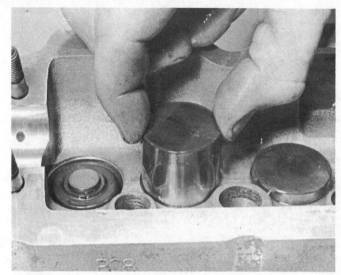

10.2 Removing the bucket tappets

10 Cylinder head – dismantling, overhaul and reassembly

1 With the head removed as described in the previous Section remove the camshaft with reference to Section 7.

2 Withdraw the bucket tappets, together with their respective shims, keeping them all identified for location (photo).

3 Disconnect the remaining leak off pipes and unscrew the injectors. Remove the special washers.

4 Disconnect the wiring and unscrew the glow plugs.

5 Unscrew the nuts and bolts, and remove the inlet and exhaust manifolds from the cylinder head. Remove the exhaust manifold gaskets.

6 Using a valve spring compressor, depress one valve spring retainer to gain access to the collets. The valves are deeply recessed, so the end of the compressor may need to be extended with a tube or box section with a 'window' for access. Remove the collets and release the compressor. Recover the retainer, large and small valve springs, and the spring seat, then withdraw the valve from the cylinder head. (photos). Repeat the procedure to remove the other seven valves, keeping each valve and components identified for position. Remove the timing probe blank if necessary.

7 Dismantling of the cylinder head is now complete. Refer to Section 11 for decarbonisation procedures.

10.6A Depress the retainer with a valve spring compressor and remove the collets, retainer, ...

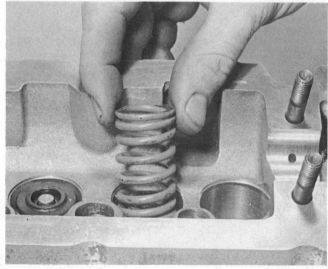

10.6B ... large valve spring ...

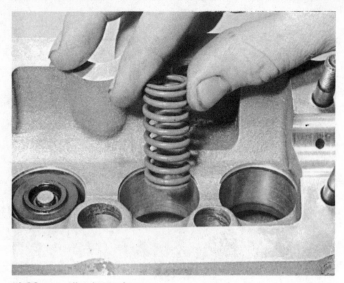

10.6C ... small valve spring ...

10.6D ... spring seat ...

10.6E ... and valve

Fig. 1.9 Checking the cylinder head for distortion (Sec 10)

8   Clean all the components and examine them for wear. Obtain new gaskets for the cylinder head, manifolds, valve cover and thermostat housing. Inspect the head for cracks or other damage.

9   Check the head gasket face for distortion (warp) using a straight-edge and feeler blades diagonally and along the edge (photo and Fig. 1.9). Do not position the straight-edge over the swirl chambers, as they may be proud of the cylinder head face. Distortion in excess of that specified may be corrected by machining ('skimming' within a specified limit. This is a specialist's job: the valve seats and swirl chambers must also be machined, and washers fitted under the valve springs. A head which cannot be reclaimed by machining, or any head in which the camshaft does not turn freely, must be renewed.

10   Inspect the valve seats and swirl chambers for burning or cracks (photo). Both can be renewed but the work should be entrusted to a specialist.

11   Using a dial test indicator check that the swirl chamber protrusion is within the limits given in the Specifications (photos).

12   Check each valve for straightness, freedom from burning or cracks, and for an acceptable fit in its guide. Excessive play in the guide may be caused by wear in either component; measure the valve stem with a micrometer, or try the fit of a new valve, if available, to establish whether it is the valve or the guide which is worn.

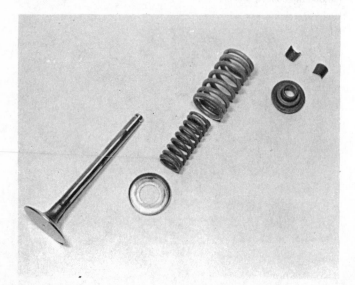

10.6F Valve components

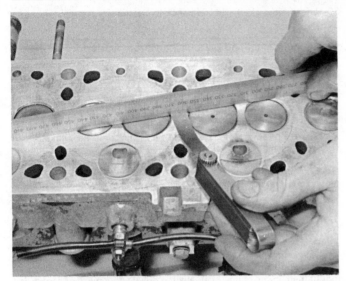

10.9 Checking the head gasket face for distortion

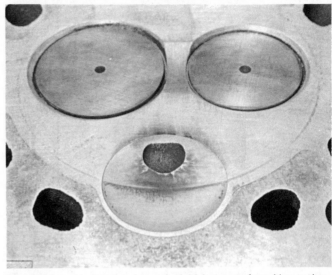

10.10 This swirl chamber shows the initial stages of cracking and burning

10.11A Zero the dial test indicator ...

13 The valve guides can be renewed, but this is a job for a specialist.

14 Minor surface pitting or carbon build-up on the valve heads and seats may be removed by grinding, but if refacing or recutting is required, consideration must be given to the final height of the valve head in relation to the cylinder head surface. A dial test indicator will be required to check that the valve head is within the specified limits (photo).

15 New or refaced valves and seats should be ground together as follows (the coarse paste may be omitted if the fit is already good).

16 Invert the head and support it securely. Smear a little coarse grinding paste around the sealing area of the valve head. Insert the valve in its guide and grind it to the seat using a valve grinding stick and rubber sucker. The stick is held between the hands and rotated first in one direction then in the opposite direction (photo). Lift the valve occasionally to redistribute the grinding paste.

10.11B ... then check the swirl chamber protrusion

10.14 Checking the valve head height

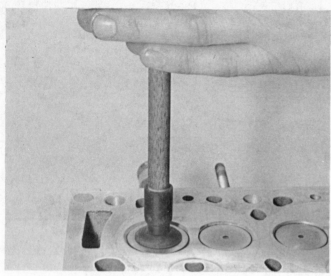

10.16 Grinding in the valves

17 Wipe the paste from the valve and seat occasionally to check progress. When the sealing faces are unbroken and all pitting is removed, repeat the procedure using fine grinding paste.

18 After all the valves have been ground in, clean away all traces of grinding paste, first with a paraffin-soaked rag then with clean dry rags, finally with compressed air if available. Do not overlook the valve guides. It will be obvious that even a small quantity of grinding paste remaining in the engine could cause extremely rapid wear.

19 Examine the valve springs for signs of fatigue and if possible compare their length with a new spring. It is worth renewing all the springs if the engine has completed a high mileage.

20 Examine the tappets and their bores for scoring or other damage.

21 Examine the camshaft bearing surfaces in the cylinder head and bearing caps. Also examine the camshaft with reference to Section 7.

22 Inspect the studs for the manifolds and camshaft bearing caps. Renew them if necessary by using a proprietary stud extractor, or lock two nuts together on the exposed threads. Studs which have come out by mistake should be cleaned up and refitted using thread locking fluid.

23 Commence reassembly by oiling a valve stem and inserting it into its guide. With the cylinder head on its side, fit the spring seat followed by the two springs (either way up) and the retainer.

24 Compress the springs with the compressor and fit the collets. A smear of grease on the collets will hold them in place on the valve stem groove. Carefully release the compressor and remove it.

25 Repeat the procedure to fit the other seven valves. Refit the timing probe blank if removed.

26 Refit the inlet and exhaust manifolds with new gaskets and progressively tighten the nuts.

27 Insert and tighten the heater plugs to the specified torque (Chapter 3). Reconnect the wiring.

28 Insert and tighten the injectors with their washers to the specified torque (Chapter 3). Reconnect the leak off pipes.

29 Oil and insert the bucket tappets, together with their respective shims, making sure that they are fitted in the correct locations, and with the size markings downwards. Make a note of the shim thickness fitted at each position, if not already done, for reference when checking the valve clearances.

30 Refit the camshaft with reference to Section 7.

11 Cylinder head and pistons – decarbonisation

1 With the cylinder head removed as described in Section 9, the carbon deposits should be removed from the valve heads and surrounding surfaces of the head. Use a blunt scraper or wire brush and take care not to damage the valve heads.

2 Where a more thorough job is to be carried out, the cylinder head should be dismantled as described in the previous Section so that the valves may be ground in and the parts cleaned, brushed and blown out after the manifolds have been removed. Also clean the manifolds, particularly the exhaust manifold where an accumulation of carbon is most likely.

3 Before grinding-in a valve, remove the carbon and deposits completely from its head and stem. With an inlet valve this is usually simply a matter of scraping off the carbon with a blunt knife and finishing with a wire brush. With an exhaust valve the deposits are much harder to remove. One method of cleaning valves quickly is to mount them in the chuck of an electric drill using a piece of card or foil to protect the surface of the stem. A scraper or wire brush may then be used carefully to remove the carbon.

4 An important part of the decarbonising operation is to remove the carbon deposits from the piston crowns. To do this, turn the crankshaft so that two pistons are at the top of their stroke and press some grease between these pistons and the cylinder walls. This will prevent carbon particles falling down into the piston ring grooves. Cover the other two bores and the cylinder block internal oil and water channels with newspaper taped down securely.

5 Using a blunt scraper remove all the carbon from the piston crowns, taking care not to score the soft alloy. Thoroughly clean the combustion spaces which are recessed in the piston crowns.

6 Remove the newspaper then rotate the crankshaft half a turn and repeat the cleaning operation on the remaining two pistons. Wipe away the grease from the top of the bores.

7 Finally clean the top surface of the cylinder block.

12 Oil seals – renewal

Note: *The procedures described here are for renewal with the engine in the vehicle – with the engine removed, the steps taken to gain access may be ignored.*

Camshaft (Timing belt end)
1 Follow the procedure given in paragraphs 1 to 12 of Section 5.

2 Remove the timing belt from the camshaft sprocket and tie it to one side without bending it excessively.

3 Unscrew the M8 bolt holding the camshaft sprocket in the timing position.

4 Hold the camshaft sprocket stationary using a suitable tool through two of the holes (Fig. 1.10). A tool may be made out of flat metal bar and two long bolts. Alternatively a strap wrench as used for removing oil filters may be used to hold the sprocket.

5 Unscrew the bolt and withdraw the sprocket from the camshaft. Do not rotate the camshaft otherwise the valves will strike the pistons of Nos 1 and 4 cylinders. Recover the Woodruff key if it is loose.

6 Pull out the oil seal using a hooked instrument.

7 Clean the oil seal seating.

8 Smear the lip of the new oil seal with oil then fit it over the end of the camshaft, open end first, and press it in until flush with the end face

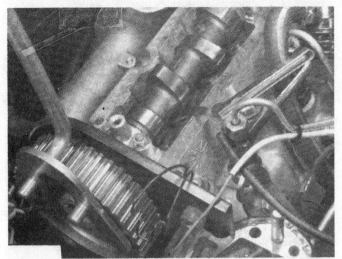

Fig. 1.10 Holding the camshaft sprocket stationary with the special tool (Sec 12)

12.8 Socket, bolt and washer for fitting the camshaft oil seals

16 Pull out the oil seal using a hooked instrument.

17 Clean the oil seal seating.

18 Smear the lip of the new oil seal with oil then fit it over the end of the camshaft, open end first, and press it in until flush with the end face of the cylinder head (photo). Use a bolt, washers and a suitable socket to press it in.

19 Refit the Woodruff key (if removed) and the pump pulley to the camshaft and tighten the centre bolt.

20 Locate the drivebelt on the camshaft pulley and pump pulley then press the pump downwards until the deflection of the belt midway between the two pulleys is approximately 5.0 mm (0.2 in) under firm thumb pressure. Tighten the adjustment bolt followed by the pivot bolt.

21 Refit the air cleaner.

22 Refit the inlet ducting.

12.18 Camshaft oil seal flush with the end face of the cylinder head

of the cylinder head. Use an M10 bolt, washers and a suitable socket to press it in (photo).

9 Fit the Woodruff key (if removed) and the camshaft sprocket to the camshaft, insert the bolt and tighten it while holding the camshaft stationary.

10 Refit the M8 timing bolt to the camshaft sprocket.

11 Refit and adjust the timing belt with reference to Section 4, paragraphs 20 to 25. The remaining procedure is a reversal of removal.

Camshaft (flywheel end)
12 Remove the air cleaner.

13 Remove the inlet ducting as necessary.

14 Loosen the pivot and adjustment bolts of the hydraulic high pressure pump (BX models), or vacuum pump (Visa models), swivel the unit upwards, and disconnect the drivebelt from the pulleys.

15 Unscrew the centre bolt and remove the pump pulley from the camshaft. If the centre bolt is very tight it will be necessary to remove the timing covers and hold the camshaft sprocket stationary while the bolt is loosened (to prevent damage to the timing belt). Recover the Woodruff key if it is loose.

Crankshaft (Timing belt end)
23 Remove the timing belt as described in Section 4.

24 Slide the timing belt sprocket from the crankshaft and recover the Woodruff key if it is loose.

25 Note the fitted depth then pull the oil seal from the housing using a hooked instrument. Alternatively drill a small hole in the oil seal and use a self-tapping screw to remove it.

26 Clean the housing and crankshaft then dip the new oil seal in engine oil and press it in (open end first) to the previously noted depth. A piece of thin plastic is useful to prevent damage to the oil seal (photo).

27 Refit the Woodruff key and timing belt sprocket.

28 Refit the timing belt with reference to Section 4.

Crankshaft (flywheel end)
29 Remove the flywheel/driveplate as described in Section 16.

30 Using vernier calipers measure the fitted depth of the oil seal and record it.

31 Pull out the oil seal using a hooked instrument. Alternatively drill a small hole in the oil seal and use a self-tapping screw to remove it.

12.26 Fitting the timing belt end oil seal to the crankshaft with a plastic protector

12.33 Fitting the flywheel end oil seal to the crankshaft with a plastic protector

2   Position a suitable container beneath the engine. Unscrew the drain plug and allow the oil to drain from the sump.

3   Wipe clean the drain plug and refit it.

4   On BX models unbolt the crossmember beneath the sump (photos).

5   Note the location of the sump bolts (see Fig. 1.16) then unscrew them.

6   Remove the sump and gasket (photo). The sump will probably be stuck in position in which case it will be necessary to cut it free using a thin knife.

7   Clean all remains of gasket from the sump and block and wipe dry.

8   Apply a little sealing compound where the front housing abuts the block on both sides.

9   Position a new gasket on the sump then lift the sump into position and insert the bolts in their correct locations.

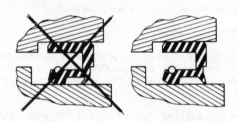

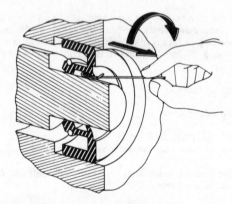

Fig. 1.11 Correct fitting of the crankshaft flywheel end oil seal (Sec 12)

32 Clean the oil seal seating and crankshaft flange.

33 Dip the new oil seal in engine oil, locate it on the crankshaft open end first, and press it in squarely to the previously noted depth using a suitable metal tube. A piece of thin plastic is useful to prevent damage to the oil seal (photo). When fitted note that the outer lip of the oil seal must point outwards; if it is pointing inwards use a piece of bent wire to pull it out (Fig. 1.11).

34 Refit the flywheel/driveplate with reference to Section 16.

13 Sump – removal and refitting

1   Chock the rear wheels then jack up the front of the car and support on axle stands.

13.4A Crossmember front bolt (arrowed) ...

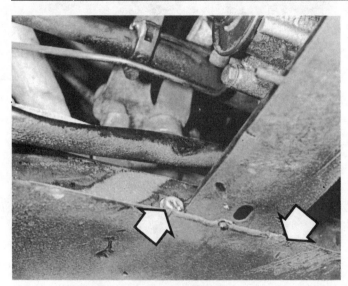

13.4B ... and rear bolts (arrowed) on BX models

6 Withdraw the L-shaped spacer from beneath the oil pump.

7 Remove the location dowel and disengage the oil pump sprocket from the chain. Withdraw the oil pump.

8 Remove the chain and sprocket from the nose of the crankshaft and recover the Woodruff key if it is loose.

9 Remove the six bolts which hold the two halves of the oil pump together. Separate the halves, being prepared for the release of the relief valve spring and plungers (photos).

10 If necessary remove the strainer by prising off the cap, then clean all components (photos).

11 Inspect the gears and the housings for wear and damage. Check the endfloat of the gears using a straight-edge and feeler blades, also check the clearance between the tip of the gear lobes and the housing (photos). If any of these clearances exceeds the specified limit, renew the pump. Note that with the exception of the relief valve spring and plunger, individual components are not available.

12 If the pump is to be renewed it is wise to renew the chain and the crankshaft sprocket also.

13.6 Removing the sump

14.9A Unscrew the oil pump bolts ...

10 Tighten the bolts evenly to the specified torque.

11 Refit the crossmember on BX models.

12 Lower the car to the ground and refill the engine with the correct quantity and grade of oil.

14 Oil pump – removal, inspection and refitting

1 Remove the timing belt as described in Section 4.

2 Slide the timing belt sprocket from the crankshaft and recover the Woodruff key if it is loose.

3 Remove the sump as described in Section 13.

4 Unscrew the bolts and remove the front oil seal housing. Remove the gasket.

5 Unscrew the three bolts securing the oil pump to the crankcase. Identify them for position as all three are of different lengths.

14.9B ... separate the halves ...

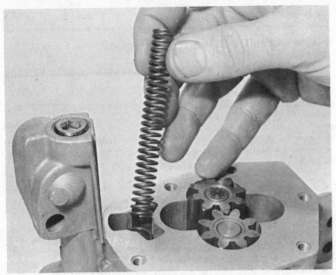

14.9C ... and remove the relief valve spring ...

14.9D ... and plunger

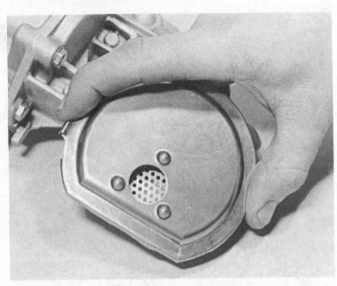

14.10A Removing the oil pump cap ...

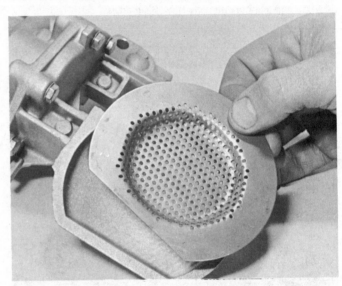

14.10B ... and strainer

14.11A Oil pump rotors and housing

14.11B Checking the rotor endfloat

14.11C Checking the rotor side clearance

13 Lubricate the gears with engine oil then reassemble the oil pump in reverse order and tighten the six bolts evenly to the specified torque.

14 Locate the Woodruff key on the nose of the crankshaft and refit the sprocket, teeth end first. Engage the chain with the sprocket.

15 Prise the oil seal from the front housing. Refit the housing to the cylinder block, together with a new gasket, and tighten the bolts evenly to the specified torque.

16 Fit a new oil seal to the housing with reference to Section 12.

17 Check that the location dowel is fitted to the block. Engage the oil pump sprocket with the chain and slide the L-shaped spacer into position, making sure that its open end engages the dowel.

18 Insert the bolts in their correct locations (Fig. 1.12). The longest bolt through the dowel and the next longest by the oil return hole. Tighten the bolts evenly to the specified torque (photo).

19 Refit the sump with reference to Section 13.

20 Refit the Woodruff key and timing belt sprocket.

21 Refit the timing belt with reference to Section 4.

Fig. 1.12 Oil pump mounting bolt locations (Sec 14)

A Longest bolt   B Next longest bolt

15 Pistons and connecting rods – removal and refitting

1 Remove the cylinder head as described in Section 9.

2 Remove the oil pump as described in Section 14.

3 If there is a pronounced wear ridge at the top of any bore, it may be necessary to remove it with a scraper or ridge reamer to avoid piston damage during removal. Such a ridge may indicate that reboring is necessary, which will entail new pistons in any case.

4 Check that each connecting rod and cap is marked for position and, if not, mark them with a centre punch on the oil filter side, number one at the flywheel end.

14.18 Tightening the oil pump mounting bolts

15.5 Removing a big-end bearing cap

5   Turn the crankshaft to bring pistons 1 and 4 to BDC (bottom dead centre). Unscrew the nuts from No 1 piston big-end bearing cap, then take off the cap and recover the bottom half bearing shell (photo).

6   Using a hammer handle push the piston up through the bore and remove it from the block. Loosely refit the shell bearings and cap to ensure correct reassembly.

7   Remove No 4 piston in the same manner then turn the crankshaft 180° to bring pistons 2 and 3 to BDC (bottom dead centre) and remove them.

8   If new piston rings are to be fitted to old bores, the bores must be deglazed to allow the new rings to bed-in properly. Protect the big-end journals by wrapping them in masking tape, then use a piece of coarse emery paper to produce a cross-hatch pattern in each bore. A flap wheel in an electric drill may be used, but beware of spreading abrasive dust. When deglazing is complete wash away all abrasive particles and unwrap the big-end journals.

9   Commence refitting by laying out the assembled pistons and rods in order, with the bearing shells, connecting rod caps and nuts.

10   Arrange the piston ring gaps 120° from each other.

11   Clean the bearing shells, caps and rods then press the shells into position so that the locating tangs engage in the grooves.

12   Oil the bores, pistons, crankpins and shells. Fit a piston ring compressor to No 1 piston. With Nos 1 and 4 crankpins at BDC insert No 1 piston in the bore nearest the flywheel, making sure that the clover leaf cut-out on the piston crown is towards the oil filter side of the engine.

13   Using a hammer handle tap the piston through the ring compressor and into the bore (photo). Guide the connecting rod onto the crankpin and fit the cap, together with its shell bearing, making sure it is the correct way round.

14   Fit the nuts and tighten them to the specified torque (photo). Turn the crankshaft to check for free movement.

15   Repeat the procedure to fit the other three pistons.

16   Refit the oil pump with reference to·Section 14.

17   Refit the cylinder head with reference to Section 9.

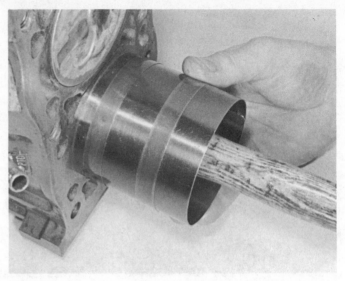

15.13 Using a hammer handle to tap the piston through the ring compressor

16 Flywheel/driveplate – removal and refitting

1   Either remove the engine and transmission and separate them (Sections 19, 20 and 21), or remove the transmission alone as described in the appropriate manual for petrol-engined vehicles.

2   On manual transmission models make alignment marks then slacken the clutch pressure plate bolts progressively and remove the pressure plate and driven plate (photo).

3   Hold the flywheel/driveplate stationary with a screwdriver or suitable bar inserted between the teeth of the starter ring gear and the transmission location dowel, then unscrew and remove the bolts and lift the flywheel/driveplate from the crankshaft. Alignment marks are not required as there is a location dowel on the crankshaft flange. Obtain new bolts for reassembly.

4   Commence refitting by cleaning the mating surfaces of the crankshaft and flywheel/driveplate.

15.14 Tightening the big-end bearing cap nuts

16.2 Removing the clutch pressure plate and driven plate

16.6A Apply locking fluid to the flywheel bolts ...

16.6B ... and tighten them to the specified torque

17.2 Right-hand engine mounting bracket (BX models)

5   Locate the flywheel/driveplate on the crankshaft dowel.

6   Apply locking fluid to the threads of the bolts, insert them, and tighten them to the specified torque while holding the flywheel/driveplate stationary (photos).

7   On manual transmission models refit the clutch driven and pressure plates.

8   Refit the transmission and the engine, if removed.

17 Engine/transmission mountings – removal and refitting

Right-hand mounting
1   Support the engine with a hoist or with a trolley jack and block of wood beneath the sump.

2   Unscrew the nuts and remove the right-hand mounting bracket (photo).

3   Unscrew the lower mounting nut from under the right-hand front wing. Also unscrew the rubber stop nuts and remove the stops, noting the location of any shims.

4   Refitting is a reversal of removal but tighten all nuts to the specified torque. With the weight of the engine on the mounting, the clearance between the mounting bracket and each rubber stop should be 1.0 ± 0.7 mm (0.04 ± 0.03 in). If necessary adjust the clearance by means of shims positioned under the stops.

Left-hand mounting
5   Support the transmission with a hoist or with a trolley jack and block of wood.

6   Remove the air cleaner and trunking.

7   Remove the battery and battery tray.

8   Unscrew the nut and remove the rubber mounting. Also unscrew the nuts or bolts and remove the mounting bracket.

9   If necessary unscrew the mounting stud from the transmission casing.

10 Refitting is a reversal of removal, but before fitting the mounting stud, clean the threads and apply a little locking fluid. Tighten the nuts and bolts to the specified torque.

Lower mounting
11 Jack up the front of the car and support on axle stands.

12 Unscrew and remove both bolts from the torque link and withdraw the link (photos).

13 Drive or press the mounting from the housing.

14 Drive or press the new mounting into position then refit the torque link and tighten the bolts to the specified torque.

15 Lower the car to the ground.

17.12A Lower engine mounting and torque link (Visa models)

17.12B Lower engine mounting torque link (BX models) – top view with engine removed

18 Engine – methods of removal

1   The engine is removed together with the transmission by lifting upwards from the engine compartment. On BX models the engine and transmission are lifted at a very steep angle and a hoist with sufficient height will therefore be necessary.

2   It is possible to remove the transmission alone from under the vehicle, after which it would, in theory, be possible to remove the engine from above. However, this method is not recommended as it involves the extra work of disconnecting the transmission which, if required is best carried out with the engine and transmission removed from the vehicle.

19 Engine and transmission (Visa models) – removal

1   Remove the bonnet.

2   Apply the handbrake then jack up the front of the vehicle and support on axle stands.

3   Drain the cooling system as described in Chapter 2.

4   Unscrew the drain plug from the rear of the differential housing, drain the oil into a suitable container, then refit and tighten the drain plug.

5   Remove the bolts securing the front track control arms to the stub axle carriers.

6   Using a lever between the anti-roll bar and track control arm, lever the balljoints from the bottom of the stub axle carriers.

7   Have an assistant pull the left-hand wheel outwards while the left-hand driveshaft is levered from the differential side gear.

8   Loosen the two nuts retaining the right-hand driveshaft intermediate bearing in the bracket bolted to the rear of the cylinder block and turn the bolt heads through 90° in order to release the bearing.

9   Have an assistant pull the right-hand wheel outwards while the right-hand driveshaft is removed from the differential side gear.

10 Unbolt the intermediate bearing bracket from the cylinder block, also unscrew and remove the bolt securing the torque link to the underbody.

11 Tie the right-hand driveshaft and intermediate bearing bracket towards the rear.

12 Remove the battery and tray, and unbolt the support.

13 Drain the engine oil if required.

14 Remove the air cleaner, together with the inlet hoses and the hose to the oil separator.

15 Unscrew and remove the exhaust manifold-to-downpipe bolts, together with the springs and collars.

16 Disconnect the coolant hoses from the engine.

17 Unbolt the securing clamp and remove the cooling system expansion tank.

18 Disconnect the gearchange control rods (photo). Also disconnect the reverse cable where fitted.

19.18 Gearchange control rods (Visa models)

19 Disconnect the vacuum hose from the brake vacuum servo unit.

20 Refer to Chapter 5 and remove the brake master cylinder.

21 Disconnect the fuel supply and return hoses from the injection pump.

22 Disconnect the wiring from the following components:

(a) Starter motor
(b) Oil pressure switch
(c) Alternator
(d) Water temperature switch
(e) Glow plugs
(f) Stop solenoid on the injection pump
(g) Diagnostic socket
(h) Transmission earth cable
(i) Reverse lamp switch

23 Disconnect the speedometer cable from the transmission.

24 Disconnect the clutch cable.

25 Disconnect the accelerator cable from the injection pump.

26 Connect a hoist to the engine lifting brackets so that the engine and transmission may be lifted in a horizontal position. Take the weight of the assembly.

27 Unscrew the nuts and remove the right-hand engine mounting bracket.

28 Unscrew the nut from the left-hand engine mounting and remove the rubber mounting. Also unbolt the support bracket.

29 Position a piece of hardboard over the radiator to protect it when the engine is being removed.

30 Raise the engine and transmission assembly, making sure that the surrounding components in the engine compartment are not damaged. When clear of the front panel withdraw the assembly and lower it to the ground.

31 If the vehicle must be moved with the engine and transmission out, reconnect the track control arms and balljoints to the stub axle carriers and support the driveshafts with wire so that they can rotate without damage.

20.8 Front anti-roll bar link rod and nut

20.9 Removing the left-hand driveshaft

20 Engine and transmission (BX models) – removal

1 Remove the bonnet.

2 Chock the rear wheels and release the handbrake.

3 Jack up the front of the vehicle and support on axle stands. Remove the front wheels.

4 Place the ground clearance control to minimum height. Loosen the hydraulic pressure regulator release screw one and a half turns to release the pressure from the hydraulic system. Do not remove the screw otherwise the sealing ball will fall out.

5 Drain the cooling system as described in Chapter 2.

6 Unscrew the drain plugs from the gearbox and differential housing and drain the oil/fluid into a suitable container, then refit and tighten the drain plugs. Also drain the engine oil if required.

7 Unscrew the nut from the left-hand front suspension lower balljoint. Using a balljoint separator tool release the suspension arm.

8 Unscrew the nut from the top of the left-hand link rod for the front anti-roll bar, then lower the suspension arm (photo).

9 Have an assistant pull the left-hand wheel outwards while the left-hand driveshaft is levered from the differential side gear (photo).

10 On models manufactured before July 1984 the left-hand differential side gear must be supported using a suitable dowel, preferably wooden. If this precaution is not taken, the side gears may become misaligned when the right-hand driveshaft is removed.

11 Remove the right-hand driveshaft completely.

12 Unscrew and remove the exhaust manifold-to-downpipe bolts, together with the springs and collars (photo).

13 Disconnect the heater hoses from the engine and bulkhead (photo).

14 Disconnect the gearchange control rods, including the rearmost rod from the intermediate lever (photos). Turn both intermediate levers so that they are parallel with the steering gear. Disconnect the reverse cable where applicable.

20.12 Exhaust manifold-to-downpipe bolts, springs and collars

20.13 Heater hose connection at the bulkhead

20.14A Disconnecting the gearchange lower rod ...

20.14B ... upper rod ...

20.14C ... and rear rod (BX models)

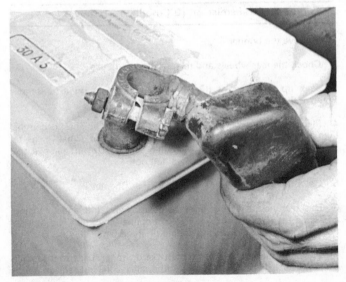

20.15A Disconnecting the battery leads

20.15B Removing the battery clamp

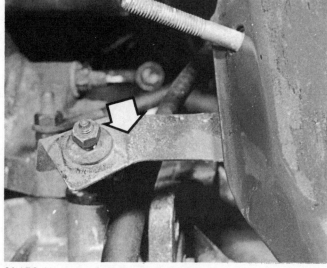

20.15C Air cleaner supporting lug (arrowed)

20.16 Disconnecting the top hose from the thermostat housing

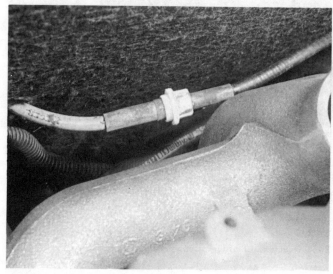

20.18 Speedometer cable connection at the bulkhead

15 Remove the battery, air cleaner and the supporting lug (photos).

16 Remove the radiator as described in Chapter 2, and disconnect the top hose from the thermostat housing (photo).

17 Disconnect the clutch cable and recover the pushrod.

18 Disconnect the speedometer cable at the bulkhead (photo).

19 Disconnect the battery earth cable from the gearbox (photo).

20 Disconnect the accelerator cable from the injection pump.

21 Pull apart the wiring connectors located beneath the battery support bracket (photo).

22 Disconnect the supply wiring from No 2 glow plug.

23 Where applicable disconnect the tachometer wiring from the harness.

24 Disconnect the fuel supply and return hoses from the injection pump (photo).

25 Unbolt and remove the fuel filter.

26 Disconnect the high pressure pump suction pipe and the return pipe from the fluid reservoir and plug the open holes to prevent the ingress of dust and dirt. Release the pipe from the clip (photo).

27 On manual steering models disconnect the fluid return pipe from the pressure regulator, also disconnect the coiled fluid supply pipe and release it from the clips (photo). Plug all pipe ends.

28 On power steering models disconnect the overflow return pipe from the pressure regulator, also disconnect the fluid supply pipe from the output distributor. Unbolt the pressure regulator and output distributor and tie the assembly to the electric cooling fan.

29 Connect a hoist to the engine lifting brackets so that the engine and transmission assembly will assume an angle of 45° when lifted (with the engine uppermost). Take the weight of the assembly.

20.19 Battery earth cable on the gearbox

20.21 Engine harness wiring connectors beneath the battery support bracket

20.24 Injection pump fuel supply hose (arrowed)

20.26 Hydraulic pipe retaining clip (BX models)

20.27 Hydraulic pressure regulator (arrowed) with return pipe port plugged (BX models)

20.30 Engine lower mounting and torque link (BX models)

30 Unscrew and remove the front bolt from the torque link beneath the engine (photo).

31 Unscrew the nut from the left-hand engine mounting and remove the rubber mounting (photo). To prevent the mounting stub subsequently falling below the mounting bracket it is advisable though not essential to position a loose fitting metal plate on the stud and refit the nut.

32 Unscrew the nuts and remove the right-hand engine mounting bracket.

33 Place a piece of hardboard over the hydraulic height corrector to the right of the torque link in order to protect the dust cover (photo).

34 Raise the engine and transmission assembly, making sure that the surrounding components in the engine compartment are not damaged (photo). When clear of the front panel withdraw the assembly and lower it to the ground.

20.31 Left-hand engine mounting (BX models)

20.33 Protect the hydraulic height corrector with a piece of hardboard

35 If the vehicle must be moved with the engine and transmission out, reconnect the left-hand front suspension lower balljoint, also temporarily refit the right-hand driveshaft. Support the driveshafts with wire so that they can rotate without damage. Note that the wheel bearings can be damaged if the vehicle is moved without the driveshafts in position.

21 Engine and transmission – separation

1 With the engine and transmission removed from the vehicle clean away all external dirt.

2 Slacken the bolts and remove the TDC sensor (photo). Remove the bolts and withdraw the sensor holder.

20.34 Lifting the engine and transmission assembly – note the support plate (arrowed) for the left-hand mounting

21.2 Removing the TDC sensor

3   Disconnect the wiring and unbolt the starter motor using a hexagon key. Also disconnect the wiring from the reversing lamp switch (photo).

4   Unbolt the bottom cover from the transmission (photo).

5   On automatic transmission models unscrew the bolts securing the torque converter to the driveplate. Turn the engine as required to bring the bolt heads into view.

6   Note the location of the hydraulic pressure pump (BX) or vacuum pump (Visa), the coolant tube, the hydraulic line, and the transmission retaining bolts. The pump adjustment link is attached to an extended hexagon, and the rearmost transmission bolt has a socket head (photos).

7   Remove the drivebelt and unbolt the hydraulic pressure pump or vacuum pump bracket. Where applicable unbolt the bracket for the hydraulic line (photos).

8   Support the engine then unscrew the bolts and lift the transmission from the engine. On automatic transmission models make sure that the torque converter is kept in full engagement with the transmission. On BX models the hydraulic pressure regulator may remain attached to the transmission.

21.3 Reversing lamp switch and wiring

21.4 Transmission bottom cover

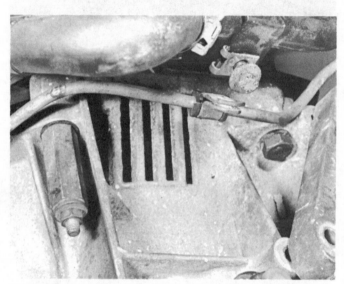

21.6A Extended hexagon for pump adjustment link (BX models)

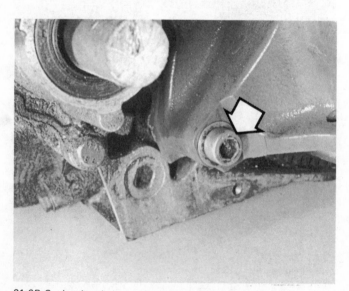

21.6B Socket-headed rear transmission bolt (arrowed)

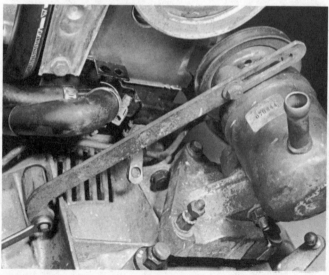

21.7A Removing the hydraulic pressure pump (BX models)

21.7B Hydraulic line and bracket (BX models)

23.2A Removing the front timing cover section ...

22 Engine dismantling – general

1   Clean the engine thoroughly using a water-soluble grease solvent or similar product. Keep dirt and water out of vulnerable components such as the fuel injection pump and the alternator.

2   When possible the engine should be dismantled on a workbench or strong table. If an engine dismantling stand is available, so much the better. Avoid working directly on a concrete floor, as grit presents a serious problem. If there is no alternative to working on the floor, cover it with an old piece of lino or carpet.

3   As well as the usual selection of tools, have available some wooden blocks for propping up the engine. A notebook and pencil will be needed, as will a couple of segmented boxes or a good supply of plastic bags and labels.

4   A waterproof marker pen is useful for making alignment marks without recourse to punches or chisels, however, take care that the marks are not erased during cleaning.

5   Whenever possible, refit nuts, washers etc to the components from which they were removed. This makes reassembly much simpler.

6   Spills of oil, fuel and coolant are bound to occur during dismantling. Have rags and newspapers handy to mop up the mess.

7   Do not throw away old gaskets immediately, but save them for comparison with new ones or for use as patterns if new gaskets have to be made.

23.2B ... and the rear timing cover section

23 Engine – complete dismantling

1   If not already done, drain the engine oil.

2   Pull up the special clip, release the spring clips, and withdraw the two timing cover sections (photos).

3   Disconnect the wiring from the following components and identify each wire for location:

    (a) Alternator
    (b) Oil pressure switch
    (c) Diagnostic socket (if fitted) (photo)
    (d) Temperature sensor(s) (photo)
    (e) Oil level sensor

23.3A Diagnostic socket wiring connector

23.3B Temperature sensors and wiring

23.4 Diagnostic socket and mounting bolt

23.5 Removing the pump pulley from the flywheel end of the camshaft

4   Unbolt and remove the diagnostic socket and bracket where fitted (photo).

5   Unscrew the bolt and withdraw the pump pulley from the flywheel end of the camshaft (photo). If it is tight due to corrosion, use a two or three-legged puller to remove it. Recover the Woodruff key.

6   Note the location of the fuel pipes from the injection pump to the injectors then unscrew the union nuts and remove the pipe assemblies. Cover the pipe ends, the injectors and the injection pump outlets to prevent entry of dust and dirt. Small plastic bags and elastic bands are ideal for this (photos).

7   Pull the leak-off hoses from the injectors.

8   Unbolt the engine lifting bracket from the cylinder head. Also unbolt the lower rear engine mounting bracket (photo).

9   Remove the alternator (Chapter 7) and bracket.

10 Unscrew the oil filter cartridge using a strap wrench if necessary.

11 On the 1.9 engine disconnect the hoses from the oil cooler. Unscrew the centre stud and remove the oil cooler from the block. Disconnect the oil cooler hoses.

12 Disconnect the bottom hose from the water pump inlet.

13 Disconnect the crankcase ventilation hoses from the valve cover and sump inlet. Remove the clip and slide the oil separator from the dipstick tube.

14 Remove the oil filler cap and ventilation hose if fitted.

15 Unscrew the bolts and remove the inlet manifold from the cylinder head. There are no gaskets.

16 Unscrew the nuts and withdraw the exhaust manifold and gaskets from the studs.

17 Slacken the bolt and remove the clamp from the end of the fast idle cable. Unscrew the locknut and remove the fast idle outer cable from the bracket on the injection pump.

18 Unscrew and remove the oil level sensor from the cylinder block (photos).

19 Unscrew and remove the oil pressure switch (photo).

20 Unbolt the thermostat housing from the cylinder head, complete with the fast idle thermo-unit and temperature sensor(s) (photos).

21 Unbolt the water pump inlet and remove the gasket. Also unbolt the coolant tube from the cylinder block (photos).

22 Unscrew the nuts securing the inlet bracket to the sump. Remove the bracket and gasket (photos).

23 Have an assistant hold the flywheel/driveplate stationary with a screwdriver or suitable bar inserted between the teeth of the starter ring gear and the transmission location dowel, then unscrew the crankshaft pulley bolt. Slide the pulley from the front of the crankshaft (photo).

24 Unbolt the bottom timing cover (photo).

25 Turn the engine by the flywheel/driveplate until the three bolt holes in the camshaft and injection pump sprockets are aligned with the corresponding holes in the engine front plate.

26 Insert an 8.0 to 8.5 mm diameter metal dowel rod or twist drill through the special hole in the left-hand rear flange of the cylinder block then carefully turn the engine either way until the rod enters the TDC hole in the flywheel/driveplate (photo).

23.6A Fuel pipe locations (arrows)

23.6B Small plastic bags can be used to protect the injectors from dust and dirt

23.8A Engine lifting bracket

23.8B Lower rear engine mounting bracket – also supports right-hand driveshaft

23.18A Oil level sensor location in the cylinder block. Coolant drain plug (arrowed) is adjacent

23.18B Removing the oil level sensor

23.19 Removing the oil pressure switch

23.20A Unscrew the bolts ...

23.20B ... and remove the thermostat housing

23.21A Removing the water pump inlet

23.21B Coolant tube mounting on the rear of the cylinder block

23.21C Coolant tube mounting on the front of the cylinder block

23.22A Unscrew the nuts ...

23.22B ... and remove the inlet bracket ...

23.22C ... and gasket

23.23 Removing the crankshaft pulley

23.24 Bottom timing cover (arrowed)

23.26 Using a twist drill to enter the TDC hole in the flywheel

27 Insert three M8 bolts through the holes in the camshaft and injection pump sprockets and screw them into the engine front plate finger tight.

28 Loosen the timing belt tensioner pivot nut and adjustment bolt, then turn the bracket anti-clockwise to release the tension and retighten the adjustment bolt to hold the tensioner in the released position.

29 Mark the timing belt with an arrow to indicate its normal direction of turning then remove it from the camshaft, injection pump, water pump, and crankshaft sprockets.

30 Unbolt and remove the valve cover. Remove the gasket.

31 With the injection pump sprocket held stationary by the timing bolts, unscrew the central nut to release the sprocket from the pump shaft taper. Remove the timing bolts and the pump sprocket with its nut and puller, and recover the Woodruff key if it is loose (photos). The puller is incorporated in the sprocket by means of the plate bolted over the nut, and the nut has an outer shoulder which bears against the plate.

32 Similarly unscrew the bolt from the camshaft sprocket and withdraw the sprocket.

33 Slide the sprocket from the crankshaft and recover the Woodruff key if it is loose.

34 Unscrew the bolts and remove the water pump from the cylinder block. Remove the gasket.

35 Mark the injection pump in relation to the mounting bracket. Unscrew the nuts and bolt and withdraw the injection pump.

36 Unbolt and remove the mounting bracket (photo).

37 Unscrew the timing belt tensioner adjustment bolt and pivot nut. A tool may now be used to hold the tensioner plunger as described in Section 5 while the tensioner arm and roller is removed. However, it is possible to remove the arm and roller by keeping the arm pressed against the plunger (photo).

38 Remove the plunger and spring (photo).

39 Unscrew the bolts and remove the engine mounting bracket and the timing belt intermediate roller and bracket (photos).

40 Unbolt the engine front plate (photo).

41 Progressively unscrew the cylinder head bolts in the reverse order to that shown in Fig. 1.8. Remove the washers.

42 Release the cylinder head from the cylinder block and location dowel by rocking it. Lift the head from the block and remove the gasket.

43 Remove the clutch if applicable then hold the flywheel/driveplate stationary with a screwdriver or suitable bar inserted between the teeth of the starter ring gear and the transmission location dowel, then unscrew and remove the bolts and lift the flywheel/driveplate from the crankshaft.

44 Invert the engine and unbolt the sump. Remove the gasket.

45 Unscrew the three bolts securing the oil pump to the crankcase. Identify them for position as all three are of different lengths.

46 Withdraw the L-shaped spacer from beneath the oil pump (photo).

47 Remove the location dowel and disengage the oil pump sprocket from the chain. Withdraw the oil pump (photo).

48 Unscrew the bolts and remove the front oil seal housing (photo). Remove the gasket.

23.31A Unscrew the nut ...

23.31B ... and remove the injection pump sprocket

23.36 Injection pump mounting bracket

23.37 Removing the tensioner arm and roller

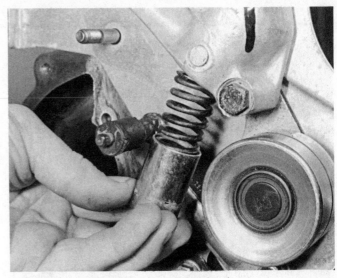

23.38 Removing the tensioner plunger and spring

23.39A Right-hand engine mounting bracket

23.39B Timing belt intermediate roller and bracket

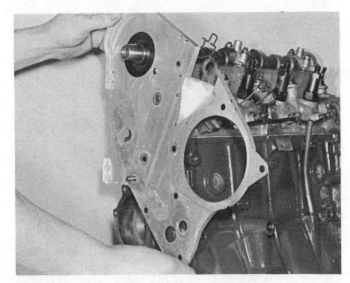

23.40 Removing the engine front plate

23.46 Withdrawing the oil pump spacer

23.47 Removing the oil pump

23.48 Removing the crankshaft front oil seal housing

23.49A Slide off the oil pump sprocket ...

23.49B ... and remove the Woodruff key

49 Remove the oil pump chain followed by the sprocket. Recover the Woodruff key if it is loose (photos).

50 Check that each connecting rod and cap is marked for position and, if not, mark them with a centre punch on the oil filter side, number one at the flywheel end.

51 Position the cylinder block either on its side or on the flywheel end.

52 Turn the crankshaft to bring pistons 1 and 4 to BDC (bottom dead centre). Unscrew the nuts from No 1 piston big-end bearing cap then take off the cap and recover the bottom half bearing shell.

53 Using a hammer handle push the piston up through the bore and remove it from the block. Loosely refit the shell bearings and cap to ensure correct reassembly.

54 Remove No 4 piston in the same manner then turn the crankshaft 180° to bring pistons 2 and 3 to BDC and remove them.

55 The main bearing caps should be numbered 1 to 5 from the flywheel end. If not mark them accordingly. Also note the fitted depth of the rear oil seal.

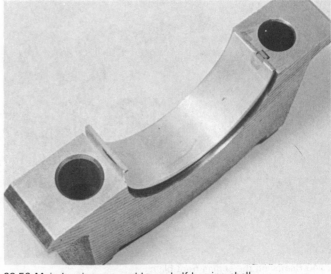

23.56 Main bearing cap and lower half bearing shell

23.57A Lift out the crankshaft ...

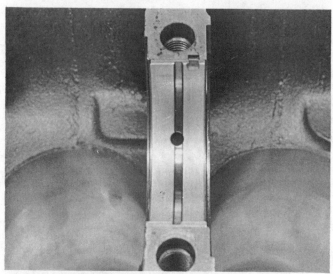

23.57B ... and remove the upper half bearing shells

56 Invert the engine then unbolt and remove the main bearing caps. Recover the lower half bearing shells keeping them with their respective caps (photo). Also recover the thrust washers.

57 Lift out the crankshaft. Discard the rear oil seal. Recover the upper half bearing shells and keep them together with their respective caps, however, identify them as the upper shells (photos). Also recover and identify the upper thrust washers.

24 Examination and renovation – general

1 With the engine completely dismantled, all components should be cleaned and examined as detailed in the appropriate Sections of this Chapter.

2 Most components can be cleaned with rags, a soft brush and paraffin, or some other solvent. Do not immerse parts with oilways in solvent since it can be very difficult to remove and if left will contaminate the oil. Clean oilways and water channels with a piece of wire and blow through with compressed air if available.

3 When faced with a borderline decision as to whether to renew a particular part, take into consideration the expected future life of the engine and the degree of trouble or expense which will be caused if the part fails before the next overhaul

4 If extensive overhauling is required, estimate the likely cost and compare it with the cost of a complete reconditioned engine. The difference may not be great, and the reconditioned engine will have a guarantee.

25 Engine components – examination and renovation

Cylinder block and bores

1 Check the cylinder block casting for any damage or cracking.

2 If necessary unscrew the two plugs from the rear of the block and from the flange beneath the oil filter location, and clean the oil gallery. Refit and tighten the plugs on completion. The water channels may be cleaned by removing the inspection plate from the rear of the block.

3 Check the core plugs for signs of leakage and if necessary renew them. It may be possible to remove the old plugs by drilling a small hole and using a self-tapping screw to pull them out. Alternatively, use a hammer to drive a chisel through the old plugs and prise them out. Clean the seating then apply a little sealing compound and tap the new plug into position with the flat face of a hammer. Spread the core plug by striking the centre with a ball face hammer.

4 If cracks in the block are suspected it may be necessary to have it crack-tested professionally. There are various ways of doing this, some involving special dyes and chemicals, some using ultrasonic or electromagnetic radiation.

5 Bore wear is indicated by a wear ridge at the top of the bore. For accurate assessment a bore micrometer is required, however, a rough measurement can be made by inserting feeler gauges between a piston (without rings) and the bore wall. Compare the clearance at the bottom of the bore, which should be unworn, with that just below the wear ridge. No wear limits are specified, but out-of-round or taper in excess of 0.1 mm (0.004 in) would normally be considered grounds for a rebore. Scuffs, scores and scratches must also be taken into account.

6 If reboring is undertaken the machine shop will normally obtain the oversize pistons and rings at the same time.

7 Where the degree of wear does not justify a rebore, the fitting of proprietary oil control rings may be considered.

Crankshaft and bearings

8 Check the crankshaft for damage or excessive wear.

9 Examine the bearing shells for wear and scratches on the working surfaces. New shells should be fitted in any case, unless the old ones are obviously in perfect condition and are known to have covered only a nominal mileage (photo). Refitting used shells is false economy.

25.9 Big-end bearing shell

10 Examine the bearing journals on the crankshaft for scoring or other damage, which if present will probably mean that regrinding or renewal is necessary. If a micrometer is available, measure the journals in several places to check for out-of-round and taper. No limits are specified but typically 0.025 mm (0.001 in) is the maximum acceptable.

11 Note that the crankshaft may already have been reground, and that the makers only specify one stage of regrinding.

12 Main and big-end bearing clearances can be measured using Plastigage thread. The journal and bearing shell are wiped dry before placing the thread across the journal. After tightening the bearing cap onto the Plastigage it is removed and a special gauge used to determine the running clearance. The makers do not specify any clearances but typically it would be between 0.025 and 0.050 mm (0.001 and 0.002 in).

13 Check the crankshaft endfloat using a feeler blade between the No 2 thrust washers and crankshaft web. If this is more than the specified amount obtain new thrust washers. Alternatively a dial gauge on the end of the crankshaft may be used for the check (photo).

25.13 Checking the crankshaft endfloat

Pistons, piston rings and connecting rods
14 The piston rings may be removed from each piston with the aid of some old feeler blades or similar thin metal strips. Carefully spread the top ring just far enough to slide the blades in between the ring and the piston, then remove the ring and blades together (photo). Be careful not to scratch the piston with the ends of the ring.

15 Repeat the process to remove the second and third rings, using the blades to stop the rings falling into the empty grooves. Note that the third ring incorporates an expander. Always remove the rings from the top of the piston. Keep each set of rings with its piston if the old rings are to be re-used.

16 Measure the end gaps of the rings by fitting them, one at a time, to their bores. Check the gaps with the rings either at the extreme top or bottom of the bores, where the wear is minimum, using feeler blades (photo).

17 If the rings are renewed the bores must be deglazed as described in Section 15.

18 Examine the pistons for damage, in particular for burning on the crown and for scores or other signs of 'picking-up' on the skirts and piston ring lands. Scorch marks on the sides show that blow-by has occurred.

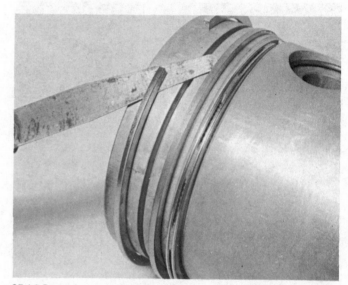
25.14 Removing the piston rings with an old feeler blade

19 If the pistons pass this preliminary inspection clean all the carbon out of the ring grooves using a piece of old piston ring. Protect your fingers – piston rings are sharp. Do not remove any metal from the ring grooves.

20 Roll each ring around its groove to check for tight spots. Any excessive clearance not due to worn rings must be due to piston wear and, unless the piston can be machined to accept special rings, renewal is required.

21 If renewing pistons without reboring make sure that the correct size is obtained. Piston class is denoted by either an 'A1' mark or no mark at all on the centre of the crown. The identical code appears also on the corner of the cylinder block at the timing belt end. The piston weight class is stamped on the crown and must be identical on all pistons in the same engine.

22 To separate a piston from its connecting rod, prise out the circlips and push out the gudgeon pin (photos). Hand pressure is sufficient to remove the pin. Identify the piston and rod to ensure correct reassembly.

23 Wear between the gudgeon pin and the connecting rod small-end bush can be cured by renewing both the pin and bush. Bush renewal, however, is a specialist job because press facilities are required and the new bush must be reamed accurately.

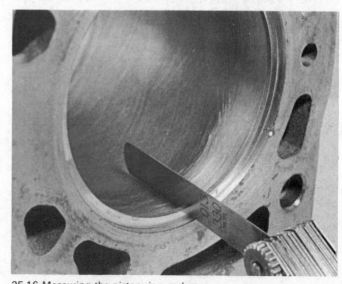
25.16 Measuring the piston ring end gaps

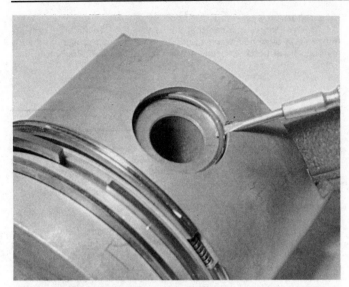
25.22A Prising out the gudgeon pin circlip

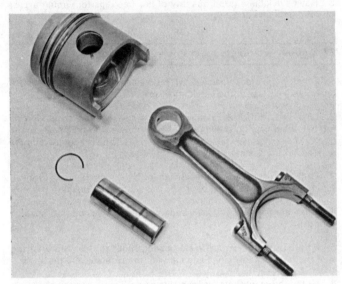
25.22B Piston and connecting rod components

24 New gudgeon pins and circlips are supplied when purchasing new pistons. The connecting rods themselves should not be in need of renewal unless seizure or some other major mechanical failure has occurred.

25 Reassemble the pistons and rods. Make sure that the pistons are fitted the right way round – the clover leaf cut-out on the crown must face the same way as the shell bearing cut-out in the connecting rod. Oil the gudgeon pins before fitting them (photos). When assembled, the piston should pivot freely on the rod.

26 Fit the piston rings using the same technique as for removal. Fit the bottom ring first and work up. When fitting the oil control ring first insert the expander then fit the ring with its gap positioned 180° from the expander's gap. Arrange the gaps of the upper two rings 120° either side of the oil control ring gap. Make sure that No 2 ring is fitted the correct way round (Fig. 1.14).

Oil pump
27 Refer to Section 14.

Timing belt and sprockets
28 Refer to Section 4 and also examine the sprockets for wear and damage.

Camshaft
29 Refer to Section 7.

Cylinder head
30 Refer to Section 10.

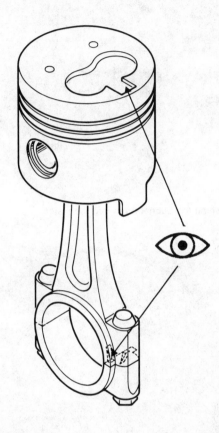
Fig. 1.13 Correct piston and connecting rod assembly (Sec 25)

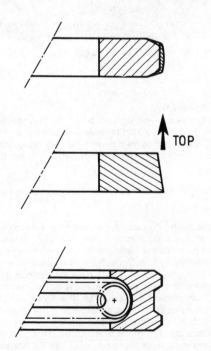
Fig. 1.14 Piston ring cross sections (Sec 25)

25.25A Pushing the gudgeon pin into the piston

25.25B Clover leaf cut-out on the piston crown

Flywheel/driveplate

31 Examine the clutch mating surface of the flywheel for scoring or cracks. Light grooving or scoring may be ignored. Surface cracks or deep grooving can sometimes be removed by specialist machining, provided not too much metal is taken off, otherwise the flywheel must be renewed.

32 Inspect the flywheel/driveplate for damage or cracks and renew it if necessary.

33 Inspect the starter ring gear for damaged or missing teeth. It is not possible to obtain a genuine Citroën ring gear separate from the flywheel/driveplate, and if damaged it may therefore be necessary to renew the complete flywheel/driveplate. However, some motor factors may be able to supply one, in which case the old ring gear should be drilled and split with a cold chisel to remove it. The new ring gear must be heated then quickly tapped onto the flywheel/driveplate and allowed to cool naturally. The temperature to which the ring gear must be heated is critical – too little heat and the ring gear may not fit or may even jam halfway on. Too much heat and the temper of the metal may be lost causing it to wear rapidly in use. The correct temperature is normally attached to the new ring gear, however, the average DIY mechanic may prefer to leave the job to a garage or engineering works.

Miscellaneous

34 The makers recommend that the flywheel/driveplate bolts only are renewed at overhaul, however, it would be prudent to also renew the cylinder head bolts especially if they have been tightened more than once.

26 Engine reassembly – general

1 Before commencing reassembly, make sure that all parts are clean and that the new components required have been obtained. A full set of oil seals and gaskets must be purchased – refer to Section 9 for selection of the correct head gasket.

2 Renew any nuts, bolts or studs with damaged threads.

3 A dial test indicator and stand (preferably magnetic) will be needed, also an oil can filled with clean engine oil to lubricate working parts as they are assembled.

4 Small quantities of grease, thread locking compound, anti-seize compound and various types of sealant will be called for.

5 Have available a good quantity of lint-free rags for wiping excess oil off hands and engine parts.

27 Engine – complete reassembly

1 Position the block upside down on the bench. Wipe clean the main bearing shell seats in the block and caps.

2 Wipe any protective coating from the new bearing shells. Fit the top half main bearing shells (with the oil grooves) to their seats in the block. Make sure that the locating tangs on the shells engage with the recesses in the seats.

3 Fit the thrust washers on each side of No 2 main bearing, grooved side outwards. Use a smear of grease to hold them in position (photo).

4 Lubricate the top half shells and lower the crankshaft into position (photo).

5 Fit the plain bottom half main bearing shells to their caps, making sure that the locating tangs engage with the recesses. Oil the shells.

6 Fit the thrust washers on each side of No 2 main bearing cap using a smear of grease to hold them in position.

7 Before fitting the caps check that the crankshaft endfloat is within the specified limits using a dial test indicator on the crankshaft nose.

8 Fit the main bearing caps Nos 2 to 5 to their correct locations (photo) and the right way round (the bearing shell tang locations in the block and caps must be on the same side). Insert the bolts loosely.

9 Apply a small amount of thread locking fluid to the No 1 main bearing cap face on the block around the sealing strip holes (photo).

10 Press the sealing strips in the grooves on each side of No 1 main bearing cap (photo). It is now necessary to obtain two thin metal strips of 0.25 mm (0.010 in) thickness or less in order to prevent the strips moving when the cap is being fitted. Citroën garages use the tool shown in Fig. 1.15 which acts as a clamp, however, metal strips can be used provided all burrs which may damage the sealing strips are first removed.

11 Oil both sides of the metal strips and hold them on the sealing strips. Fit the No 1 main bearing cap, insert the bolts loosely, then carefully pull out the metal strips with a pair of pliers in a horizontal direction (photos).

12 Tighten the main bearing bolts evenly to the specified torque (photo).

27.3 No 2 main bearing and thrust washers

27.4 Oiling the main bearing shells

27.8 Fitting No 5 main bearing cap

27.9 Applying thread locking fluid to the No 1 main bearing cap joint face

27.10 Sealing strips fitted to No 1 main bearing cap

Fig. 1.15 Using the special tool to fit No 1 main bearing cap (Sec 27)

27.11A Slide the No 1 main bearing cap and metal strips into position ...

27.11C ... then carefully pull out the metal strips

27.12 Tightening the main bearing bolts

27.11B ... insert the bolts ...

13 Check that the crankshaft rotates freely – there must be no tight spots or binding.

14 Dip the new rear oil seal in engine oil, locate it on the crankshaft open end first, and press it squarely to the previously noted depth using a metal tube slightly less than 102 mm (4.0 in) in diameter. A piece of thin plastic is useful to prevent damage to the oil seal (photo). Make sure that the outer lip of the oil seal points outwards and if necessary use a piece of bent wire to pull it out.

15 Position the cylinder block either on its side or on the flywheel end.

16 Lay out the assembled piston and rods in order with the bearing shells, connecting rod caps and nuts.

17 Check that the piston ring gaps are arranged 120° from each other.

18 Clean the bearing shells, caps and rods then press the shells into position so that the locating tangs engage in the grooves.

19 Oil the bores, pistons, crankpins and shells. Fit a piston ring compressor to No 1 piston. With Nos 1 and 4 crankpin at BDC insert No 1 piston in the bore at the flywheel end, making sure that the clover leaf cut-out on the piston crown is towards the oil filter side of the engine.

27.14 Fitting the crankshaft rear oil seal with a plastic protector

20 Using a hammer handle tap the piston through the ring compressor and into the bore. Guide the connecting rod onto the crankpin and fit the cap, together with its shell bearing, making sure it is the correct way round.

21 Fit the nuts and tighten them to the specified torque. Turn the crankshaft to check for free movement.

22 Repeat the procedure to fit the other three pistons.

23 Temporarily refit the pulley bolt to the nose of the crankshaft then, using a torque wrench, check that the torque required to turn the crankshaft does not exceed 41 Nm (30 lbf ft) (photo). Any excessive tightness must be investigated before proceeding.

24 Using feeler blades and a knife, cut the sealing strips on No 1 main bearing cap to 1.0 mm (0.040 in) above the sump gasket mating surface (photo).

25 Fit the Woodruff key to the groove in the crankshaft and refit the oil pump sprocket, teeth end first. Engage the chain with the sprocket and tie it up or to one side so that it remains engaged (photo).

26 Prise the oil seal from the front housing. Check that the two dowels are located in the front of the cylinder block then refit the front housing, together with a new gasket, and tighten the bolts evenly to the specified torque (photo).

27 Check that the dowel is fitted to the bottom of the block. Engage the oil pump sprocket with the chain and slide the L-shaped spacer under the pump, making sure that its open end engages the dowel.

28 Insert the oil pump bolts in their correct location, the longest bolt through the dowel and the next longest by the oil return hole. Tighten the bolts evenly to the specified torque.

29 Dip the front oil seal in engine oil then press it into the front housing until flush with the outer face.

30 Apply a little sealing compound where the front housing abuts the block on both sides. Position a new gasket on the block and refit the sump (photos). Note the correct location of the bolts as shown in Fig. 1.16. Tighten the bolts evenly to the specified torque. Remove the sump drain plug, renew the washer, then refit and tighten the plug.

31 Locate the flywheel/driveplate on the crankshaft dowel.

32 Apply locking fluid to the threads of the bolts, insert them, and tighten them to the specified torque while holding the flywheel/driveplate stationary with a screwdriver or suitable bar inserted between the teeth of the starter ring gear and the transmission location dowel.

33 Position the cylinder block upright on the bench.

34 Check that the cylinder head bolt holes in the block are clear preferably using a 12 x 150 tap (photo).

35 Locate the correct cylinder head gasket (see Section 9) in the block the right way round with the identification notches or holes at the flywheel/driveplate end. Check that the location dowel is fitted (photo)

36 Turn the crankshaft clockwise (from timing belt end) until pistons 1 and 4 pass BDC and commence to rise, then position them halfway up their bores. Pistons 2 and 3 will also be at their mid-way positions, but descending their bores. The Woodruff key groove on the nose of the crankshaft will be at the 9 o'clock position.

37 Check that the camshaft is set to TDC with the Woodruff key position facing upwards and the tips of cams 4 and 6 resting on the bucket tappets.

38 Lower the cylinder head onto the block (photo).

39 Grease the threads and contact faces of the cylinder head bolts,

then insert them and tighten them in the sequence shown in Fig. 1.8 in three stages as given in Specifications (photo).

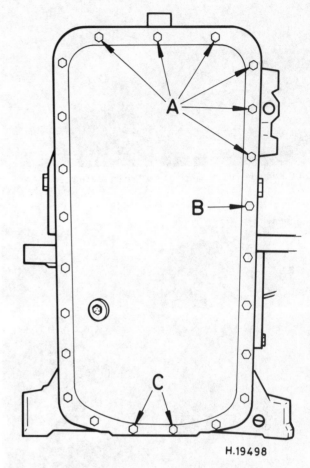

H.19498

Fig. 1.16 Sump bolt locations (Sec 27)

A   6 socket-head bolts
B   15 bolts (16 mm length)
C   2 bolts (14 mm length)

27.23 Checking the crankshaft turning torque

27.24 Cutting the sealing strips on No 1 main bearing cap

27.25 Fitting the chain to the oil pump sprocket

27.26 Tightening the front oil seal housing bolts

27.30A Apply sealing compound here ...

27.30B ... then fit the new sump gasket

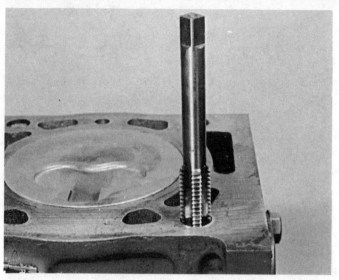

27.34 Cleaning the cylinder head bolt holes with a tap

27.35 Head gasket fitted to cylinder block with location dowel arrowed

27.38 Lowering the cylinder head onto the block

40 Recheck the valve clearances with reference to Section 8 and adjust them if necessary. Do this even if the clearances have been adjusted with the cylinder head removed as there may be minor differences.

41 Refit the engine front plate followed by the timing belt intermediate roller and bracket, and the engine mounting bracket. Tighten all the bolts. Do not forget the mounting bracket bolt on the inside face of the engine front plate (photo).

42 Insert the timing belt tensioner spring and plunger in the mounting bracket. Press the tensioner arm against the plunger and refit the bracket and roller onto the pivot stud. Alternatively compress the plunger with the tool described in Section 5. Fit the adjustment bolt and pivot nut, and tighten the bolt with the tensioner in the released position (ie spring compressed) (photos).

43 Refit the injection pump mounting bracket and tighten the bolts.

44 Refit the injection pump, align the previously made marks then tighten the nuts followed by the bolt.

45 Refit the water pump together with a new gasket and tighten the bolts to the specified torque (Chapter 2).

46 Locate the Woodruff key in the groove then slide the sprocket onto the front of the crankshaft (photo).

47 Fit the camshaft sprocket to the camshaft. Apply locking fluid to the threads then insert and tighten the bolt to the specified torque. The sprocket may be held stationary by fitting the timing bolt through the special hole (photo).

48 Unbolt the special puller from the injection pump sprocket. Check that the Woodruff key is in place then refit the sprocket and tighten the nut (photo).

49 Bolt the special puller onto the sprocket (photo).

50 Refit the valve cover, together with a new gasket, and tighten the bolts.

51 Insert the three M8 timing bolts through the holes in the camshaft and injection pump sprockets and screw them into the engine front plate fingertight.

52 Insert on 8.0 to 8.5 mm diameter metal dowel rod through the special hole in the left-hand rear flange of the cylinder block, then turn the crankshaft slowly clockwise (from the timing belt end) until the rod

27.39 Tighten the cylinder head bolts to the specified torque

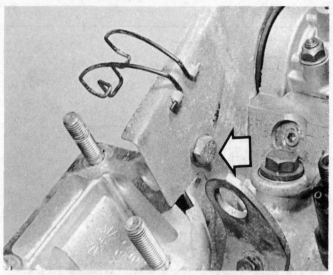

27.41 Inner bolt location for the engine mounting bracket (arrowed)

27.42A Turn the tensioner bracket anti-clockwise ...

27.42B ... and tighten the bolt to hold the tensioner in the released position

27.46 Fitting the sprocket to the crankshaft

27.47 Tightening the camshaft sprocket bolt with the timing bolt in position

27.48 Tightening the injection pump sprocket bolt with the timing bolts in position

27.49 Tightening the special puller to the injection pump sprocket

27.54A Fitting the timing belt over the injection pump sprocket ...

27.54B ... the camshaft sprocket ...

enters the TDC hole in the flywheel/driveplate. It is only necessary to turn the crankshaft a quarter turn as Nos 1 and 4 pistons are already halfway up their bores. Do not turn the crankshaft more than this otherwise pistons 2 and 3 will strike valves 4 and 6.

53 Locate the timing belt on the crankshaft sprocket making sure where applicable that the rotation arrow is facing the correct way.

54 Hold the timing belt engaged with the crankshaft sprocket then feed it over the roller and onto the injection pump, camshaft, and water pump sprockets and over the tensioner roller. To ensure correct engagement locate only a half width on the injection pump sprocket before feeding the timing belt onto the camshaft sprocket, keeping the belt taut and fully engaged with the crankshaft sprocket (photos). Locate the timing belt fully onto the sprockets.

55 With the pivot nut loose, slacken the tensioner adjustment bolt while holding the bracket against the spring tension, then slowly release the bracket until the roller presses against the timing belt. Retighten the adjustment bolt (photo).

56 Remove the bolts from the camshaft and injection pump sprockets. Remove the metal dowel rod from the cylinder block.

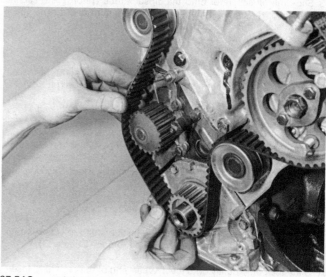

27.54C ... and the water pump sprocket

57 Rotate the engine two complete turns in its normal direction. Do not rotate the engine backwards as the timing belt must be kept tight between the crankshaft, injection pump and camshaft sprockets.

58 Loosen the tensioner adjustment bolt to allow the tensioner spring to push the roller against the timing belt, then tighten both the adjustment bolt and pivot nut.

59 Recheck the engine timing by turning the engine until the sprocket bolt holes are aligned, and check that the metal dowel rod can be inserted into the flywheel/driveplate.

60 Refit the bottom timing cover and tighten the bolts (photo).

61 Fit the pulley to the front of the crankshaft over the Woodruff key.

62 Apply locking fluid to the threads of the pulley bolt then insert it and tighten to the specified torque while an assistant holds the flywheel/driveplate stationary with a screwdriver inserted between the teeth of the starter ring gear and the transmission location dowel. Note that after tightening to the initial torque, the bolt must be angle tightened a further 60° which is the equivalent of one flat on the bolt head. Alternatively mark the flat extremities on the socket together with a starting datum on the pulley (photos).

63 Locate a new gasket on the side of the sump, refit the inlet bracket, and tighten the nuts evenly.

64 Refit the water pump inlet together with a new gasket and tighten the bolts.

65 Bolt the coolant tube to the cylinder block and fit the hoses.

66 Refit the thermostat housing, together with a new gasket, and tighten the bolts.

67 Insert the oil pressure switch in the block and tighten

68 Insert the oil level sensor and tighten.

69 Refit the fast idle cable to the injection pump with reference to Chapter 3.

70 Refit the exhaust manifold, together with new gaskets, and tighten the nuts evenly.

71 Refit the inlet manifold and tighten the bolts evenly. There are no gaskets.

72 Refit the oil filler cap and ventilation hose if fitted.

73 Slide the oil separator onto the dipstick tube (photo) and secure with the clip. Reconnect the crankcase ventilation hoses to the valve cover and sump inlet.

74 Reconnect the bottom hose to the water pump inlet.

75 On the 1.9 engine reconnect the oil cooler hoses and refit the oil cooler, tightening the centre stud to the specified torque (photos).

76 Smear a little engine oil on the sealing ring of the oil filter cartridge then refit it and tighten by hand only.

77 Refit the alternator (Chapter 7).

78 Refit the engine lifting bracket to the cylinder head, also refit the lower rear engine mounting bracket.

79 Reconnect the leak off hoses to the injectors.

80 Refit the fuel pipe assemblies to the injectors and injection pump and tighten the union nuts to the specified torque (Chapter 3).

81 Slide the pump pulley onto the flywheel end of the camshaft. Insert the bolt and tighten it to the specified torque (photo).

27.55 Tightening the tensioner adjustment bolt

27.60 Bottom timing cover fitted

27.62A Apply locking fluid to the crankshaft pulley bolt before fitting it

27.62B Tightening the crankshaft pulley bolt

27.62C Markings necessary in order to angle-tighten the crankshaft pulley bolt by 60°

27.73 Oil separator located on the dipstick tube (1.9 engine)

27.75A Oil cooler ...

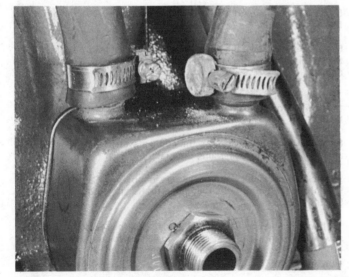

27.75B ... and coolant hose connections

27.81 Tightening the pump pulley bolt on the camshaft

82 Where applicable refit the diagnostic socket and bracket and tighten the bolt.

83 Reconnect the wiring harness to the following components:

  (a) Alternator
  (b) Oil pressure switch
  (c) Diagnostic socket (if fitted)
  (d) Temperature sensor(s)
  (e) Oil level sensor

84 Refit the two timing cover sections and press down the special clip and spring clips to secure.

85 Refit the clutch on manual transmission models.

28 Engine and transmission – reconnection

1 On automatic transmission models make sure that the torque converter is fully engaged with the transmission and remains so during the reconnection procedure.

2 Support the engine then lift the transmission into position. On manual transmission models turn the unit as required until the splined input shaft enters the clutch driven plate.

3 Push the transmission onto the location dowels and insert the bolts in their correct locations as previously noted. Tighten the bolts to the specified torque (Chapter 4).

4 Refit the hydraulic pressure pump or vacuum pump bracket and tighten the bolts. Refit the adjustment link. Slip the drivebelt over the pulleys then swivel the pump to tension the drivebelt and tighten the link bolt and pivot bolt. When correctly tensioned the belt deflection under firm thumb pressure mid-way between the pulleys should be approximately 5.0 mm (0.2 in).

5 Where applicable, refit the hydraulic line bracket and tighten the bolt.

6 On automatic transmission models align the driveplate and torque converter bolt holes, and insert and tighten the bolts.

7 Refit the bottom cover and tighten the bolts.

8 Refit the starter motor, tighten the bolts, and reconnect the wiring.

9 Refit the TDC sensor and holder and tighten the bolts. When the TDC sensor is fitted new it incorporates three legs which are 1.0 mm (0.04 in) long and these automatically set the sensor 1.0 mm from the flywheel/driveplate. When fitting an old sensor the legs should be filed off – the unit can then be fully inserted until it touches the flywheel/driveplate and then withdrawn by 1.0 mm (0.04 in) before tightening the bolts.

29 Engine and transmission (Visa models) – refitting

1 Reverse the procedure in Section 19 but note the following additional points:

  (a) Use a final drive oil seal protector (Chapter 4) when inserting the right-hand driveshaft. Remove the protector when the driveshaft is fitted
  (b) Refill the transmission and engine with oil
  (c) Adjust the accelerator and fast idle cables with reference to Chapter 3
  (d) Tighten the exhaust manifold-to-downpipe bolts with reference to Section 9, paragraph 43

  (e) Refit the engine/transmission mountings with reference to Section 17
  (f) Adjust the clutch cable
  (g) Refill the cooling system (Chapter 2)
  (h) Check the injection pump timing if necessary

30 Engine and transmission (BX models) – refitting

1 Reverse the procedure given in Section 20 but note the following additional points:

  (a) Use a final drive oil seal protector (Chapter 4) when inserting the right-hand driveshaft. Remove the protector when the driveshaft is fitted
  (b) Refill the transmission and engine with oil
  (c) Adjust the accelerator and fast idle cables with reference to Chapter 3
  (d) Refit the engine/transmission mountings with reference to Section 17
  (e) On manual transmission models adjust the clutch cable
  (f) Refill the cooling system (Chapter 2)
  (g) Prime the hydraulic high pressure pump as described in the BX petrol manual
  (h) Check the injection pump timing if necessary

31 Engine – initial start-up after overhaul

1 Check that the oil, coolant and fuel have all been replenished and that the battery is well charged.

2 On early models fitted with a Roto-Diesel fuel filter unscrew the pump plunger.

3 Switch on the ignition to energize the stop solenoid then actuate the pump on the fuel filter until resistance is felt. Retighten the plunger where necessary.

4 Fully depress the accelerator pedal, turn the ignition key to position 'M' and wait for the preheating warning light to go out.

5 Start the engine. Additional cranking may be necessary to bleed the fuel system before the engine starts.

6 Once started keep the engine running at a fast tickover. Check that the oil pressure light goes out, then check for leaks of oil, fuel and coolant.

7 If all is well, continue to run the engine at 3000 rpm for 10 minutes then switch off the ignition and let the engine cool for at least $3^{1/2}$ hours.

8 Remove the filler cap from the cooling system expansion tank to release any remaining pressure, then refit it.

9 Working on each cylinder head bolt in turn in the correct sequence first loosen the bolt 90° then retighten to the final torque given in the Specifications.

10 If many new parts have been fitted, the engine should be treated as new and run in at reduced speeds and loads for the first 600 miles (1000 km) or so. After this mileage it is beneficial to change the engine oil and oil filter.

11 Have the injection pump timing and idling speed checked and adjusted as described in Chapter 3.

32 Fault diagnosis – engine

Faults in the fuel injection system can produce noises suggesting bearing failure. To locate such a fault, slacken each injector union in turn with the engine running. The noise will disappear when the union on the faulty injector is slackened, however, to prove conclusively that the injector is faulty, fit it to another cylinder and carry out the test again. Air or other contaminants in the fuel can also cause knocking noises.

Symptom	Reason(s)
Engine will not turn over when starter switch is operated	Flat battery Battery connections corroded or loose Starter solenoid connections loose Engine/transmission earth cable loose or broken Starter motor defective
Engine turns normally, but will not start	Incorrect starting procedure Injection pump stop solenoid faulty or wire disconnected Wax in fuel (very cold conditions only) Timing belt broken Fuel system fault Poor compression (see below) Injection pump timing incorrect
Engine idles unevenly.	Fuel system fault Incorrect valve clearance Burnt out valves Blown head gasket
Poor compression	Burnt out valves Valve clearances too small Blown head gasket Worn piston rings/cylinder bores Cylinder head or block cracked
Lack of power	Poor compression (see above) Injection pump timing incorrect Worn or dirty injectors Air cleaner clogged
Excessive oil consumption	Oil leaks from crankshaft or camshaft oil seals Worn piston rings/cylinder bores (smoky exhaust is an indication) External leakage
Unusual noises	Peripheral component fault (eg water pump or alternator) Worn or damaged timing belt or alternator drivebelt Piston ring(s) broken Big-end bearings worn (worst when off load) Main bearings worn (worst when on load) Injector or injection pump fault (see Chapter 3)
Excessive smoke in exhaust	Oil being burnt (blue smoke) Fuel system fault (white or black smoke) – see Chapter 3

Chapter 2 Cooling system

For modifications, and information applicable to later models, see Supplement at end of manual

Contents

Specifications

General

System type .... Pressurised, front-mounted radiator (with integral expansion tank on BX models), coolant pump and thermostat. Electric cooling fan(s)

Capacity:
    Visa models .... 7.5 litres (13.2 pints)
    BX models .... 7.0 litres (12.3 pints)
Antifreeze content:
    28% for protection down to −15°C (5°F)
    50% for protection down to −30°C (−22°F)
Thermostat:
    Starts to open at .... 82°C (180°F)
    Fully open at .... 93°C (199°F)
    Minimum travel .... 7.5 mm (0.295 in)
Radiator cap pressure .... 1 bar (14.5 lbf/in²)
Temperature warning switch operating temperature .... 103 to 107°C (217 to 225°F)
Emergency temperature warning switch (yellow connector)
operating temperature .... 110 to 114°C (230 to 237°F)
Electric cooling fan:
    Cut-in temperature:
        1st speed .... 86 to 90°C (187 to 194°F)
        2nd speed .... 90 to 94°C (194 to 201°F)

Torque wrench settings	Nm	lbf ft
Water pump	12	9

1 General description

The cooling system is pressurised with a front-mounted radiator and a water pump driven by the engine timing belt. The thermostat is located on the flywheel end of the cylinder block, and enables the engine to achieve a fast warm-up period by initially restricting the coolant flow within the engine and heater circuits. Thereafter, the coolant flows through the radiator to provide additional cooling. The main engine temperature control is provided by one or two electric cooling fans mounted in front of the radiator. Visa models have two separate fans and BX models a single twin-speed fan. In both cases a twin action sensor in the radiator activates the fan(s) according to the coolant temperature.

Essential to the operation of the system is the expansion tank, integral with the radiator on BX models or separate on Visa models. This tank provides a reservoir to allow for expansion and contraction of the coolant with changes in temperature. It also incorporates a filler/pressure relief valve cap.

The radiator is of the crossflow type, with plastic side tanks. A temperature warning switch is provided on the water outlet from the cylinder head to warn the driver of excessive temperature. An additional warning switch is also provided on BX models which operates at the 'emergency' temperature and causes the warning lamp to remain on permanently as against the flashing warning lamp activated at the lower temperature.

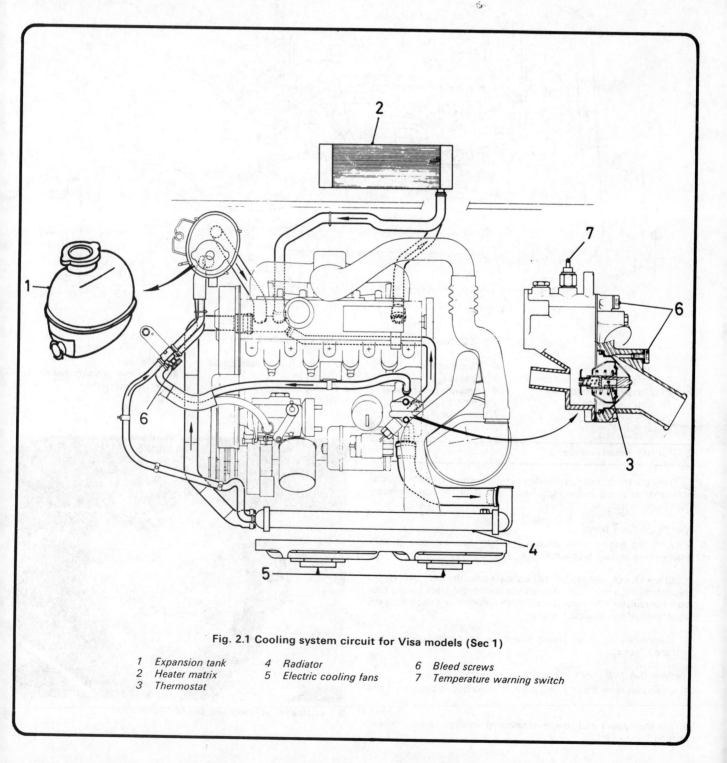

Fig. 2.1 Cooling system circuit for Visa models (Sec 1)

1 Expansion tank
2 Heater matrix
3 Thermostat
4 Radiator
5 Electric cooling fans
6 Bleed screws
7 Temperature warning switch

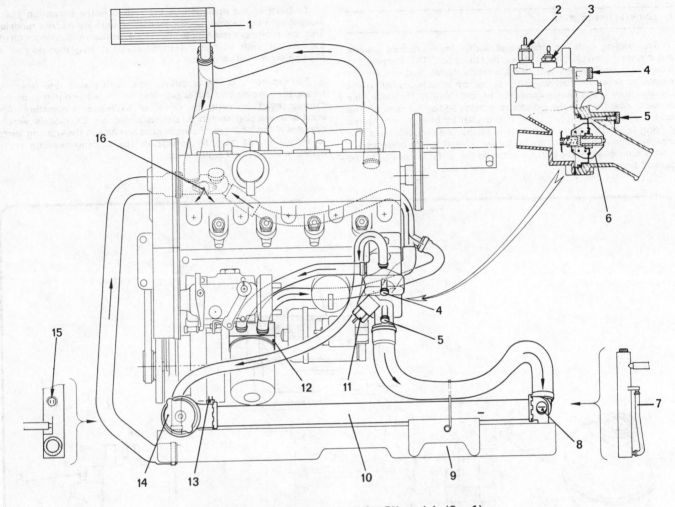

Fig. 2.2 Cooling system circuit for BX models (Sec 1)

1   Heater matrix
2   Temperature warning switch
3   Emergency temperature
    warning switch
4 and 5 Bleed screws

6   Thermostat
7   Drain pipe
8   Radiator bleed screw
9   Electric cooling fan
10 Radiator

11 Fast idle temperature sensor
12 Oil cooler
13 Electric cooling fan thermal
    switch

14 Filler cap
15 Low level warning switch
16 Water pump inlet

2   Routine maintenance

Carry out the following procedures at the intervals given in Routine
Maintenance at the beginning of this manual or the corresponding
petrol engine manual.

Check coolant level

1   With the engine cold, depress the filler cap and turn it anti-
clockwise to remove it (photo).

2   Check that on Visa models the coolant is up to the level plate visible
through the filler neck. On BX models withdraw the black plastic tube
from the radiator filler neck and check that the coolant level is on the
upper limit of the 'threaded' section.

3   If necessary top up the system with the recommended coolant then
refit the filler cap.

Renew the antifreeze mixture

4   Drain and flush the cooling system as described in Sections 4 and
5.

5   Fill the system with the recommended coolant as described in
Section 6.

2.1 Expansion tank and filler cap on Visa models

3 Cooling system – pressure test

1 In cases where leakage is difficult to trace a pressure test can prove helpful. The test involves pressurising the system by means of a hand pump and an adaptor which is fitted to the expansion tank or radiator in place of the filler cap. The resourceful home mechanic may be able to improvise the apparatus using an old filler cap and a tyre valve, alternatively the test can be performed by a Citroën garage.

2 Fit the test equipment to the expansion tank or radiator then run the engine to normal operating temperature and switch it off.

3 Apply 1.4 bar (20.3 lbf/in²) pressure and check that this pressure is held for at least 10 seconds. If the pressure drops prematurely there is a leak in the cooling system which must be traced and rectified.

4 Besides leaks from hoses, pressure can also be lost through leaks in the radiator and heater matrix. A blown head gasket or a cracked head or block can cause an 'invisible' leak, but there are usually other clues to this condition such as poor engine performance, regular misfiring, or combustion gases entering the coolant.

5 After completing the test, allow the engine to cool then remove the test equipment.

6 The condition of the filler cap must not be overlooked. Normally it is tested with similar equipment to that used for the pressure test. The release pressure is given in the Specifications and is also usually stamped on the cap itself. Renew the cap if it is faulty.

4 Cooling system – draining

1 If the engine is hot allow it to cool for at least 10 minutes after switching off.

2 Depress the filler cap and slowly turn it anti-clockwise until it can be removed. If the engine is hot cover the cap with a thick cloth before removing it as a precaution against scalding.

3 Position a suitable container beneath the left-hand side of the radiator then unscrew the drain plug and allow the coolant to drain. If there is no drain plug fitted, disconnect the drain pipe on the left-hand side of the radiator or disconnect the bottom hose from the right-hand side.

4 When the radiator is completely drained refit the drain plug, pipe or hose then drain the block by unscrewing the drain plug located on the rear of the engine at the flywheel end (see Chapter 1, photo 23.18A). Refit the drain plug on completion.

5 Cooling system – flushing

1 If the coolant is contaminated with rust and scale the complete system should be flushed as follows.

2 Drain the system as described in the previous Section.

3 Remove the thermostat as described in Section 8.

4 If not already done disconnect the bottom hose from the radiator.

5 Insert a garden hose into the thermostat housing so that the water runs through the engine in the reverse direction to normal flow and comes out of the bottom hose. Continue until the water emerges clean.

6 Run the water through the radiator in the normal direction of flow by inserting the garden hose in the top hose. In severe cases of contamination it may be helpful to remove the radiator and reverse-flush it.

7 Chemical descalers or flushing agents should only be used as a last resort, in which case follow the instructions given by the manufacturers.

8 When flushing is complete, refit the thermostat and reconnect the hoses.

6 Cooling system – filling

1 Make sure that the drain plugs are secure and that all hoses are in good condition and their clips tight.

2 Loosen or remove the bleed screws located on the thermostat housing cover, on the radiator on BX models and, on Visa models only, the expansion tank return pipe (photos).

3 Fill slowly with coolant via the filler neck and at the same time keep an eye on the bleed screw holes (photo). As soon as coolant free of air bubbles emerges refit and tighten the bleed screws.

6.2A Bleed screws (arrowed) on the thermostat housing

6.2B Bleed screw (arrowed) on the radiator (BX models)

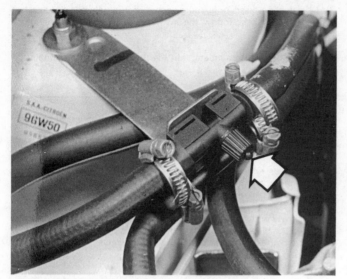

6.2C Bleed screw (arrowed) on the expansion tank return pipe (Visa models)

6.3 Filling the radiator on BX models

6.6 Removing the coolant level tube on BX models

4   Top up the radiator or expansion tank until it is full to the filler cap seating. There still remains air in the system which must be purged as follows.

5   Start the engine and run at a fast idle speed for several minutes. Stop the engine.

6   Top up the coolant level as follows. On Visa models top up to the level plate visible through the filler neck. On BX models withdraw the black plastic tube from the radiator filler neck and note the coolant level on the 'threaded' section (photo). The bottom of the tube indicates the minimum level and the upper limit of the 'threaded' section indicates the maximum level. Top up to the maximum level, then refit the tube.

7   Fit the filler cap.

8   Start the engine and run to normal operating temperature indicated by the electric cooling fan(s) cutting in then out after a few minutes.

9   Stop the engine and allow to cool for at least 1 hour.

10 Recheck the coolant level as described in paragraph 6 and top up as necessary.

7   Radiator – removal and refitting

1   Drain the cooling system as described in Section 4.

2   Remove the air cleaner as described in Chapter 3.

3   Loosen the clips and disconnect the top hose, bottom hose, and bypass hose from the radiator.

4   On Visa models disconnect the bonnet release cable from its catch and unbolt the crossmember. Lift the crossmember from the top of the radiator.

5   Disconnect the wiring from the thermal switch on the right-hand side of the radiator. Also disconnect the coolant level warning switch (when fitted).

6   On Visa models remove the front grille panel then remove one headlamp unit and detach the fan cowl.

7   On BX models unscrew the bolts and lift the crossmember from the top of the radiator (photos).

7.7A Radiator top crossmember retaining bolt – arrowed (BX models)

7.7B Removing the radiator top crossmember (BX models)

7.8 Removing the radiator on BX models

8.3A Unscrewing the thermostat housing cover bolts

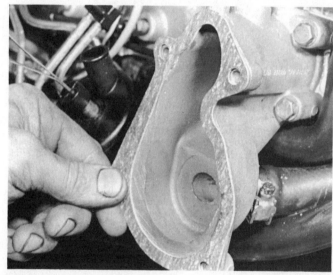

8.3B Removing the thermostat housing cover gasket

8   Carefully lift the radiator from the engine compartment (photo).

9   Refitting is a reversal of removal. Refill the system as described in Section 6.

8 Thermostat – removal, testing and refitting

1   Drain the cooling system as described in Section 4.

2   Loosen the clip and disconnect the top hose from the thermostat housing cover.

3   Unscrew the four bolts and remove the thermostat housing cover from the cylinder head water outlet. There is no need to disconnect the fast idle cable. Remove the gasket (photos).

4   Using circlip pliers, extract the circlip from the cover and lift out the thermostat (photo).

5   If necessary pull the rubber seal from the thermostat (photo).

8.4 Thermostat and retaining circlip

8.5 Removing the rubber seal from the thermostat

9.5A Unscrew the bolts ...

6   To test the thermostat place it in a pan of cold water and check that it is initially closed. Heat the water and check that it commences to open at the temperature given in Specifications. Continue to heat the water and check the fully open temperature and minimum travel. Finally allow the water to cool and check that it fully closes. Discard it if it is faulty.

7   Refitting is a reversal of removal, but when inserting the thermostat in the cover, position the vent hole uppermost and also fit a new gasket. Refill the system as described in Section 6.

9   Water pump – removal and refitting

1   Disconnect the battery negative lead.

2   Remove the timing belt as described in Chapter 1, Section 4.

3   Drain the cooling system as described in Section 4 of this Chapter.

4   To provide additional working room loosen the clips and remove the bottom hose.

5   Unscrew the bolts and withdraw the water pump from the cylinder block (photos). Remove the gasket.

6   Clean the mating faces of the water pump and block.

7   Fit the water pump together with a new gasket, insert the bolts, and tighten them evenly to the specified torque.

8   Reconnect the bottom hose if removed.

9   Refit the timing belt as described in Chapter 1, Section 4.

10 Reconnect the battery negative lead.

11 Refill the cooling system as described in Section 6 of this Chapter.

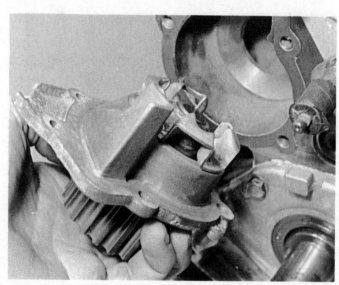

9.5B ... and withdraw the water pump

9.5C Water pump showing impellor vanes

Chapter 3 Fuel and exhaust systems

For modifications, and information applicable to later models, see Supplement at end of manual

Contents

Specifications

General

System type	Rear-mounted fuel tank, injection pump with integral transfer pump, indirect injection
Firing order	1-3-4-2 (No 1 at flywheel end)
Fuel:	
Type	Commercial diesel fuel for road vehicles (DERV)
Tank capacity:	
Visa	43 litres (9.5 gallons)
BX	52 litres (11.4 gallons)

Injection pump (Roto-Diesel)

Static advance .... 2.26 ± 0.05 mm (0.089 ± 0.002 in) BTDC (equivalent to 16° BTDC)

Dynamic advance:

    Visa .... 14 ± 1° BTDC at 800 rpm

    BX17 .... 14 ± 1° BTDC at 800 rpm

    BX19 with injection pump code DPCR 844 3161 A .... 17 ± 1° BTDC at idle speed

    BX19 with injection pump code DPCR 844 3261 C .... 14 ± 1° BTDC at idle speed

Idle speed:

    Visa .... 750 rpm

    BX .... 750 $+50 \atop -0$ rpm

Maximum engine speed (no load) .... 5100 ± 100 rpm

Rotation .... Clockwise from sprocket end

Injection pump (Bosch)

Static advance:

    Visa .... 0.72 ± 0.03 mm (0.028 ± 0.001 in) BTDC

    BX17 .... 0.80 ± 0.03 mm (0.031 ± 0.001 in) BTDC

    BX19 .... 0.57 ± 0.03 mm (0.022 ± 0.001 in) BTDC

Dynamic advance:

    Visa .... 14 ± 1° BTDC at 800 rpm

    BX17 .... 14 $+1° \atop -0$ BTDC at 800 rpm

    BX19 .... 13 to 14° BTDC at idle speed

Idle speed:

    Manual gearbox .... 750 to 800 rpm

    Automatic transmission .... 800 to 850 rpm

Maximum engine speed .... 5100 ± 100 rpm

Fast idle speed (automatic transmission only) .... 1150 to 1250 rpm

Rotation .... Clockwise from sprocket end

Injectors

Type .... Pintle

Opening pressure:

    Roto-Diesel .... 115 ± 5 bar (1668 ± 73 lbf/in²)

    Bosch .... 130 ± 5 bar (1885 ± 73 lbf/in²)

Heater plugs

Type .... Champion CH 68

Torque wrench settings

	Nm	lbf ft
Injector:		
Roto-Diesel	130	96
Bosch	90	66
Injector pipe union nuts	20	15
Heater plug	22	16
Injection pump	18	13
Cylinder head blanking plug	30	22
Injection pump (Bosch) blanking plug	20	15
Fuel filter through-bolt	10	7
Injection pump sprocket nut	50	37

1 General description

The fuel system consists of a rear-mounted fuel tank, a fuel filter, a fuel injection pump, injectors and associated components. The exhaust system is similar to that used on petrol-engined vehicles.

Fuel is drawn from the tank by a vane-type transfer pump incorporated in the delivery head of the injection pump. Before reaching the pump the fuel passes through a fuel filter where foreign matter and water are removed. The injection pump is driven at half crankshaft speed by the timing belt. The high pressure required to inject the fuel into the compressed air in the swirl chambers is achieved by two opposed pistons forced together by rollers running on a cam ring. The fuel passes through a central rotor with a single outlet drilling which aligns with ports leading to the injector pipes and injectors. Fuel metering is controlled by a centrifugal governor which reacts to accelerator pedal position and engine speed. The governor is linked to the metering valve which moves the rotor sleeve to increase or decrease the amount of fuel transferred to the high pressure chamber. Injection timing is varied by turning the cam ring to suit the prevailing engine speed.

There are four precision-made injectors which inject a homogeneous spray of fuel into the swirl chambers located in the cylinder head. The injectors are calibrated to open and close at critical pressures to provide efficient and even combustion. The injector needle is lubricated by fuel which accumulates in the spring chamber and is channelled to the injection pump return hose by leak-off pipes.

Preheater or 'glow' plugs are fitted to each swirl chamber to facilitate cold starting and, additionally, a thermostatic sensor in the cooling system operates a fast idle lever to increase the idling speed and supply additional fuel when the engine is cold.

A stop solenoid cuts the fuel supply to the injection pump rotor when the ignition is switched off, and there is also a hand-operated stop lever for use in an emergency.

Servicing of the injection pump and injectors is very limited for the home mechanic, and any dismantling other than that described in this Chapter must be entrusted to a Citroën dealer or fuel injection specialist.

Warning: *It is necessary to take certain precautions when working on the fuel system components, particularly the fuel injectors. Before carrying out any operations on the fuel system, refer to the precautions given in 'Safety first!' at the beginning of this manual, and to any additional warning notes at the start of the relevant Sections.*

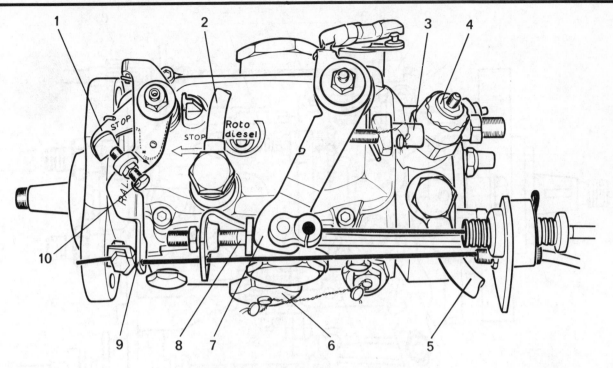

Fig. 3.1 Roto-Diesel injection pump (Sec 1)

1 Manual stop lever
2 Fuel return to tank
3 Engine maximum speed
   adjustment screw
4 Stop solenoid
5 Fuel inlet
6 Timing inspection plug
7 Accelerator lever
8 Anti-stalling adjustment
   screw
9 Fast idle lever
10 Idling adjustment screw

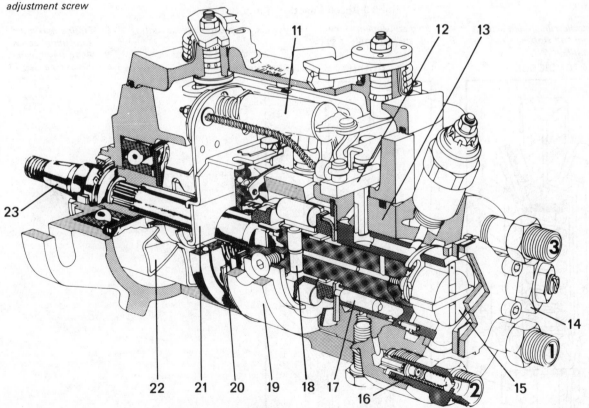

Fig. 3.2 Cutaway view of the Roto-Diesel injection pump (Sec 1)

11 MIN-MAX speed regulator
12 Fuel metering valve
13 Hydraulic head
14 Transfer pressure adjustment
15 Transfer pump
16 High pressure outlet and
    recirculation valve
17 Overload ram
18 Pistons
19 Cam ring
20 Overload springs
21 Control lever
22 Centrifugal governor
23 Driveshaft

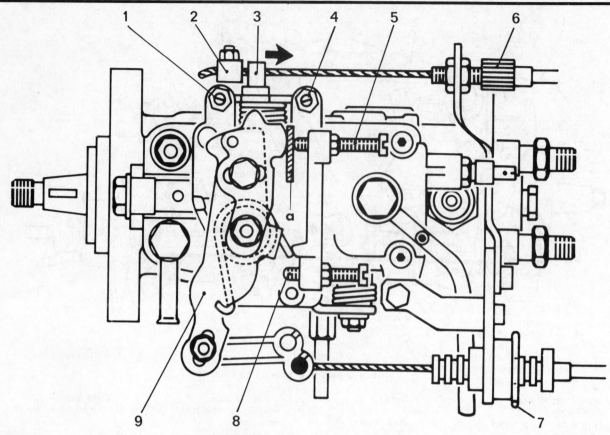

Fig. 3.3 Bosch injection pump (Sec 1)

1 Fast idle adjustment screw
2 Cable end stop
3 Fast idle lever
4 Idling adjustment screw
5 Anti-stall adjustment screw
6 Fast idle cable adjustment ferrule
7 Accelerator cable adjustment ferrule
8 Engine maximum speed adjustment screw
9 Accelerator lever
a Shim (see Sec 11)

ROTO DIESEL   BOSCH

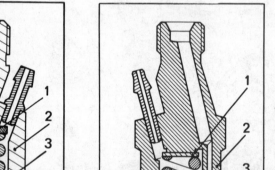
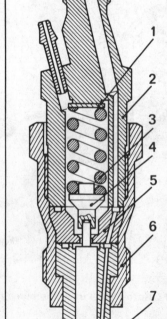
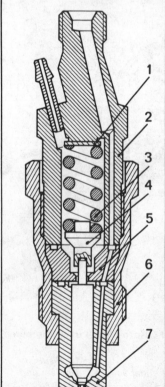

Fig. 3.4 Cross-section of the injectors (Sec 1)

1 Adjustment shim
2 Upper body
3 Spring
4 Pushrod
5 Spacer
6 Nut
7 Lower body and needle

I

II

Modifications to the Bosch pump

In 1987 the Bosch injection pump was modified to increase the length of the pump shaft front bearing. At the same time, the pump sprocket, timing belt tensioner roller and timing belt covers were modified. Old and new components are not interchangeable. Maintenance and adjustment procedures are unchanged.

2 Routine maintenance

Carry out the following procedures at the intervals given in Routine Maintenance at the beginning of this manual on the corresponding petrol engine manual.

Renew the fuel filter

1   This job may be carried out leaving the filter head *in situ*. However due to limited access and the possibility of spilling fuel over the engine, it is recommended that the filter head is removed, together with the cartridge.

2   Unscrew the union bolts and disconnect the inlet and outlet fuel unions from the filter head (photo). Recover the union washers.

3   Unbolt the filter head from the bracket and withdraw it, together with the cartridge (photo).

4   With the assembly in a container to catch spilled fuel, unscrew the through-bolt. On the Roto-Diesel filter this will release the end cap and enable the cartridge and seals to be removed (photos). On the Bosch filter remove the chamber followed by the element and seals.

5   Clean the filter head and end cap or chamber.

6   Locate the new seals in position then fit the new cartridge or element using a reversal of the removal procedures.

7   Finally prime the fuel injection system as described in Section 17.

Drain water from the fuel filter

8   Position a small container beneath the filter.

9   Loosen the bleed screw on the bottom of the filter and allow any water to drain into the container. Where fitted, also loosen the air bleed screw on the filter head or inlet union bolt.

10 Tighten the lower bleed screw when fuel free of water flows. Retighten the air bleed screw where fitted.

11 Prime the fuel injection system as described in Section 17.

Renew the air cleaner element

12 Refer to Section 3.

2.2 Inlet (1) and outlet (2) unions on the Bosch fuel filter

2.3 Removing the Roto-Diesel filter head and cartridge

2.4A Unscrew the through-bolt ...

2.4B ... and remove the Roto-Diesel filter cartridge

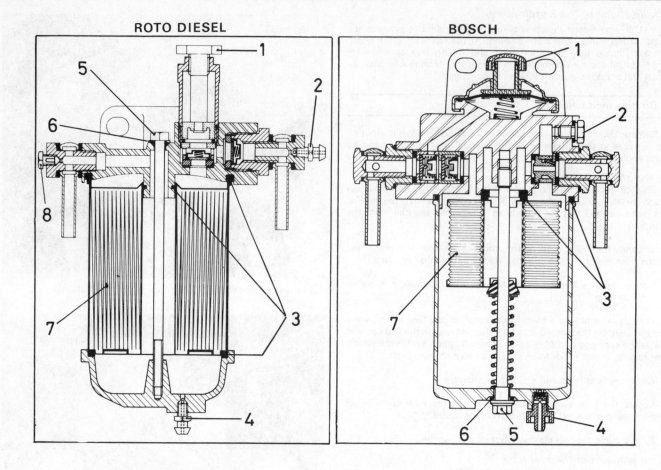

Fig. 3.5 Cross-section of the fuel filters (Sec 2)

1 Priming plunger	3 Seals	5 Through-bolt	7 Cartridge/element
2 Fuel bleed screw	4 Water bleed screw	6 Through-bolt seal	8 Air bleed screw

3 Air cleaner and element – removal and refitting

Visa models

1 Unscrew and remove the through-bolt from the top of the air cleaner.

2 Release the spring clips and lift off the cover (photo).

3 Remove the element and wipe clean the inside surfaces of the main body and cover.

4 Loosen the clips and disconnect the inlet ducting. Leave the bracket for the rear duct attached to the duct, but unbolt the bracket from the inlet manifold. Disconnect the ventilation hose from the oil separator (photos).

5 Unscrew the nut from the base of the main body then slide the body rearwards from the two mounting rubbers (photo).

6 Refitting is a reversal of removal.

BX models

7 Unscrew the wing nut and lift the cover from the air cleaner (photos).

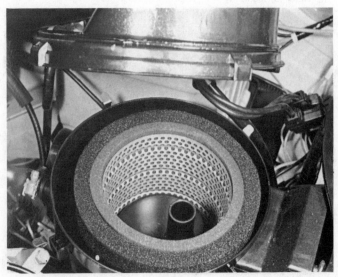

3.2 Air cleaner element (Visa models)

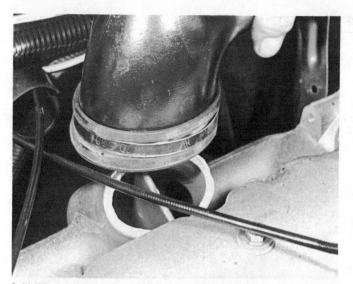

3.4A Disconnecting the air duct from the inlet manifold

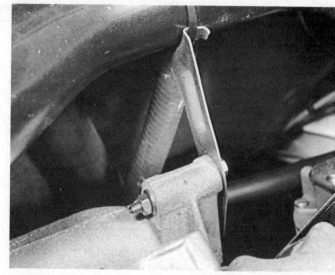

3.4B Air duct support bracket (Visa models)

3.4C Disconnecting the ventilation hose (arrowed) from the oil separator (Visa models)

3.5 Removing the air cleaner from the mounting rubbers (Visa models)

3.7A Unscrew the wing nut ...

3.7B ... and lift off the air cleaner cover (BX models)

8 Move the inlet duct to one side and remove the element. Wipe clean the inside surfaces of the main body and cover.

9 Check the sealing ring for the cover and renew it if necessary.

10 Loosen the clips and disconnect the inlet ducting.

11 Unscrew the nut securing the base of the main body to the bracket below the battery, then slide the body rearwards from the mounting rubbers in the bracket over the radiator (photos).

12 Refitting is a reversal of removal.

4 Fuel injection pump – removal and refitting

1 Disconnect the battery negative lead.

2 Cover the alternator with a plastic bag as a precaution against spillage of diesel fuel.

3 On Visa models apply the handbrake. On BX models chock the rear wheels and release the handbrake.

4 On manual transmission models, jack up the front right-hand corner of the vehicle until the wheel is just clear of the ground. Support the vehicle on an axle stand and engage 4th or 5th gear. This will enable the engine to be turned easily by turning the right-hand wheel. On automatic models the engine must be turned by using a spanner on the crankshaft pulley bolt. It may be advantageous to remove the heater plugs.

5 Pull up the special clip, release the spring clips, and withdraw the two timing cover sections.

6 Open the accelerator lever on the injection pump and disconnect the cable by passing it through the special slot. Disconnect the cable adjustment ferrule from the bracket.

7 Note the position of the end stop on the fast idle cable then loosen the screw and disconnect the inner cable. Unscrew the adjustment locknut and remove the cable and ferrule from the bracket.

8 Loosen the clip and disconnect the fuel supply hose.

9 Disconnect the main fuel return pipe and the injector leak off return pipe from the union tube (photo).

10 Disconnect the wire from the stop solenoid (photo).

11 Unscrew the union nuts securing the injector pipes to the injection pump (photo).

12 On BX models remove the clip securing the hydraulic pipes to the engine front plate.

13 Turn the engine by means of the front right-hand wheel or crankshaft pulley bolt until the two bolt holes in the injection pump sprocket are aligned with the corresponding holes in the engine front plate.

14 Insert two M8 bolts through the holes and hand tighten them. Note that the bolts must retain the sprocket while the injection pump is removed thereby making it unnecessary to remove the timing belt.

15 Mark the injection pump in relation to the mounting bracket using a scriber or felt tip pen (photo). This will ensure the correct timing when refitting. If a new pump is being fitted transfer the mark from the old pump to give an approximate setting.

16 Unscrew the three mounting nuts and remove the plates. Unscrew and remove the rear mounting bolt and support the injection pump on a block of wood (photos).

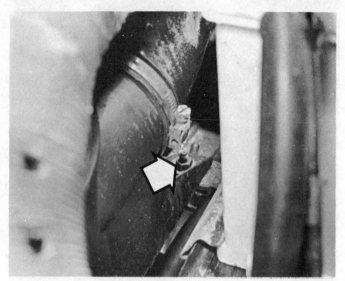

3.11A Air cleaner mounting nut – arrowed (BX models)

3.11B Air cleaner mounting rubbers – arrowed (BX models)

4.9 Main fuel return pipe (1) and injector leak off return pipe (2) (Roto-Diesel)

4.10 Disconnecting the stop solenoid wire (Roto-Diesel)

4.11 Injector pipe union nuts on the Roto-Diesel injection pump

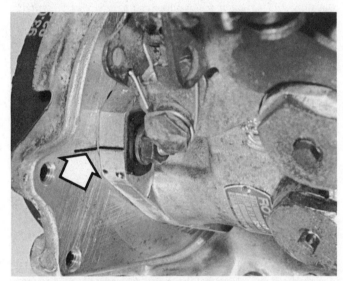

4.15 Mark the injection pump in relation to the mounting bracket (arrow)

4.16A Injection pump mounting nut and plate (arrowed)

4.16B Injection pump mounting bolt (arrowed)

17 Unscrew the sprocket nut until the shaft taper is released from the sprocket. The nut acts as a puller, together with the plate bolted to the sprocket.

18 Continue to unscrew the sprocket nut and withdraw the injection pump from the mounting bracket (photo). Recover the Woodruff key from the shaft groove if it is loose.

19 Commence refitting the injection pump by fitting the Woodruff key to the shaft groove (if removed).

20 Unbolt the puller plate from the injection pump sprocket.

21 Insert the injection pump from behind the sprocket, making sure that the shaft key enters the groove in the sprocket. Screw on the nut and hand tighten it.

22 Fit the mounting nuts, together with their plates, and hand tighten the nuts.

23 Tighten the sprocket nut to the specified torque then refit the puller plate and tighten the bolts.

4.18 Removing the injection pump from its mounting bracket

24 Unscrew and remove the two bolts from the injection pump sprocket.

25 If the original injection pump is being refitted, align the scribed marks and tighten the mounting nuts. If fitting a new pump, the timing must now be set as described in Sections 5 or 6.

26 Refit the rear mounting bolt and special nut, tightening the nut slowly to allow the bush to align itself as shown in Fig. 3.6.

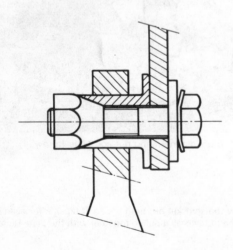

Fig. 3.6 Cross-section of injection pump rear mounting (Sec 4)

27 On BX models refit the clip securing the hydraulic pipes.

28 Refit the injector pipes to the injection pump and tighten the union nuts.

29 Reconnect the wire to the stop solenoid.

30 Refit the fuel supply and return pipes.

31 Refit the fast idle cable and accelerator cable, and adjust them with reference to Sections 7 and 8.

32 Refit the two timing cover sections and secure with the spring clips.

33 Lower the vehicle to the ground and apply the handbrake (BX models).

34 Remove the plastic bag from the alternator and reconnect the battery negative lead.

35 Prime the fuel circuit by first switching on the ignition to energize the stop solenoid, then actuating the pump on the fuel filter until resistance is felt. On early models fitted with a Roto-Diesel filter the pump plunger must first be unscrewed then retightened after priming.

36 Turn the ignition key to position M and wait for the preheating warning light to go out. Start the engine and adjust the idling speed with reference to Section 9.

5 Fuel injection pump (Roto-Diesel) – checking and adjusting the static timing

Caution: *The maximum engine speed and transfer pressure settings, together with timing access plugs, are sealed by the manufacturers at the factory using locking wire and lead seals. Do not disturb the wire if the vehicle is still within the warranty period otherwise the warranty will be invalidated. Also do not attempt the timing procedure unless accurate instrumentation is available.*

1   Disconnect the battery negative lead.

2   Cover the alternator with a plastic bag as a precaution against spillage of diesel fuel.

3   On Visa models apply the handbrake. On BX models chock the rear wheels and release the handbrake.

4   On manual gearbox models jack up the front right-hand corner of the vehicle until the wheel is just clear of the ground. Support the vehicle on an axle stand and engage 4th or 5th gear. This will enable the engine to be turned easily by turning the right-hand wheel. On automatic transmission models use an open-ended spanner on the crankshaft pulley bolt.

5   Disconnect the wire and unscrew the heater plug from cylinder No 4 (timing belt end). Note that the engine is timed with **No 4** piston at TDC compression (ie No 1 piston at TDC with valves 'rocking').

6   Two dial test indicators are now necessary for checking the positions of the No 4 piston and the injection pump. Magnetic type stands will be found helpful or alternatively brackets may be made for fitting to appropriate positions on the engine.

7   Unscrew and remove the blanking plug from the cylinder head next to No 4 injector (photo).

8   Turn the engine forwards until pressure is felt in No 4 cylinder indicating that No 4 piston is commencing its compression stroke.

9   Position the dial test indicator over the blanking hole and fit the probe (photo).

10 Turn the engine forwards until the maximum lift of piston No 4 is registered on the dial test indicator. Turn the engine slightly back and forth to determine the exact point of maximum lift then zero the indicator.

11 On BX models remove the clip securing the hydraulic pipes to the engine front plate and move the pipes to one side.

12 Loosen the lower of the two large side plugs on the side of the injection pump. Position a small container beneath the plug then remove the plug and catch the escaping fuel in the container (photo).

5.7 Removing the blanking plug from No 4 cylinder

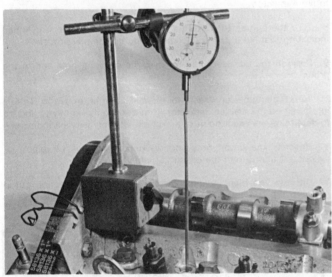
5.9 Setting No 4 piston timing position with a dial test indicator

5.12 Roto-Diesel injection pump with the timing plug removed

13 Inside the plug aperture there is a probe guide. Insert the probe and connect it to the dial test indicator directly over the hole (photo). Refer to Fig. 3.7 and note that the end of the probe must be pointed in order to fully engage the groove in the pump rotor.

14 Turn the engine backwards approximately 1/8th of a turn or until the No 4 piston has moved 4.0 mm (0.158 in) down the cylinder. Now turn the engine slowly forwards while watching the dial test indicator on the injection pump. After the probe has reached the bottom of the timing groove then risen by 0.01 to 0.02 mm (0.0004 to 0.0008 in), check that the upper dial test indicator reads 2.26 ± 0.05 mm (0.089 ± 0.002 in) before TDC. If the timing is incorrect proceed as follows.

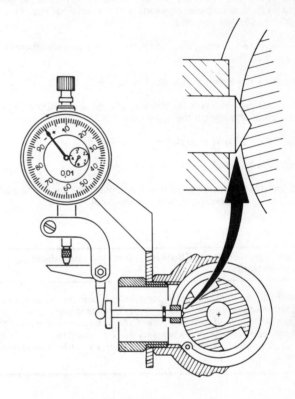
Fig. 3.7 Checking the timing on the Roto-Diesel fuel injection pump (Sec 5)

5.13 Timing the Roto-Diesel injection pump with a dial test indicator

15 Check the zero setting of the upper dial test indicator by repeating the procedure given in paragraph 10.

16 Turn the engine backwards approximately $\frac{1}{8}$th of a turn or until No 4 piston has moved 4.0 mm (0.158 in) down the cylinder. Now turn the engine slowly forwards until No 4 piston is 2.26 ± 0.05 mm (0.089 ± 0.002 in) before TDC.

17 Unscrew the union nuts and disconnect the injector pipes from the injection pump. Loosen the injection pump mounting nuts and bolt.

18 Turn the pump body until the probe is at the bottom of the timing groove in the rotor. Zero the dial test indicator. Now turn the pump clockwise (from the injector pipe end) until the probe has risen by 0.01 to 0.02 mm (0.0004 to 0.0008 in).

19 Tighten the mounting nuts and bolts making sure that there is no movement on the dial test indicator.

20 Recheck the timing as described in paragraph 14.

21 Remove the dial test indicators and refit the plugs. Reconnect the injector pipes and tighten the union nuts.

22 Refit the hydraulic pipe clip on BX models.

23 Refit the heater plug and connect the wire.

24 Lower the car to the ground and reconnect the battery negative lead. Remove the plastic bag from the alternator.

6 Fuel injection pump (Bosch) – checking and adjusting the static timing

Caution: *Some of the injection pump settings and access plugs may be sealed by the manufacturers at the factory using locking wire and lead seals. Do not disturb the wire if the vehicle is still within the warranty period otherwise the warranty will be invalidated. Also do not attempt the timing procedure unless accurate instrumentation is available.*

1 Disconnect the battery negative lead.

2 Cover the alternator with a plastic bag as a precaution against spillage of diesel fuel.

3 On Visa models apply the handbrake. On BX models chock the rear wheels and release the handbrake.

4 On manual gearbox models jack up the front right-hand corner of the vehicle until the wheel is just clear of the ground. Support the vehicle on an axle stand and engage 4th or 5th gear. This will enable the engine to be turned easily by turning the right-hand wheel. On automatic transmission models use an open ended spanner on the crankshaft pulley bolt.

5 Disconnect the wire and unscrew the heater plug from cylinder No 4 (timing belt end). Note that the engine is timed with **No 4** piston at TDC compression (ie No 1 piston at TDC with valves 'rocking').

6 Two dial test indicators are now necessary for checking the positions of the No 4 piston and the injection pump. Magnetic type stands will be found helpful or alternatively brackets may be made for fitting to appropriate positions on the engine.

7 Unscrew and remove the blanking plug from the cylinder head next to No 4 injector.

8 Turn the engine forwards until pressure is felt in No 4 cylinder, indicating that No 4 piston is commencing its compression stroke.

9 Position the dial test indicator over the blanking hole and fit the probe.

10 Turn the engine forwards until the maximum lift of piston No 4 is registered on the dial test indicator. Turn the engine slightly to and fro to determine the exact point of maximum lift then zero the indicator.

11 Unscrew the union nuts and disconnect the injector pipes for cylinders 1 and 2 from the injection pump.

12 Unscrew the blanking plug from the end of the injection pump between the injector pipe connections. Be prepared for the loss of some fuel.

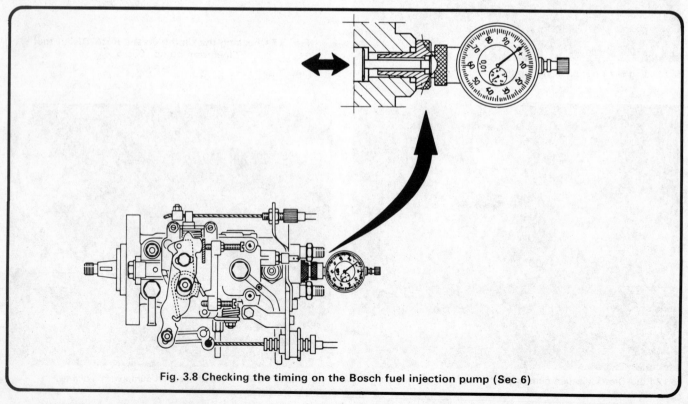

Fig. 3.8 Checking the timing on the Bosch fuel injection pump (Sec 6)

13 Insert the probe and connect it to the dial test indicator positioned directly over the hole. The fixture used by Citroën technicians is shown in Fig. 3.8.

14 Turn the engine backwards approximately $1/8$th of a turn or until the No 4 piston has moved 4.0 mm (0.157 in) down the cylinder.

15 Zero the dial test indicator on the injection pump.

16 Turn the engine slowly forwards until the dial test indicator on the injection pump reads 0.30 mm (0.012 in), then check that the upper dial test indicator reads 0.72 ± 0.03 mm (0.028 ± 0.001 in) before TDC for Visa models, or 0.80 ± 0.03 mm (0.031 ± 0.001 in) before TDC for BX17 models or 0.57 ± 0.03 mm (0.022 ± 0.001 in) before TDC for BX19 models. If the timing is incorrect proceed as follows.

17 Check the zero setting of the upper dial test indicator by repeating the procedure given in paragraph 10.

18 Turn the engine backwards approximately $1/8$th of a turn or until the No 4 piston had moved 4.0 mm (0.158 in) down the cylinder. Now turn the engine slowly forwards until the upper dial test indicator reads 0.72 ± 0.03 mm (0.028 ± 0.001 in) before TDC for Visa models, 0.80 ± 0.03 mm (0.031 ± 0.001 in) before TDC for BX17 models, or 0.57 ± 0.03 mm (0.022 ± 0.001 in) before TDC for BX19 models.

19 Unscrew the union nuts and disconnect the remaining injector pipes from the injection pump. Loosen the injection pump mounting nuts and bolt.

20 Turn the pump body anti-clockwise (from the injector pipe end) and check that the dial test indicator is zeroed. Now turn the pump body slowly clockwise until the dial test indicator reads 0.30 mm (0.012 in).

21 Tighten the mounting nuts and bolts, making sure that there is no movement on the dial test indicator.

22 Recheck the timing as described in paragraphs 14 to 16.

23 Remove the dial test indicators and refit the plugs. Reconnect the injector pipes and tighten the union nuts.

24 Refit the heater plug and connect the wire.

25 Lower the car to the ground and reconnect the battery negative lead. Remove the plastic bag from the alternator.

7 Fast idle control – removal, refitting and adjustment

1 Loosen the clamp screw or nut and remove the end fitting from the inner cable (photo).

2 Unscrew the locknut and remove the adjustment ferrule and outer cable from the bracket on the injection pump (photo).

3 Drain the cooling system as described in Chapter 2.

4 Unscrew the thermostatic sensor from the thermostat housing cover and recover the washer.

5 Fit the new thermostatic sensor and washer.

6 Insert the cable and ferrule in the bracket and screw on the locknut finger tight.

7 Fit the end fitting on the inner cable.

8 With the engine cold, push the fast idle lever fully towards the flywheel end of the engine then tighten the clamp screw or nut with the end fitting touching the lever.

9 Adjust the ferrule to ensure that the fast idle lever is touching its stop then tighten the locknuts.

10 Measure the exposed length of the inner cable between the ferrule and end fitting.

7.1 Fast idle inner cable and end fitting (arrowed) on the Bosch injection pump

7.2 Fast idle cable adjustment ferrule on the Roto-Diesel injection pump

11 Refill the cooling system as described in Chapter 2, and run the engine to normal operating temperature.

12 With the engine hot, check that the length of the inner cable has increased by at least 6.0 mm (0.236 in) indicating that the thermostatic sensor is functioning correctly.

13 Switch off the engine.

8 Accelerator cable – removal, refitting and adjustment

1 Open the accelerator lever on the injection pump and disconnect the inner cable by passing it through the special slot (photos).

2 Disconnect the cable adjustment ferrule and outer cable from the bracket (photo).

3 Working inside the vehicle, remove the lower facia panel where necessary then release the inner cable end fitting from the top of the accelerator pedal.

4 Pull the spring shock absorber from the bulkhead and withdraw the accelerator cable from inside the engine compartment.

8.1A Accelerator cable on the Roto-Diesel injection pump

8.1B Accelerator cable attachment on the Bosch injection pump

8.2 Accelerator cable adjustment ferrule on the Bosch injection pump

5   Refitting is a reversal of removal, but adjust the cable as follows. Have an assistant fully depress the accelerator pedal then check that the accelerator lever on the injection pump is touching the maximum speed adjustment screw. If not, pull the spring clip from the adjustment ferrule, reposition the ferrule and fit the spring clip in the groove next to the metal washer. With the accelerator pedal fully released check that the accelerator lever is touching the anti-stall (deceleration) adjustment screw.

9   Idle speed – checking and adjustment

1   The usual type of tachometer (rev counter), which works from ignition system pulses, cannot be used on diesel engines. A diagnostic socket is provided for use of Citroën test equipment, but this will not normally be available to the home mechanic. If it is not felt that adjusting the idle speed 'by ear' is satisfactory, one of the following alternatives may be used:

(a)   *Purchase or hire of an appropriate tachometer*
(b)   *Delegation of the job to a Citroën dealer or other specialist*
(c)   *Timing light (strobe) operated by a petrol engine running at the desired speed. If the timing light is pointed at a mark on the camshaft pump pulley the mark will appear stationary when the two engines are running at the same speed (or multiples of that speed). The pulley will be rotating at half the crankshaft speed but this will not affect the adjustment (photos) (in practice it was found impossible to use this method on the crankshaft pulley due to the acute viewing angle)*

2   Before making adjustments warm up the engine to normal operating temperature.

3   Check that the engine idles at the specified speed.

4   If adjustment is necessary on the Roto-Diesel pump, loosen the locknut on the fast idle lever then turn the adjustment screw as required and retighten the locknut (photo).

5   If adjustment is necessary on the Bosch pump, first loosen the locknut and unscrew the anti-stall adjustment screw until it is clear of the accelerator lever. Loosen the locknut and turn the idle speed adjustment screw as required then retighten the locknut (see Fig. 3.3)

6   Adjust the anti-stall adjustment screw as described in Section 10 or 11.

7   Stop the engine and disconnect the instrument as appropriate.

9.1A Mark on the pump pulley for checking the idle speed ...

9.1B ... with a timing light operated by a petrol engine

9.4 Idle speed adjustment screw (arrowed) on the Roto-Diesel injection pump

10.3 Anti-stall adjustment on the Roto-Diesel injection pump showing feeler blades (1) and twist drill (2)

10 Fuel injection pump (Roto-Diesel) – anti-stall adjustment

Note: *This adjustment requires the use of a tachometer – refer to Section 9 for alternative methods.*

1   Run the engine to normal operating temperature then switch it off.

2   Insert a 3.0 mm (0.118 in) shim or feeler blade between the accelerator lever and the anti-stall adjustment screw.

3   Turn the stop lever clockwise until it is clear of the hole in the fast idle lever then insert a 3.0 mm (0.118 in) dowel rod or twist drill (photo).

4   Start the engine and allow it to idle. The engine speed should be 900 ± 100 rpm.

5   If adjustment is necessary loosen the locknut, turn the anti-stall adjustment screw as required, then tighten the locknut.

6   Remove the feeler blade and twist drill and adjust the idling speed as described in Section 9.

7   Turn the accelerator lever to increase the engine speed to 3000 rpm then quickly release the lever. If the deceleration is too fast and the engine stalls turn the anti-stall adjustment screw 1/4 turn anti-clockwise (viewed from flywheel end of engine). If the deceleration is too slow, resulting in poor engine braking, turn the screw 1/4 turn clockwise.

8   Retighten the locknut after making an adjustment then recheck the idling speed as described in Section 9.

9   With the engine idling check the operation of the manual stop control by turning the stop lever clockwise. The engine must stop instantly.

10 Switch off the ignition switch.

11 Fuel injection pump (Bosch) – anti-stall adjustment

Note: *This adjustment requires the use of a tachometer – refer to Section 9 for alternative methods.*

1   Run the engine to normal operating temperature. Note the exact idling speed then switch off the engine.

2   Insert a 1.0 mm (0.039 in) shim or feeler blade between the accelerator lever and the anti-stall adjustment screw (see Fig. 3.3).

3   Start the engine and allow it to idle. The engine speed should exceed the normal idling speed by 50 rpm.

4   If adjustment is necessary loosen the locknut and turn the anti-stall adjustment screw as required. Retighten the locknut.

5   Remove the feeler blade and allow the engine to idle.

6   Move the fast idle lever fully towards the flywheel end of the engine and check that the engine speed increases to 950 ± 50 rpm. If necessary loosen the locknut and turn the stop adjusting screw as required, then retighten the locknut.

7   With the engine idling, check the operation of the manual stop control by turning the stop lever. The engine must stop instantly.

8   Switch off the ignition switch.

12 Maximum engine speed – checking and adjustment

Caution: *On Roto-Diesel injection pumps the maximum speed setting is sealed by the manufacturers at the factory using locking wire and a lead seal. Do not disturb the wire if the vehicle is still within the warranty period otherwise the warranty will be invalidated. This adjustment requires the use of a tachometer – refer to Section 9 for alternative methods.*

1   Run the engine to normal operating temperature.

2   Have an assistant fully depress the accelerator pedal and check that the maximum engine speed is as given in the Specifications. Do not keep the engine at maximum speed for more than two or three seconds.

3   If adjustment is necessary stop the engine then loosen the locknut, turn the maximum engine speed adjustment screw as necessary, and retighten the locknut (photo).

4   Repeat the procedure in paragraph 2 to check the adjustment.

5   Switch off the ignition switch.

12.3 Maximum engine speed adjustment screw on the Roto-Diesel injection pump

13.3 Disconnecting the leak off pipes from the injectors

13.5 Disconnecting the injector pipes

13 Fuel injectors – removal, testing and refitting

Warning: *Exercise extreme caution when working on the fuel injectors. Never expose the hands or any part of the body to injector spray, as the high working pressure can cause the fuel to penetrate the skin, with possibly fatal results. You are strongly advised to have any work which involves testing the injectors under pressure, carried out by a dealer or fuel injection specialist.*

1   On BX models remove the air duct between the air cleaner and inlet manifold.

2   Clean around the injectors and injector pipe union nuts.

3   Pull the leak off pipes from the injectors (photo).

4   Loosen the injector pipe union nuts at the injection pump.

5   Unscrew the union nuts and disconnect the pipes from the injectors (photo). If required the injector pipes may be completely removed.

6   Unscrew the injectors and remove them from the cylinder head (photos).

13.6A Removing an injector

13.6B An injector

13.7A Removing an injector copper washer ...

13.7B ... fire-seal washer ...

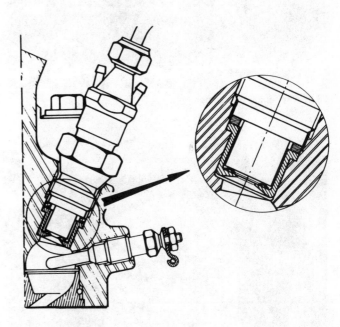

Fig. 3.9 Cross-section of cylinder head showing location of injector and heater plug (Sec 13)

Note fire-seal washer position in inset

7   Recover the copper washers, fire-seal washers, and sleeves from the cylinder head (photos).

8   Obtain new copper washers and fire-seal washers.

9   Take care not to drop the injectors or allow the needles at their tips to become damaged. The injectors are precision-made to fine limits and must not be handled roughly, in particular do not mount them in a bench vice.

10 Accurate testing and calibration of the injectors must be left to a specialist.

13.7C ... and sleeve

11 Commence refitting by inserting the sleeves followed by the fire-seal washers (convex face uppermost), and copper washers.

12 Insert the injectors and tighten them to the specified torque (photo).

13 Refit the injector pipes and tighten the union nuts to the specified torque.

14 Reconnect the leak off pipes (photo).

15 On BX models refit the air duct.

13.12 Tightening an injector

13.14 A leak off pipe connected between two injectors

14 Preheater system – description and testing

1 Each swirl chamber has a preheater plug (commonly called a glow plug) screwed into it. The plugs are electrically operated before, during and immediately after starting a cold engine. Preheating is not required on a hot engine.

2 If the system malfunctions, testing is ultimately by substitution of known good units, but some preliminary checks may be made as follows.

3 Disconnect the main supply cable from the No 1 heater plug (counting from the flywheel) on Visa models, or No 2 plug on BX models.

4 Connect a voltmeter between the supply cable and earth making sure that the cable is kept clear of the engine and bodywork. Have an assistant switch on the preheater and check that there is a 12 volt supply for several seconds before the system cuts out. Typically there should be a 7 second supply at an ambient temperature of 20°C (68°F), but this will increase with colder temperatures and decrease with higher temperatures. If there is no supply, the relay or associated wiring is at fault. Switch off the ignition.

5 Connect an ammeter between the supply cable and the heater plug inter-connecting wire. Have the assistant switch on the preheater and check that the current draw after 20 seconds is 12 amps per working plug, ie 48 amps if all four plugs are working.

6 If one or more heater plugs appear to be not drawing the expected current, disconnect the inter-connecting wire and check them individually or use an ohmmeter to check them for continuity and equal resistance.

15 Heater plugs and relay – removal and refitting

Heater plugs
1 Check that the ignition switch is off.

2 On BX models remove the air duct between the air cleaner and inlet manifold.

3 Prise the plastic clips from the heater plugs (photo).

4 Unscrew the nuts from the heater plug terminals. Remove the main supply cable from No 1 plug (counting from the flywheel) on Visa models, or No 2 plug on BX models, then remove the inter-connecting wire from all the plugs (photos).

5 Unscrew the heater plugs and remove them from the cylinder head (photos).

6 Refitting is a reversal of removal but tighten the heater plugs to the specified torque (photo).

Relay
7 The relay is located on the left-hand side of the engine compartment near the battery (photos).

15.3 Plastic clips (arrowed) on heater plug terminals

15.4A Heater plug terminal and inter-connecting wire

15.4B Removing the heater plug main supply cable (arrowed)

15.5A Removing a heater plug

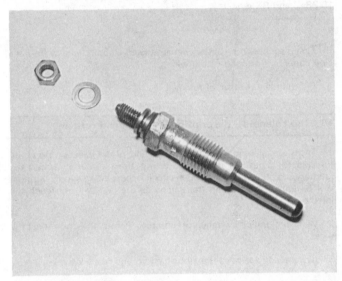

15.5B Heater plug and terminal nut

15.6 Tightening a heater plug

15.7A Heater plug control relay on Visa models ...

15.7B ... and BX models

8   First disconnect the battery negative lead. Unbolt the relay from the side panel and disconnect the wiring.

9   Refitting is a reversal of removal.

16 Stop solenoid – description, removal and refitting

1   The stop solenoid is located on the end of the injection pump by the injector pipes. Its purpose is to cut the fuel supply when the ignition is switched off. If an open circuit occurs in the supply wiring it will be impossible to start the engine as the fuel will not reach the injectors.

2   With the ignition switched off unscrew the nut and disconnect the wire.

3   Unscrew and remove the stop solenoid and recover the washer.

4   Refitting is a reversal of removal.

17 Fuel injection system – priming

1   After disconnecting part of the fuel injection system or running out of fuel it is necessary to carry out the priming procedure prior to starting the engine.

2   Loosen the bleed screw on the fuel filter head two or three turns. On the Roto-Diesel filter a plastic drain tube may be fitted to the bleed screw and a small container positioned to catch the fuel.

3   Actuate the plunger until fuel free from air bubbles flows from the bleed screw. On some Roto-Diesel filter heads the plunger must first be unscrewed, and with this type the plunger may become detached from the internal piston. If this happens, unscrew the housing and press the piston back onto the plunger. Refit the housing and operate the plunger slowly.

4   Tighten the bleed screw.

5   Turn on the ignition so that the stop solenoid is energised then activate the plunger until resistance is felt.

6   Where applicable on Roto-Diesel filters retighten the plunger.

7   Turn the ignition switch to position 'M' and wait for the preheater warning light to go out.

8   Fully depress the accelerator pedal and start the engine. Additional cranking may be necessary to finally bleed the fuel system before the engine starts.

18 Manifolds – removal and refitting

Inlet
1   Disconnect the battery negative lead.

2   Disconnect and remove the air duct from the inlet manifold and air cleaner. On Visa models unbolt the support bracket.

3   Using a hexagon key, unscrew the bolts and remove the inlet manifold from the cylinder head (photos). There are no gaskets.

4   Refitting is a reversal of removal, but tighten the bolts evenly.

Exhaust
5   Jack up the front of the car and support on axle stands. Apply the handbrake on Visa models, or chock the rear wheels on BX models.

18.3A Inlet manifold bolts (arrowed)

18.3B Removing the inlet manifold (engine removed from car)

6   Unscrew and remove the exhaust manifold-to-downpipe bolts, together with the springs and collars (photo). Tie the downpipe to one side.

7   Unscrew the nuts and withdraw the exhaust manifold from the studs in the cylinder head. Recover the gaskets (photo).

8   Refitting is a reversal of removal, but clean the mating faces and fit new gaskets. Tighten the nuts evenly (photo).

19 Exhaust system – inspection, removal and refitting

1   Inspect the exhaust system periodically for leaks, corrosion and damage, and check the security and condition of the mountings. Small leaks are more easily detected if an assistant temporarily blocks the tailpipe with a wad of cloth whilst the engine is idling.

2   Proprietary pastes and bandages are available for the repair of holes and splits. They work well in the short term, but renewal of the section concerned will probably prove more satisfactory in the long run.

3   Check the rubber mountings for deterioration, and renew them if necessary (photo).

4   The removal and refitting procedures are the same as for petrol versions as described in the Visa or BX Owners Workshop Manuals.

18.6 Exhaust manifold resonator and downpipe bolts (arrowed) on a 1.7 engine

18.7A Removing the exhaust manifold on a 1.9 engine

18.7B Exhaust manifold gasket

18.8 Tightening the exhaust manifold nuts

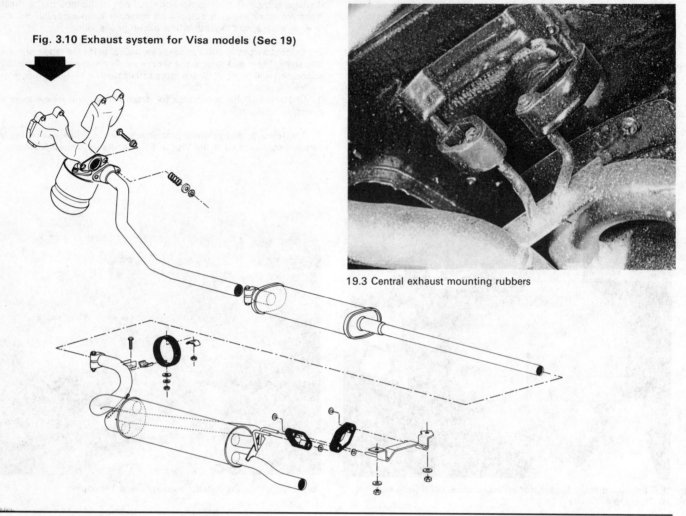

Fig. 3.10 Exhaust system for Visa models (Sec 19)

19.3 Central exhaust mounting rubbers

20 Fault diagnosis – fuel injection system

Symptom	Reason(s)
Engine turns normally but will not start	Fuel tank empty
	Incorrect starting procedure
	Fuel filter blocked
	Wax in fuel (in very cold conditions)
	Stop solenoid disconnected or defective
	Preheater system faulty
	Fast idle cable broken or thermostatic sensor faulty
	Injection pump timing incorrect
	Injection pump defective
	Poor compression (see Chapter 1)
Erratic idling	Idle speed adjustment incorrect
	Injector(s) defective
Lack of power	Fuel filter blocked
	Air cleaner blocked
	Air or water in fuel
	Injection pump timing incorrect
	Injector(s) defective
Excessive fuel consumption	Fuel leakage
	Air cleaner blocked
	Injector(s) defective
	Injection pump timing incorrect
Excessive knocking	Injector(s) defective (sticking)
	Injection pump timing incorrect
	Excessive carbon deposit

Chapter 4 Clutch, transmission and driveshafts

For modifications, and information applicable to later models, see Supplement at end of manual

Contents

Specifications

Clutch

Type .... Single dry plate with diaphragm spring. Cable operated
Friction plate diameter .... 200 mm (7.87 in)
Lining thickness .... 7.7 ± 0.3 mm (0.303 ± 0.012 in)
Release bearing type .... Sealed ball
Pedal free play .... Nil
Pedal travel:
    Visa .... 120.0 mm (4.7 in) minimum
    BX .... 130.0 to 150.0 mm (5.12 to 5.91 in)

Manual transmission

Type .... Four or five forward speeds and one reverse, synchromesh on all forward gears

Designation and type:
    Visa Van BE1 (BM61) 5-speed
    Visa 17D and 17RD .... BE1 (BM60) 4-speed or BE1 (BL04) 5-speed
    BX 17D BE1 (BL03) 5-speed
    BX 19D and 19RD .... BE1 (BL04) 5-speed or BE1 (BL62) 5-speed

Ratios (overall):

	BM60	BM61	BL03	BL04	BL62
1st	3.31:1	3.31:1	3.31:1	3.31:1	3.31:1
2nd	1.88:1	1.88:1	1.88:1	1.88:1	1.88:1
3rd	1.15:1	1.15:1	1.28:1	1.28:1	1.28:1
4th	0.80:1	0.80:1	0.97:1	0.97:1	0.97:1
5th	–	–	0.76:1	0.76:1	0.76:1
Reverse	3.33:1	3.33:1	3.33:1	3.33:1	3.33:1
Final drive	3.59:1	3.81:1	4.19:1	3.94:1	4.06:1

Oil type/specification .... Gear oil, viscosity SAE 75W/80W (Duckhams Hypoid 75W/90S)
Oil capacity .... 1.8 litres (3.2 pints)

Automatic transmission

Type .... Four forwards and one reverse gear
Designation .... ZF 4 HP14

Ratios (overall):

	Up to 1988	From 1988
1st	0.564	0.606
2nd	0.321	0.344
3rd	0.234	0.251
4th	0.174	0.186
Reverse	0.663	0.711
Final drive ratio	51/59	49/51

Oil type/specification .... Dexron II type ATF (Duckhams D-Matic)
Oil capacity (drain and refill) .... 2.5 litres (4.4 pints)

Driveshafts

Type .... Solid shaft with inner tri-axe joints and outer six-ball constant velocity joints

Grease capacity:
    Inner (tri-axe) joint .... 150 grams
    Outer (CV) joint .... 100 grams

Torque wrench settings

	Nm	lbf ft
Driveshaft nut	250	185
Right-hand driveshaft intermediate bearing retaining bolts	10	7
Left-hand engine mounting stud to gearbox	35	26
Left-hand engine mounting nut	35	26
Engine-to-gearbox bolts	40	30

1 General description

Clutch components are virtually identical to those used in petrol-engined models. For Visa models refer to the Supplement of the Visa petrol manual as the clutch is identical to that fitted to the petrol GTi model.

A BE1 type manual gearbox is fitted. On Visa models the procedures for the five-speed version are described in the Supplement of the petrol-engined model manual. The differences applicable to the four-speed gearbox are described in this Chapter. For BX models the procedures are identical to those for the BL type gearbox given in the petrol-engined model manual.

2 Routine maintenance

Carry out the following procedures at the intervals given in Routine Maintenance at the beginning of the manual.

Check the clutch adjustment
1 Refer to the relevant manual for petrol-engined models.

Renew the manual gearbox oil
2 Jack up the front of the vehicle and support on axle stands. Chock the rear wheels.

3 Two drain plugs are provided on early models – one for the gearbox and one for the differential (photo). On later models the gearbox drain plug is deleted and it is important not to confuse the reverse gear shaft clamping screw with a drain plug.

4 Unscrew the drain plug(s) and drain the oil into a suitable container. On completion refit and tighten the drain plug(s).

5 There is no provision for a level plug so the correct quantity of oil must be measured before refilling the gearbox through the filler plug hole.

6 Lower the vehicle to the ground.

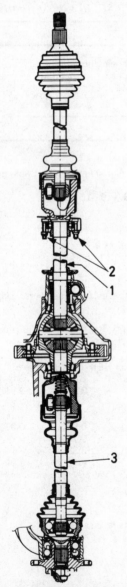

Fig. 4.1 Sectional view of the driveshaft (Sec 1)

1 *Right-hand driveshaft*   3 *Left-hand driveshaft*
2 *Support bearing retaining bolts*

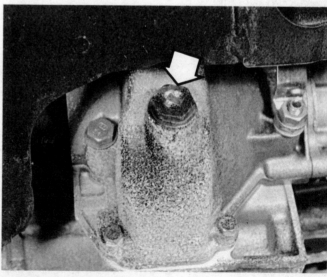

2.2 Differential drain plug (arrowed)

Renew the automatic transmission fluid (BX models)
7 Refer to the petrol-engined model manual.

Check the driveshaft rubber bellows
8 Jack up the front of the vehicle and support on axle stands. Chock the rear wheels.

9 Thoroughly check the driveshaft rubber bellows for splits and damage by turning the appropriate front wheel slowly. If necessary renew the bellows.

10 Remove the axle stands, lower the vehicle to the ground, and remove the chocks from the rear wheels.

3 Manual gearbox – removal and refitting

1 Jack up the front of the vehicle and support on axle stands. Also jack up the rear of the vehicle and support on axle stands so that the vehicle is level.

2 Remove the air cleaner (Chapter 3).

3 Remove the battery and its tray.

4 Unscrew the drain plug(s) and drain the gearbox oil into a suitable container. On completion refit and tighten the plug(s).

5 Unbolt the earth cable from the gearbox.

6 Unbolt the high pressure pump on BX models from the gearbox, leaving the lines attached. Remove the vacuum pump completely on Visa models (Chapter 5).

7 Unbolt the cable guide where fitted.

8 Disconnect the clutch cable and position it to one side. Recover the pushrod and, if fitted, the balance weight and the return spring (photos).

9 Disconnect the gearchange control rods (and cable if fitted).

10 Pull out the rubber cotter and disconnect the speedometer cable. Position it to one side.

11 Remove the left-hand front roadwheel.

12 Unbolt the inner shield from the wheel arch (where fitted).

13 Disconnect the wiring from the reversing lamp switch.

14 Disconnect the front track control arms from the stub axle carriers and, on BX models, unscrew the nut and separate the left-hand link rod from the anti-roll bar.

15 Have an assistant pull the left-hand strut outwards while the left-hand driveshaft is levered from the differential side gear. Hold the strut outwards with a block of wood.

16 On BX models manufactured before July 1984 the left-hand differential side gear must be supported using a suitable dowel, preferably wooden. If this precaution is not taken, the side gears may become misaligned when the right-hand driveshaft is removed.

17 Loosen the two nuts retaining the right-hand driveshaft intermediate bearing in the bracket bolted to the rear of the cylinder block and turn the bolt heads through 90° in order to release the bearing.

18 Have an assistant pull the right-hand wheel outwards while the right-hand driveshaft is removed from the differential side gear. Hold the wheel and strut out with a block of wood.

19 Position a piece of thin board over the radiator to protect it from possible damage.

20 Remove the starter motor.

3.8A Clutch cable and lever return spring

3.8B Removing the balance weight from the clutch cable

3.8C Feeding the clutch cable through the bracket

21 On BX models unbolt the hydraulic pressure regulator from the gearbox leaving the pressure lines attached.

22 Unbolt and remove the gearbox-to-engine lower cover.

23 Support the engine under the sump with a trolley jack and block of wood.

24 Unscrew the nut from the left-hand engine mounting and remove the rubber mounting.

25 On Visa models unbolt the support bracket.

26 Unscrew the left-hand mounting stud from the gearbox.

27 Lower the engine two or three inches, or on BX models until it touches the crossmember.

28 Unscrew and remove the four engine-to-gearbox bolts.

29 Lift the gearbox directly from the engine keeping it horizontal until clear of the clutch, then lower it to the ground.

30 Refitting is a reversal of removal, but before lifting the gearbox onto the engine, temporarily hold the clutch release arm in position using wire as shown in Fig. 4.2. Remove the wire after fitting the mounting bolts. Make sure that the two dowels are in place on the mating face of the gearbox. When fitting the left-hand mounting stud apply locking fluid to its threads before tightening to the specified torque. Tension the hydraulic pump or vacuum pump drivebelt with reference to Chapter 5 of this manual for Visa models or Chapter 8 of the petrol version manual for BX models. Refill the gearbox with oil as described in Section 2.

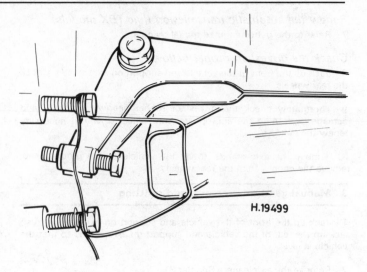

Fig. 4.2 Using two bolts and wire to hold the clutch release arm while refitting the gearbox (Sec 3)

engage a gear then immobilise the input shaft using an old clutch disc to which a metal bar has been welded (Fig. 4.3). It is unwise to attempt to grip the input shaft splines with any other tool as damage may be caused.

3 With the input and output shaft nuts slackened proceed as described for the five-speed gearbox.

4 When reassembling the gearbox use the same method described in paragraph 2 to tighten the shaft nuts. Remember to stake the nuts after tightening them.

5   Driveshaft rubber bellows – renewal

1 With the driveshaft removed (refer to the relevant manual for petrol-engined models for removal procedure) loosen the clips on the outer rubber bellows. If plastic straps are fitted cut them free with snips (photo).

2 Prise the bellows large diameter from the outer joint housing (photo), then tap the centre hub outwards using a soft metal drift in order to release it from the retaining circlip. Slide the outer joint complete from the driveshaft splines.

3 Extract the circlip from the groove in the driveshaft (photo).

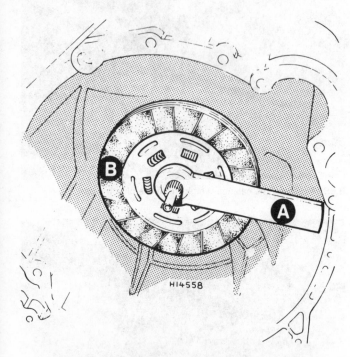

Fig. 4.3 Tool for locking the gearbox input shaft (Sec 4)

Lever (A) welded to old clutch disc (driven plate) (B)

4   Manual gearbox (4-speed) – dismantling and reassembly

1 The four-speed and five-speed manual gearboxes differ only in respect of the 5th gear and its associated components.

2 To remove the components the input and output shafts must be locked before unscrewing the end nuts. The best way to do this is to

5.1 Plastic straps on the outer rubber bellows

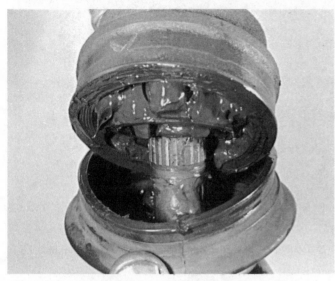

5.2 Removing the rubber bellows from the outer joint housing

5.3 Driveshaft outer joint retaining circlip (arrowed)

4   Prise off the rubber bellows. If necessary remove the plastic seating from the recess in the driveshaft (photos).

5   Loosen the clips on the inner rubber bellows. If plastic straps are fitted cut them free.

6   Prise the bellows large diameter from the inner joint housing and slide the rubber bellows off the outer end of the driveshaft (photo).

7   Mark the driveshaft and inner joint housing in relation to each other then separate them, keeping the rollers engaged with their respective spigots (photo).

8   Clean away the grease then retain the rollers using adhesive tape (photo).

9   Remove the pressure pad and spring from inside the inner joint housing (photo).

10 Clean away the grease then commence reassembly by inserting the pressure pad and spring into the inner joint housing with the housing mounted upright in a soft-jawed vice.

11 Inject half the required amount of grease into the inner joint housing (photo).

12 Locate the new inner rubber bellows halfway along the driveshaft (photo).

13 Remove the adhesive tape and insert the driveshaft into the housing.

14 Inject the remaining amount of grease in the joint.

15 Keeping the driveshaft pressed against the internal spring, refit the rubber bellows and tighten the clips. Metal type clips can be tightened using two pliers, by holding the buckle and pulling the clip through. Cut off the excess and bend the clip back under the buckle (photos).

16 Fit the plastic seating in the driveshaft recess and refit the new rubber bellows small diameter on it.

17 Refit the circlip in the driveshaft groove.

18 Inject the required amount of grease in the outer joint then insert the driveshaft, engage the splines, and press in until the circlip snaps into the groove.

19 Ease the rubber bellows onto the outer joint, and fit the two clips, tightening them as previously described.

5.4A Removing the outer rubber bellows from the driveshaft

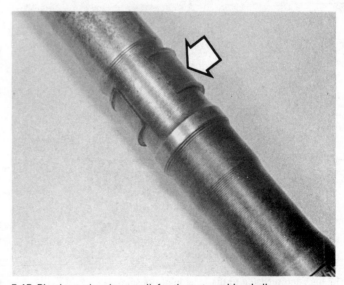

5.4B Plastic seating (arrowed) for the outer rubber bellows

5.6 Removing the inner rubber bellows

5.7 Separating the driveshaft and rollers from the inner joint housing

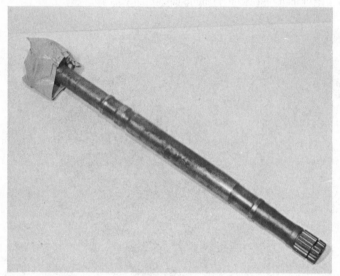
5.8 Left-hand driveshaft with rollers retained with adhesive tape

5.9 Removing the pressure pad and spring from the inner joint housing

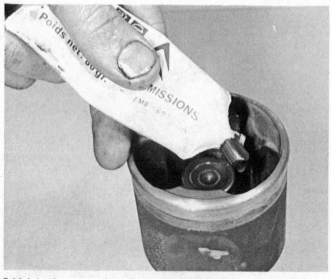
5.11 Injecting grease into the inner joint housing

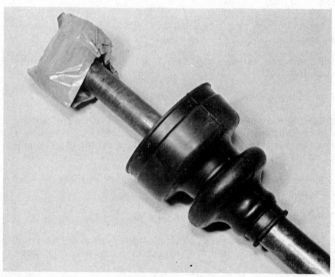
5.12 Inner rubber bellows located on the driveshaft

7 Have an assistant pull the right-hand wheel outwards while the right-hand driveshaft is removed from the differential side gear. Hold the strut out with a block of wood.

8 Using a screwdriver lever the oil seals from the gearbox (photo).

9 Clean the oil seal seatings in the gearbox.

10 Press the new left-hand oil seal squarely into the gearbox until flush using a block of wood.

11 The new right-hand oil seal is supplied with a protector to be used when fitting the driveshaft. First remove the protector and press the oil seal squarely into the gearbox until flush using a block of wood. Refit the protector having applied a little grease to the seal lips (photos).

12 Insert the right-hand driveshaft while guiding the intermediate bearing in the bracket (photo).

13 Pull out the protector and discard it. The protector is split so that it will pass over the driveshaft.

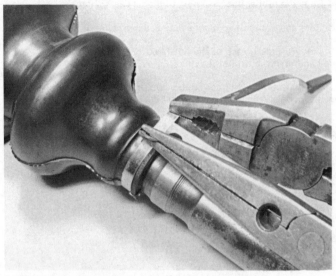

5.15A Tighten the metal clip ...

5.15B ... and bend it back under the buckle

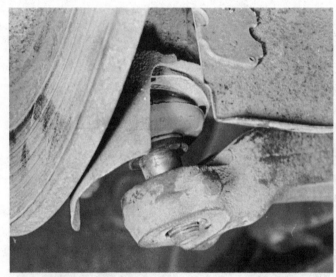

6.3 Disconnecting a front track control arm (BX model)

6 Driveshaft oil seals – renewal

1 Jack up the front of the vehicle and support on axle stands. Apply the handbrake on Visa models or chock the rear wheels on BX models.

2 Unscrew the drain plug(s) and drain the gearbox oil into a suitable container. On completion refit and tighten the plug(s).

3 Disconnect the front track control arms from the stub axle carriers (photo), and, on BX models, unscrew the nuts and separate the link rods from the anti-roll bar.

4 Have an assistant pull the left-hand wheel outwards while the left-hand driveshaft is levered from the differential side gear. Hold the strut outwards with a block of wood.

5 On BX models manufactured before July 1984 the left-hand differential side gear must be supported using a suitable dowel, preferably wooden. If this precaution is not taken, the side gears may become misaligned when the right-hand driveshaft is removed.

6 Loosen the two nuts retaining the right-hand driveshaft intermediate bearing in the bracket bolted to the rear of the cylinder block and turn the bolt heads through 90° in order to release the bearing.

6.8 Levering a driveshaft and oil seal from the gearbox

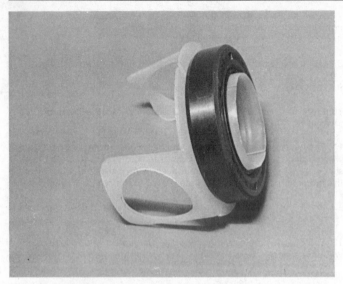

6.11A The right-hand driveshaft oil seal is supplied with a protector

14 Slide the rubber dust seal next to the oil seal (photo).

15 Refit and tighten the intermediate bearing bolts.

16 Apply a little grease to the left-hand oil seal lips then insert the left-hand driveshaft (photo).

17 Reconnect the front track control arms to the stub axle carriers and, on BX models, reconnect the anti-roll bar links.

18 Lower the vehicle to the ground and refill the gearbox with oil as described in Section 2.

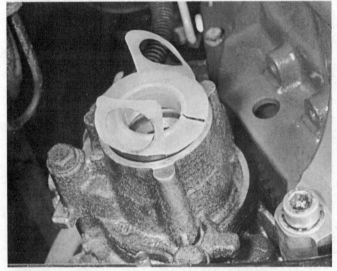

6.11B Right-hand driveshaft oil seal installed ready for driveshaft refitting

6.12 Refitting the right-hand driveshaft

6.14 Right-hand driveshaft rubber dust seal

6.16 Refitting the left-hand driveshaft

Chapter 5 Braking and hydraulic systems

Contents

Specifications

General

System type .... Discs front, drums rear on Visa models. Discs all round on BX models. Cable-operated handbrake on rear wheels for Visa models and front wheels for BX models.

Hydraulic fluid type/specification

BX models .... Green LHM fluid (Duckhams LHM fluid)
Visa models (braking system) .... Hydraulic fluid to SAE J1703 C (Duckhams Universal Brake and Clutch Fluid)

Front brakes (Visa models)

Disc diameter .... 247.0 mm (9.724 in)
Minimum disc thickness .... 8.0 mm (0.315 in)
Maximum disc run-out .... 0.07 mm (0.003 in)
Maximum variation of disc thickness .... 0.02 mm (0.0008 in)
Minimum disc pad lining thickness .... 2.0 mm (0.079 in)

Rear brakes (Visa models)

Maximum drum internal diameter:
  Saloon .... 181.0 mm (7.126 in)
  Van .... 229.6 mm (9.039 in)
Minimum rear brake shoe lining thickness .... 1.0 mm (0.04 in)
Brake limiter adjustment (Van models):
  Cable clamp-to-lever contact faces clearance .... 4.0 to 5.0 mm (0.158 to 0.197 in)

Vacuum pump (Visa models)

Drivebelt tension .... Approx 5.0 mm (0.2 in) deflection midway between pulleys
Oil capacity .... 40 cc
Oil grade .... SAE 10W 30

Torque wrench settings (Visa models)

	Nm	lbf ft
Master cylinder	8	6
Servo unit	8	6
Cross-tube brackets	14	10
Rear hub nut (Saloon models)	190	140

1 General description

On Visa models the braking system is similar to that for petrol engine models, but there is insufficient vacuum for a vacuum servo unit. A vacuum pump, belt-driven from the camshaft, is therefore employed. The vacuum servo unit and master cylinder are located on the left-hand side of the bulkhead. A cross-tube mounted inside the passenger compartment links the brake pedal to the vacuum servo unit.

On BX models the braking system is virtually identical to that on petrol engine models.

2 Routine maintenance

The Routine Maintenance procedures are as for petrol engine models but including the following:

Check vacuum pump oil level (Visa models)

1 With the vehicle on level ground, unscrew the filler/level plug and check that the oil level is up to the bottom of the hole (see photo 10.5). If not, top up with the correct grade of oil then refit and tighten the plug.

Check vacuum pump drivebelt tension (Visa models)

2 Depress the drivebelt midway between the pulleys. If the deflection is not as given in the Specifications, loosen the pivot and adjustment bolts, reposition the vacuum pump, then tighten the bolts.

3 Hydraulic system (BX models) – general

1 The high pressure pump is belt-driven from a pulley attached to the end of the camshaft. The pump mounting bracket is bolted to the top of the gearbox as also is the adjusting link (photos).

2 Apart from the different location of the high pressure pump, the hydraulic system components and procedures are as described for the petrol engine model.

3.1A HP pump adjusting bolt on BX models

3.1B HP pump pivot bolt on BX models

3.1C HP pump mounting bracket on BX models

3.1D Checking HP pump drivebelt tension on BX models

4 Handbrake (Visa models) – adjustment

1 Chock the front wheels then jack up the rear of the vehicle and support on axle stands.

2 Fully depress the footbrake pedal several times.

3 Apply the handbrake lever to the third notch. Turn each rear wheel separately and check that there is a slight resistance to movement, indicating that the brake shoes are just touching the drums.

4 If necessary adjust the cable with the handbrake lever still on the third notch. On Van models loosen the locknut on the primary cable, turn the adjustment nut as required, then tighten the locknut. On Saloon models turn the outer cable adjusters where they emerge from the vehicle floor. Check that there is equal resistance to both rear wheels.

5 Apply the handbrake lever to the fifth notch and check that both rear wheels are locked.

6 Lower the vehicle to the ground.

5 Rear brake drum (Visa Saloon models) – removal and refitting

1 Jack up the rear of the car and support on axle stands. Chock the front wheels. Remove the rear wheel.

2 Prise the dust cap from the centre of the drum.

3 Unscrew the hub nut, recover the washer and withdraw the brake drum. If difficulty is experienced due to the drum being excessively worn, insert a screwdriver through a wheel bolt hole and prise the spring tensioned sector from the automatic adjustment lever (see Fig. 5.2).

4 Before refitting the drum, ensure that the bearings and the space between them are greased.

5 Refit the drum on the stub axle, followed by the washer and a new hub nut.

6 Tighten the hub nut to the specified torque then lock the collar into the stub axle groove using a round-ended drift.

7 Tap the dust cap into position.

8 Refit the rear wheel and lower the car to the ground. Apply the footbrake pedal several times to reset the automatic adjuster.

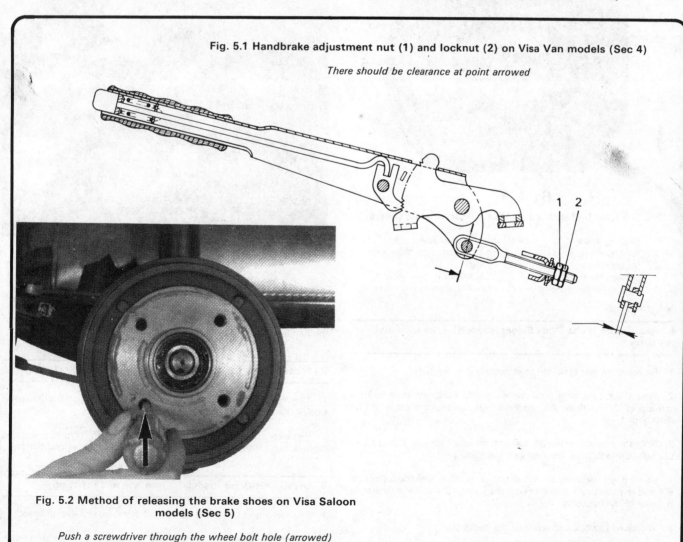

Fig. 5.1 Handbrake adjustment nut (1) and locknut (2) on Visa Van models (Sec 4)

There should be clearance at point arrowed

Fig. 5.2 Method of releasing the brake shoes on Visa Saloon models (Sec 5)

Push a screwdriver through the wheel bolt hole (arrowed)

Fig. 5.3 Backplate access hole (1) on Visa Saloon models
(Sec 6)

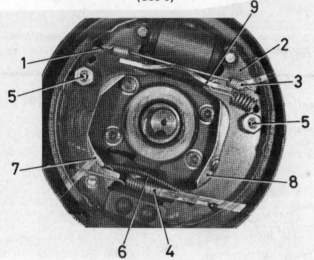

Fig. 5.4 Rear brake shoes on Visa Saloon models (Sec 6)

1	Leading shoe	6	Handbrake cable
2	Trailing shoe		(disconnected to show end
3	Upper return spring		fitting)
4	Lower return spring	7	Self-adjusting mechanism
5	Anti-rattle springs	8	Handbrake lever
		9	Strut

6 Rear brake shoes (Visa Saloon models) – removal and refitting

1   Remove the rear brake drum as described in Section 5.

2   Prise the rubber plug from the rear of the backplate then insert a screwdriver and actuate the handbrake lever so that the cable can be disengaged.

3   Note the position of the top and bottom return springs. Using a pair of pliers, unhook them from the brake shoes.

4   Using pliers, depress the anti-rattle spring cups, turn them through 90° and remove them, together with the springs. Extract the pins from the rear of the backplate.

5   Withdraw the brake shoes from the backplate.

6   Disengage the strut and detach the self-adjusting levers from the leading shoe.

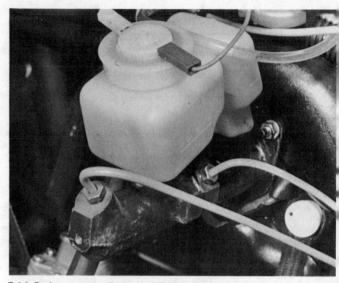

7.1A Brake master cylinder on Visa models

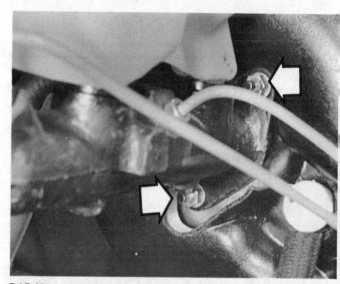

7.1B Master cylinder mounting nuts (arrowed) on Visa models

7   Refitting is a reversal of removal, but before fitting the return springs, actuate the self-adjusting mechanism to set the brake shoes to slightly less than the internal diameter of the brake drum. Finally adjust the handbrake as described in Section 4.

7 Master cylinder (Visa models) – removal and refitting

1   The master cylinder is located on the servo unit on the left-hand side of the bulkhead (photos).

2   Removal and refitting procedures are as given for petrol-engined models, but before starting work remove the air cleaner and battery.

8 Servo unit (Visa models) – removal and refitting

1   The servo unit is located on the left-hand side of the bulkhead.

2   Removal and refitting procedures are as given for petrol engine models, but access to the mounting nuts is gained by extracting the cross-head screws and removing the left-hand side shelf (photos).

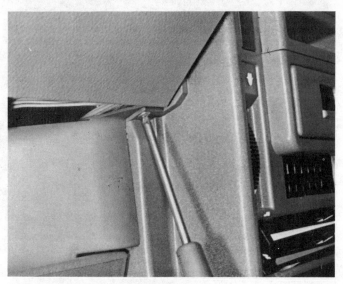

8.2A Extract the shelf cross-head screws ...

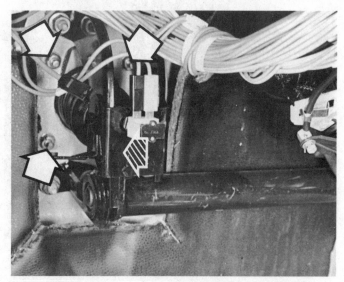

8.2B ... for access to the servo unit mounting nuts (arrowed)

9 Pedal cross-tube (Visa models) – removal and refitting

1 Disconnect the battery negative lead.

2 Extract the cross-head screws and remove the right-hand side shelf (photos). Similarly remove the left-hand side shelf.

3 Remove the steering column as described for petrol engine models.

4 Disconnect the accelerator cable from the pedal.

5 Disconnect the clutch cable from the pedal.

6 Remove the clevis pin and disconnect the servo unit pushrod from the cross-tube.

7 Disconnect the wiring from the stop-lamp switch.

8 Unscrew the nuts and detach the left and right-hand brackets from the bulkhead.

9 Extract the spring clips and disconnect the link from the brake pedal and cross-tube.

10 Withdraw the brackets from each end of the cross-tube, then withdraw the cross-tube from the vehicle.

11 Refitting is a reversal of removal, but adjust the clutch and accelerator cables.

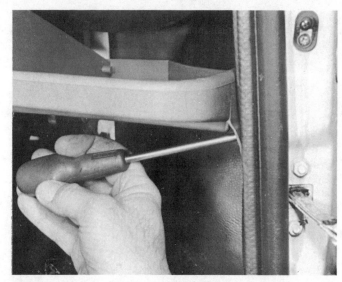

9.2A Removing the right-hand shelf side ...

10 Vacuum pump (Visa models) – removal and refitting

1 Remove the air cleaner and ducting.

2 Disconnect the inlet and outlet hoses.

3 Loosen the pivot and adjustment link bolts and nuts, swivel the vacuum pump upwards and slip the drivebelt from the pulleys.

4 Unscrew the bolts and remove the vacuum pump from the mounting bracket and adjustment link.

5 Refitting is a reversal of removal, but swivel the pump downwards until the drivebelt tension is as given in the Specifications before tightening the pivot and adjustment link bolts and nuts. With the vehicle on level ground, unscrew the filler/level plug (photo) and check that the oil level is up to the bottom of the hole. If not, top up with the correct grade of oil then refit and tighten the plug.

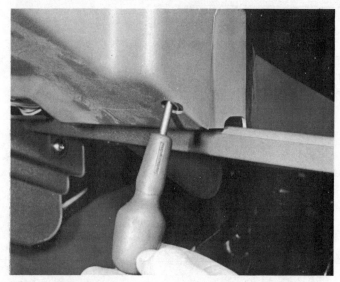

9.2B ... and centre screws

9.2C Brake pedal and cross-tube with shelf removed

10.5 View of vacuum pump with air cleaner removed showing filler/level plug (arrowed)

Chapter 6 Suspension and steering

Contents

Specifications

Front suspension

Type:

Visa models .... Independent, MacPherson strut and coil spring, with anti-roll bar. Front subframe carries track control arms, steering gear and anti-roll bar

BX models .... Independent, with upper and lower arms, hydropneumatic cylinders

Wheel alignment:

	Visa	BX
Camber	0°16′ ± 30′	0° ± 30′
Castor	To Aug '85 1°20′ ± 30′	2° ± 35′
	From Aug '85 1° 33′ ± 30′	
Steering axis inclination	9°16′ ± 40′	12°
Toe setting	To Aug '85 2.0 ± 1 mm	0 to 3.0 mm (0 to 0.118 in)
	(0.079 ± 0.039 in) toe-out	toe-out
	From Aug '85 0 to 2.0 mm	
	(0 to 0.079 in) toe-in	

Rear suspension

Type:

Visa models .... Independent, trailing arms and hydraulic dampers with coil springs

BX models .... Independent, trailing arms, hydropneumatic cylinders

Wheel alignment:

	Visa	BX
Camber	1°30′	0° 09′ ± 20′
Toe setting	1.0 to 4.0 mm (0.039 to 0.157 in) toe-in	0 to 5.0 mm (0 to 0.197 in) toe-in

Steering

Type .... Rack and pinion with safety column

Turning circle (between kerbs):

Visa .... 10.06 m (33 ft 0 in)

BX:

Manual steering .... 10.17 m (33 ft 4 in)

Power steering .... 10.37 m (34 ft 0 in)

Wheels

Type .... Pressed steel

Size:

Visa .... 4.50 B 13 FH 4.35 or 4.30

BX .... 5.00 B 14 FH 4.25

Tyres

Size:

Visa .... 145 SR 13 or 155 SR 13

BX .... 165/70 R 14

Pressures – bar (lbf/in²):	Front	Rear
Visa:		
145 SR 13 tyres	2.2 (32)	2.0 (29)
155 SR 13 tyres	2.3 (33)	2.6 (38)
BX:		
Saloon	2.1 (30)	2.1 (30)
Estate	2.3 (33)	2.5 (36)

Torque wrench settings (Visa models)

	Nm	lbf ft
Anti-roll bar to track control arm	75	55
Track control arm pivot bolt	35	26
Anti-roll bar mounting	35	26
Anti-roll guide bar to anti-roll bar	30	22
Anti-roll guide bar to subframe	25	18
Steering gear mounting	35	26
Track rod end nut	35	26
Steering shaft to pinion	15	11

1 General description

On Visa models the front subframe differs from that fitted to petrol engine models in that it carries the track control arm inner pivots, the steering gear and the anti-roll bar which is mounted from the rear. In all other respects the components and work procedures are similar to those described for the GTi model in the Supplement of the petrol-engined models manual.

The suspension and steering components fitted to BX models are identical to those on petrol engine models.

2 Front track control arm (Visa models) – removal, overhaul and refitting

1 Jack up the front of the vehicle and support on axle stands. Apply the handbrake and remove the roadwheel.

2 Unscrew the nut from the inner pivot bolt (photo).

3 Have an assistant hold the suspension strut pressed inwards then remove the bolt and release the strut. Note that the bolt head faces to the rear.

4 Unscrew the clamp bolt securing the lower balljoint to the hub carrier, then drive a suitable wedge into the slot and release the lower suspension arm. Remove the balljoint protector where fitted.

5 Unscrew the nut from the end of the anti-roll bar, remove the washer, and withdraw the track control arm.

6 The rubber bushes may be renewed if necessary. Lever or drive out the anti-roll bar bushes. Ideally, the pivot bush should be pressed out using a bench press or flypress. However, it is possible to remove and insert the bush using a long bolt, nut and washers and a suitable metal tube.

2.2 Front track control arm inner pivot bolt (arrowed) on Visa models

7 Refitting is a reversal of removal, but tighten the bolts to the specified torque with the weight of the vehicle on the front suspension. On completion check and if necessary adjust the steering angles and front wheel alignment.

3 Front anti-roll bar (Visa models) – removal and refitting

1 Jack up the front of the vehicle and support on axle stands. Apply the handbrake and remove both roadwheels.

2 Remove one track control arm with reference to Section 2.

3 Unscrew the nut securing the remaining end of the anti-roll bar to the other track control arm and recover the washer.

4 Unbolt the guide bar from the subframe.

5 Unscrew the mounting clamp bolts (photo) and withdraw the anti-roll bar over the subframe. If necessary disconnect the gearchange rods to provide additional working room.

6 Examine the rubber bearings for damage and deterioration, and renew them if necessary.

7 Refitting is a reversal of removal, but delay fully tightening the clamp bolts until the full weight of the vehicle is on the suspension. The guide bar bolt (photo) should also remain loosened until after the bearing clamp bolts have been tightened and its length should be suitably adjusted (see Fig. 6.2).

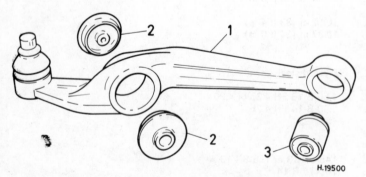

H.19500

Fig. 6.1 Front track control arm components for Visa models (Sec 2)

1 *Track control arm*   3 *Pivot bush*
2 *Anti-roll bar bushes*

3.5 Anti-roll bar mounting clamp bolts (arrowed) on Visa models

3.7 Guide bar adjustment clamp for the anti-roll bar on Visa models

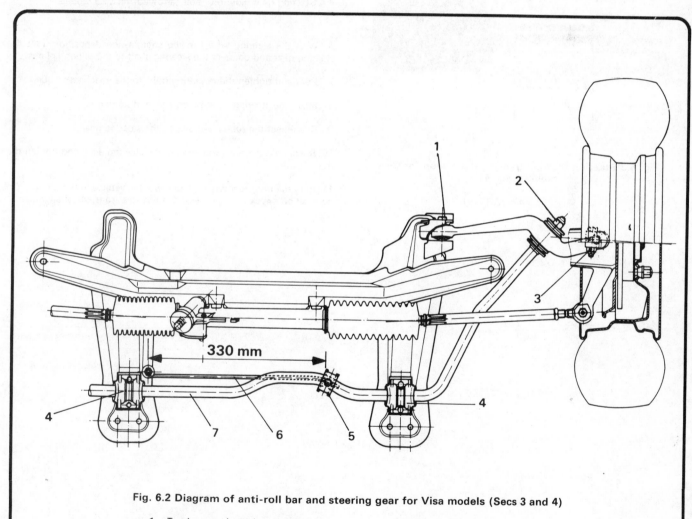

330 mm

Fig. 6.2 Diagram of anti-roll bar and steering gear for Visa models (Secs 3 and 4)

1   Track control arm inner pivot bolt
2   Anti-roll bar front mounting nut
3   Lower balljoint pinch-bolt
4   Rear mounting clamps

5   Guide bar adjustment clamp
6   Guide bar
7   Anti-roll bar

4 Steering gear (Visa models) – removal and refitting

1   Jack up the front of the vehicle and support on axle stands. Apply the handbrake. Remove the front roadwheels.

2   Unscrew the nuts from the track rod end balljoint studs and, with a suitable balljoint splitter, disconnect the balljoints from the steering arms.

3   Unscrew and remove the pinch-bolt securing the bottom of the steering shaft to the steering gear pinion splines.

4   Unscrew the mounting bolts (photo), and withdraw the steering gear sideways from the subframe.

5   Commence refitting by centralising the rack. To do this, disconnect the rubber bellows and set the rack to the dimension shown in Fig. 6.3.

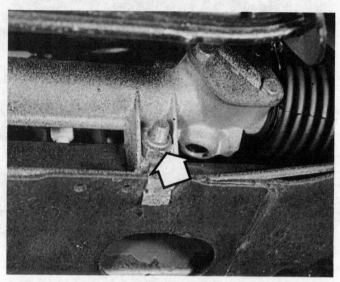

4.4 Steering gear mounting bolt (arrowed) on Visa models

6   With the steering wheel in the straight-ahead position, refit the steering gear and connect the steering shaft to the pinion splines.

7   Refit and tighten the mounting bolts to the specified torque.

8   Insert the steering shaft pinch-bolt and tighten it.

9   Reconnect the rubber bellows to the steering gear.

10 Reconnect the track rod ends to the steering arms and tighten the nuts.

11 Refit the front roadwheels and lower the vehicle to the ground. On completion check and if necessary adjust the front wheel alignment.

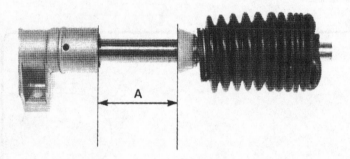

Fig. 6.3 Steering rack centralising dimension for Visa models (Sec 4)

A = 72.5 mm (2.85 in)

Chapter 7 Electrical system

For modifications, and information applicable to later models, see Supplement at end of manual

Contents

Specifications

General

System type	12 volt, negative earth, with alternator and pre-engaged starter motor
Battery capacity:	
Visa	42Ah
BX	50Ah or 83Ah

Alternator

	Visa	**BX**
Make	Bosch, Melco or Paris-Rhone	Melco or Bosch
Output	47 amps	50 amps
Regulated voltage (warm)	13.5 volts	13.8 to 14.5 volts

Starter motor

Make	Bosch or Mitsubishi/Melco

Fuses (Visa models)

No	Amps	Circuits protected
1	10	RH side and tail lamps, RH number plate lamp, ignition switch lighting
2	16	LH and RH direction indicators, rear screen wash/wipe, electric window relay, instrument lighting, all warning lamps
3	20	Stop-lamps, heated rear screen, electric cooling fan, windscreen wiper and washer
4	16	Cigar lighter, interior lamps, radio, horn, clock, hazard warning
5	10	Rear foglamps
6	10	Reversing lamps
7	20	Front electric windows, central door locking
8	10	LH side and tail lamps, LH number plate lamp, switch illumination

Fuses (BX models)

No	Amps	Circuits protected
1	10	Reversing lamps, electric cooling fan relay, water temperature control, oil pressure gauge, tachometer, water level warning
2	25	Heater motor, air conditioning, direction indicators, instrument lighting, all warning lamps
3	25	Heated rear screen relay, power window relays, stop-lamps, door warning, front and rear wash/wipe, glovebox lamp, spotlamps, lighting rheostat, clock, ABS warning, sunroof
4	30	Electric cooling fans
5	10	Hazard warning lamps
6	30	Electric rear window winders
7	30	Central door locking, interior lamps, glovebox lamp, cigar lighter, radio, clock
8	25	Heated rear screen, horn
9	30	Electric front window winders
10	5	Rear fog lamps
11	5	RH rear lamp
12	5	LH rear lamp; rear number plate lamp
13	5	LH and RH sidelamps, digital clock, lighting dimmer, illumination for hazard warning switch, heated rear screen, rear fog-lamps and screen wiper, sidelamp indicator
14		ABS system

Bulbs (watts)

	Visa	BX
Headlamps	45/40 (17D) 60/55 (17 RD)	55/60
Sidelamps	4	4
Direction indicators	21	21
Side repeaters	4	4
Stop-lamps	21	21
Tail lamps	5	5
Reversing lamps	21	21
Number plate lamps	5	5
Rear foglamp	21	21
Interior lamps	7	7
Map reading lamp	7	7
Glovebox lamp	2	2
Boot lamp	5	5

Torque wrench settings

	Nm	lbf ft
Alternator mountings	35	26
Starter motor bolts	34	25

1 General description

The electrical system is of 12 volt negative earth type. The main components are a 12 volt battery, an alternator with integral voltage regulator, and a pre-engaged starter motor (with reduction gears on some models). The starter motor incorporates a one-way clutch on its pinion shaft in order to prevent the engine driving the motor when it starts.

It is important to disconnect the battery leads before charging the battery, removing the alternator, or working on wiring circuits which are permanently live. Additionally the alternator wiring must be disconnected before using electric arc welding equipment.

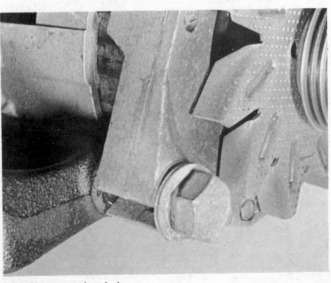

3.2 Alternator wires (arrowed)

2 Routine maintenance

The procedures are as described for petrol models, but refer to Section 3 of this Chapter when adjusting the alternator drivebelt tension.

3 Alternator – removal and refitting

1 Disconnect the battery negative lead.

2 Disconnect the wiring from the back of the alternator (photo).

3 Loosen the pivot bolt and adjustment locknut (photos).

4 Unscrew the adjustment bolt to release the tension then slip the drivebelt from the pulleys.

5 Remove the adjustment locknut, swivel the alternator outwards, and lift it from the engine. Note that the alternator is slotted to allow removal without removing the pivot bolt.

6 Refitting is a reversal of removal, but tension the drivebelt so that there is approximately 6.0 mm (0.23 in) deflection under moderate thumb pressure midway between the pulleys (photo).

3.3A Alternator pivot bolt

3.3B Alternator adjustment locknut (1) and adjustment bolt (2)

3.6 Checking tension of alternator drivebelt

4.3A Starter motor solenoid wiring (Bosch)

4 Starter motor – removal and refitting

1   Disconnect the battery negative lead.

2   Remove the air cleaner (Chapter 3).

3   Unscrew the nut and disconnect the large cable from the solenoid. Also disconnect the small trigger wire (photos).

4   Using a hexagon key, unscrew the three mounting bolts. On BX models note the location of the hydraulic pipe support bracket (photo).

5   Withdraw the starter motor from the gearbox (photo).

6   Refitting is a reversal of removal, but tighten the bolts evenly to the specified torque.

4.3B Starter motor solenoid wiring (Mitsubishi/Melco)

4.4 Removing the starter motor mounting bolts on BX models

4.5 Removing the starter motor (Mitsubishi/Melco)

5.3 Removing the through-bolts

5   Starter motor (Mitsubishi/Melco) – dismantling and reassembly

1   Clean the starter motor exterior surfaces.

2   Mark the yoke, drive end bracket and commutator end cover in relation to each other.

3   Unscrew and remove the through-bolts (photo). Unscrew the small screws and lift off the commutator end cover.

4   Remove the spacer from the end bearing (photo).

5   Using a hooked instrument, lift the springs in turn and extract the field brushes from the brush holder (photo).

6   Similarly lift the springs and extract the armature brushes. Remove the brush holder (photo).

7   Unscrew the nut and disconnect the main cable from the solenoid terminal.

8   Withdraw the yoke over the armature (photo).

9   Lift the armature and bearing from the intermediate bracket (photo).

10 Turn the drive end bracket over. Using a suitable metal tube, tap the stop ring clear of the spring clip. Extract the spring clip followed by the stop ring, pinion and spring (photo).

11 Remove the two screws and lift off the pinion shaft end cover (photo).

12 Prise out the C-clip and remove the thrust washer (photos).

13 Unscrew the cross-head screws securing the solenoid to the drive end bracket (photo).

14 Unhook the solenoid from the fork and remove the gasket (photo).

15 Unscrew the bolt and lift the intermediate bracket from the drive end bracket (photos).

16 Prise out the rubber plug and spring from the fork pivot (photo).

17 Remove the thrust washer from the pinion shaft, followed by the reduction gear (photos).

5.4 End bearing spacer removal

5.5A Brush holder prior to removal

5.5B Field brush (1) and armature brush (2)

5.6 Brush holder removed from starter motor

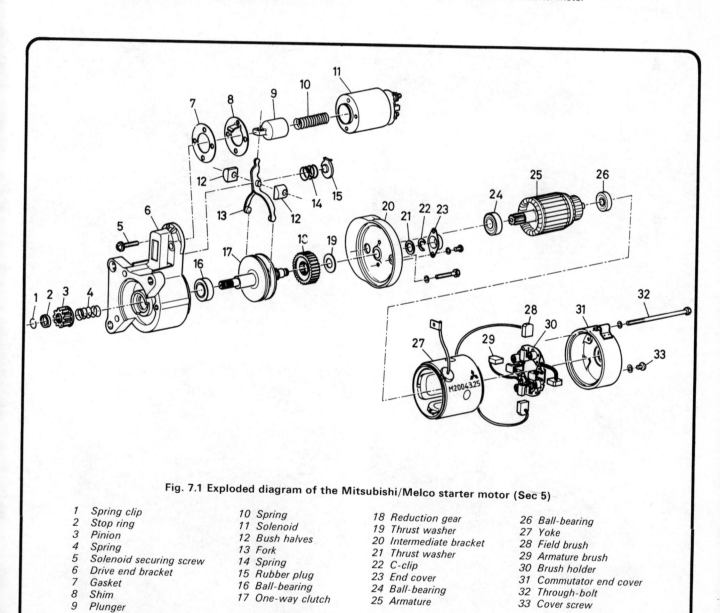

Fig. 7.1 Exploded diagram of the Mitsubishi/Melco starter motor (Sec 5)

1	Spring clip	10	Spring	18	Reduction gear	26	Ball-bearing
2	Stop ring	11	Solenoid	19	Thrust washer	27	Yoke
3	Pinion	12	Bush halves	20	Intermediate bracket	28	Field brush
4	Spring	13	Fork	21	Thrust washer	29	Armature brush
5	Solenoid securing screw	14	Spring	22	C-clip	30	Brush holder
6	Drive end bracket	15	Rubber plug	23	End cover	31	Commutator end cover
7	Gasket	16	Ball-bearing	24	Ball-bearing	32	Through-bolt
8	Shim	17	One-way clutch	25	Armature	33	Cover screw
9	Plunger						

5.8 Removing the yoke

5.9 Armature and bearing removal

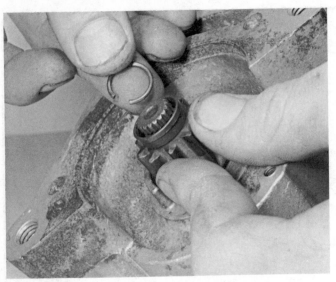

5.10A Extract the spring clip ...

5.10B ... followed by the stop ring ...

5.10C ... pinion ...

5.10D ... and spring

5.11 Removing the pinion shaft end cover

5.12A Prise out the C-clip ...

5.12B ... and remove the thrust washer

5.13 Solenoid mounting screws

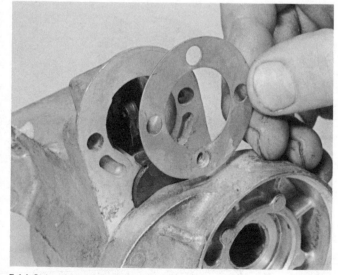

5.14 Solenoid gasket removal

5.15A Unscrew the bolt ...

5.15B ... and remove the intermediate bracket

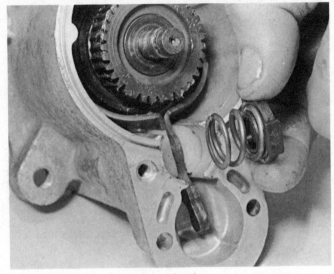

5.16 Removing the rubber plug and spring

5.17A Remove the thrust washer ...

18 Lift out the pinion shaft and fork then release the fork from the engagement groove (photos).

19 Remove the pivot bush halves from the fork (photo).

20 Clean all the components and examine them for wear and damage. Spin the ball-bearings on the armature shaft and in the drive end bracket and renew them if they feel rough or have excessive play. A puller will be required to remove the shaft bearings, and a suitable metal tube to drive out the bearing from the drive end bracket (photo).

21 Commence reassembly by fitting the new bearings. Use a metal tube on the inner track when fitting the bearings to the armature shaft, and a metal tube on the outer track when fitting the bearing to the drive end bracket.

22 Lightly grease the pivot bush halves and fit them to the fork.

23 Grease the fork ends and engage the fork with the groove in the pinion shaft. Locate the assembly in the drive end bracket.

24 Fit the reduction gear and thrust washer.

25 Locate the spring and rubber plug over the fork in the drive end bracket.

5.17B ... and reduction gear

5.18A Pinion shaft and fork in the drive end bracket

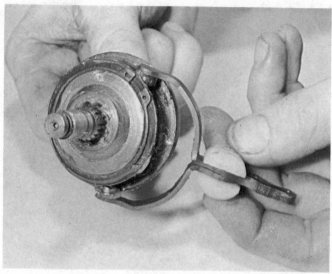

5.18B Separating the fork from the engagement groove

26 Grease the shaft then refit the intermediate bracket and secure with the bolt.

27 Locate the gasket, hook the solenoid onto the fork, and secure with the cross head screws (photos).

28 Push the pinion shaft into the drive end bracket and fit the thrust washer and C-clip (photo).

29 Refit the end cover then insert and tighten the screws.

30 Locate the spring, pinion, and stop ring on the pinion shaft. Insert the spring clip in the groove and draw the stop ring back over it.

31 Grease the gear teeth and refit the armature and bearing into the intermediate bracket.

32 Refit the yoke with the previously made marks aligned.

33 Reconnect the main cable to the solenoid terminal and tighten the nut.

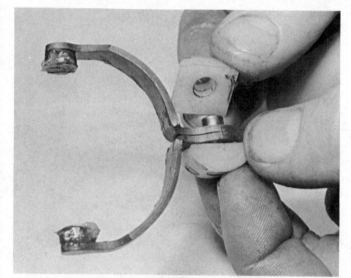

5.19 Dismantling the pivot bush halves

5.20 Drive end bracket bearing (arrowed)

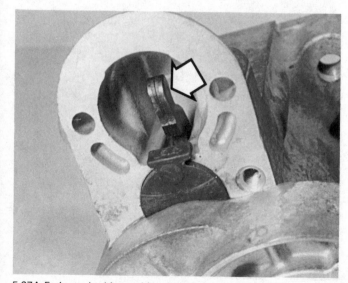

5.27A Fork arm in drive end bracket (arrowed)

5.27B Refitting the solenoid and gasket

5.28 Inserting the C-clip into the pinion shaft groove

34 Refit the brush holder. Lift the springs and insert the brushes then release the springs.

35 Locate the spacer on the end bearing.

36 Refit the commutator end cover with the previously made marks aligned. Insert and tighten the through-bolts and small screws.

6 Stop-lamp switch (Visa models) – removal and refitting

1 Extract the cross-head screws and withdraw the left-hand side shelf inside the vehicle.

2 Disconnect the wiring from the stop lamp switch (photo).

3 Unscrew the locknuts and remove the switch from the bracket.

4 Refitting is a reversal of removal, but adjust the switch so that the brake pedal has free movement of 2.5 mm (0.098 in).

7 Speedometer cable – removal and refitting

1 The procedure is similar to that described for petrol models, but to disconnect the speedometer cable from the gearbox pull out the rubber cotter (photo). Access may be found easier from beneath the vehicle.

8 Fuses and relays (Visa models) – general

1 The fuses are located on the bulkhead as on petrol models (photo).

2 Relays are located under a polythene cover beside the preheater relay on the left-hand side of the engine compartment (photo).

9 Washer pump – removal and refitting

1 The washer pump is located near the fluid reservoir on the bulkhead (photo). First note the location of the two wires then disconnect them from the terminals.

2 Note the location of the inlet and outlet pipes, and disconnect them.

3 Unbolt and remove the pump.

4 Refitting is a reversal of removal.

6.2 Stop-lamp switch – Visa models (arrowed)

7.1 Disconnecting the speedometer cable from the gearbox

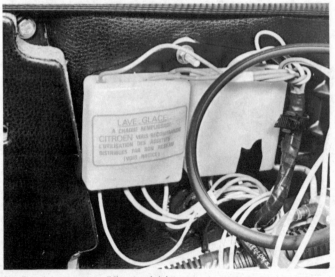

8.1 Fusebox location (Visa models)

8.2 Relay location (Visa models)

9.1 Washer pump (Visa models)

Wiring diagrams commence overleaf

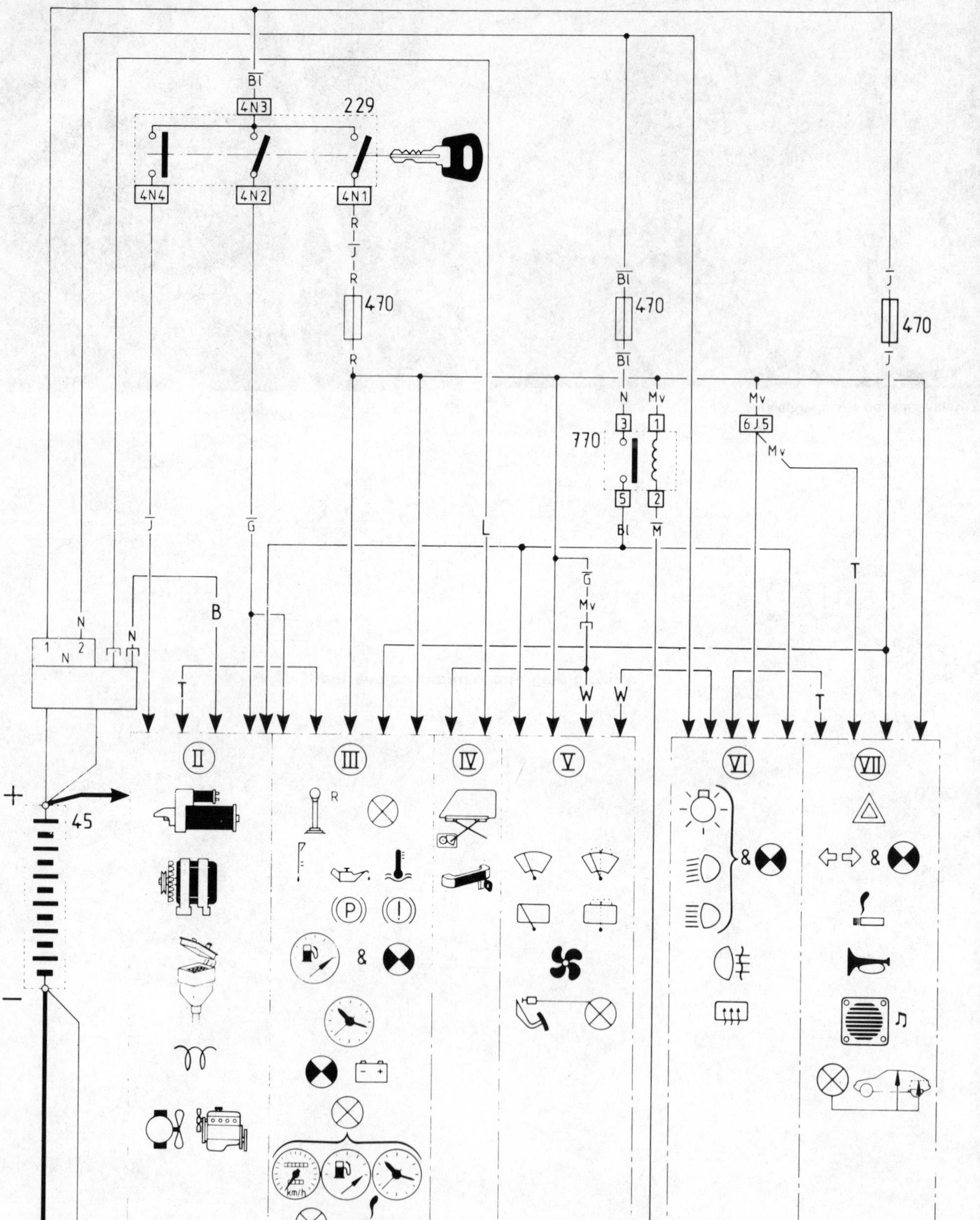

Fig. 7.2 Wiring diagram for Visa Diesel Saloons

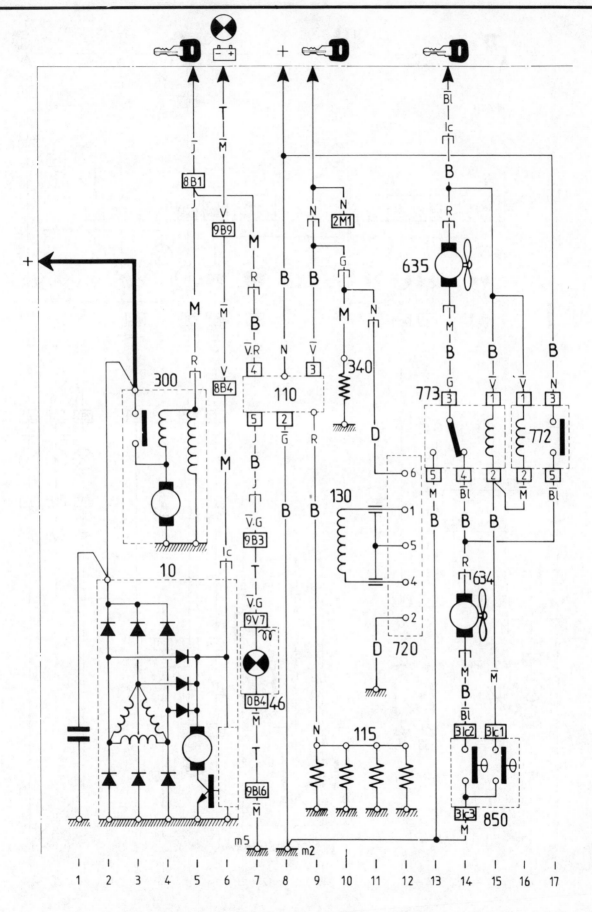

Fig. 7.2 Wiring diagram for Visa Diesel Saloons (continued)

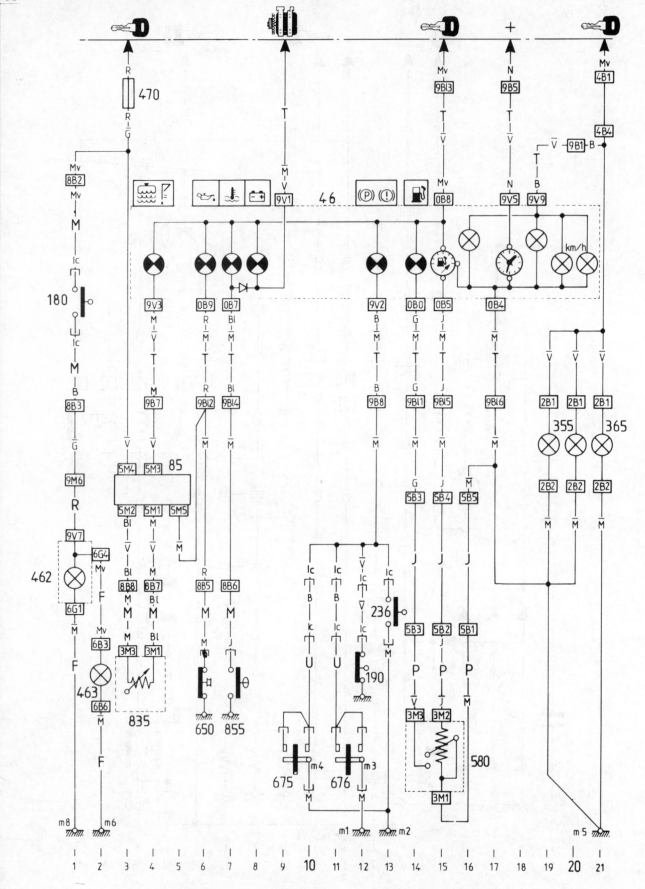

Fig. 7.2 Wiring diagram for Visa Diesel Saloons (continued)

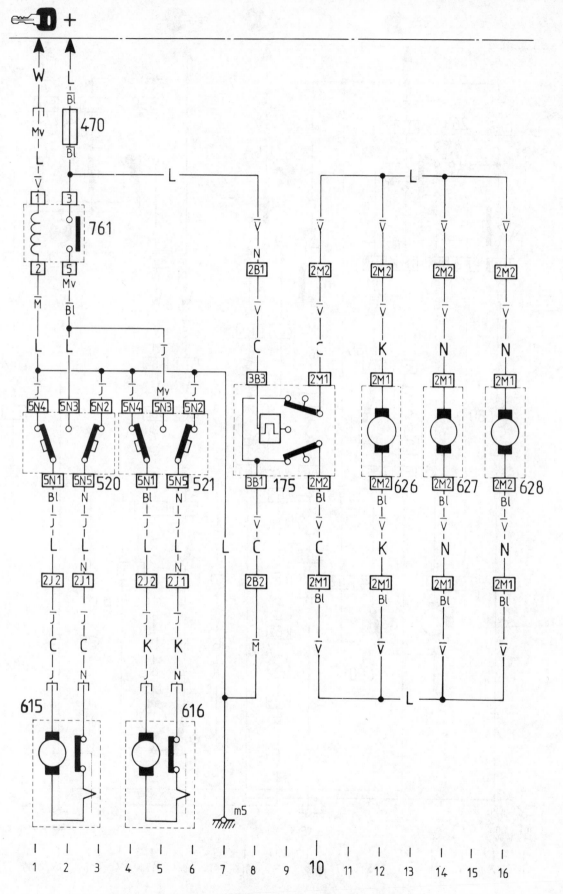

Fig. 7.2 Wiring diagram for Visa Diesel Saloons (continued)

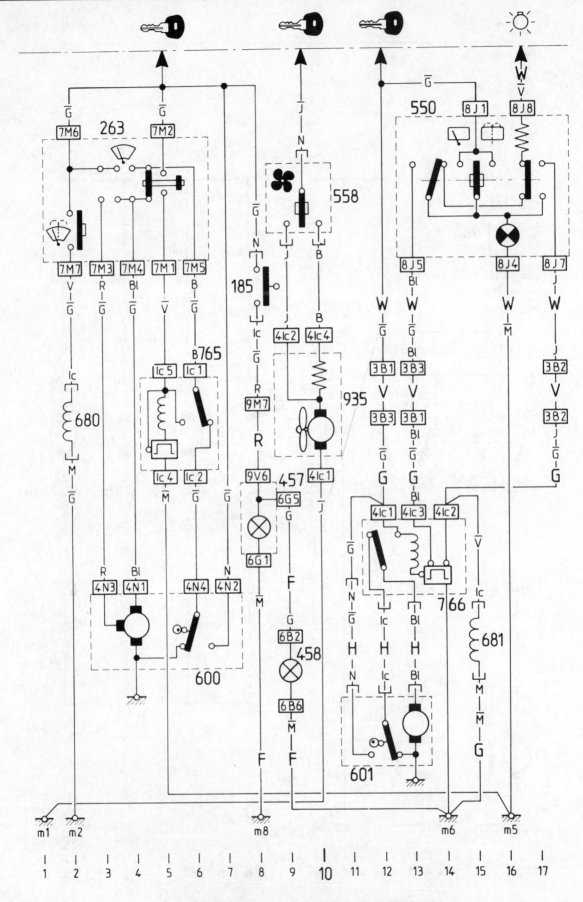

Fig. 7.2 Wiring diagram for Visa Diesel Saloons (continued)

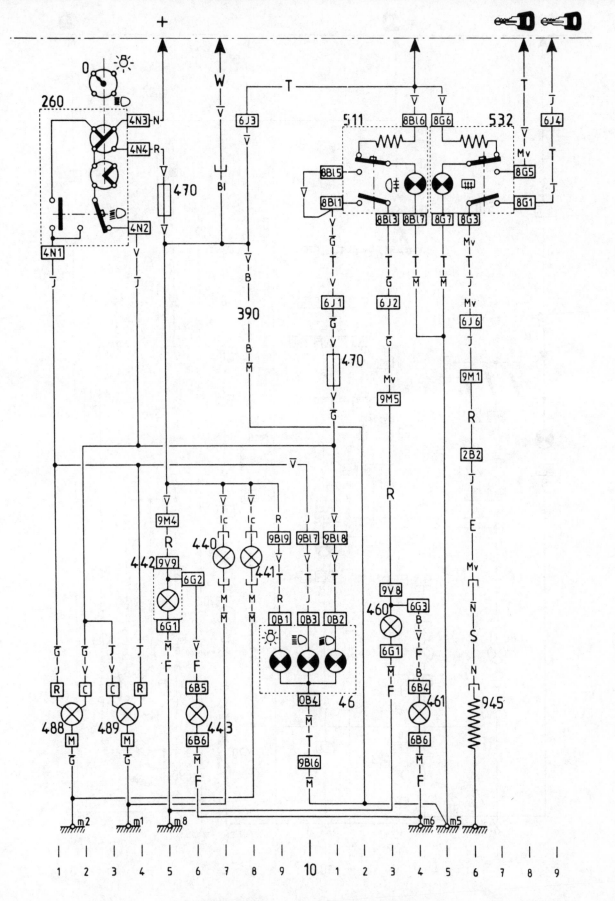

Fig. 7.2 Wiring diagram for Visa Diesel Saloons (continued)

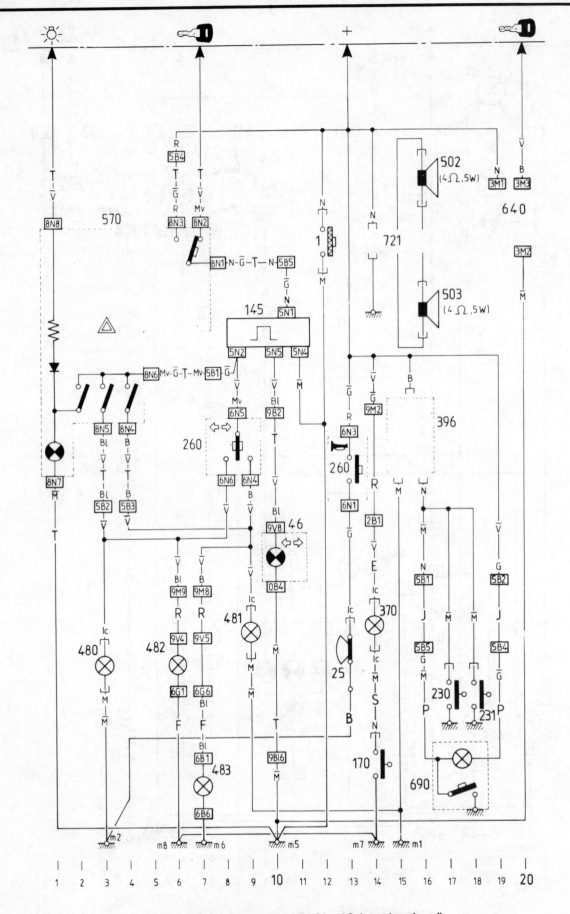

Fig. 7.2 Wiring diagram for Visa Diesel Saloons (continued)

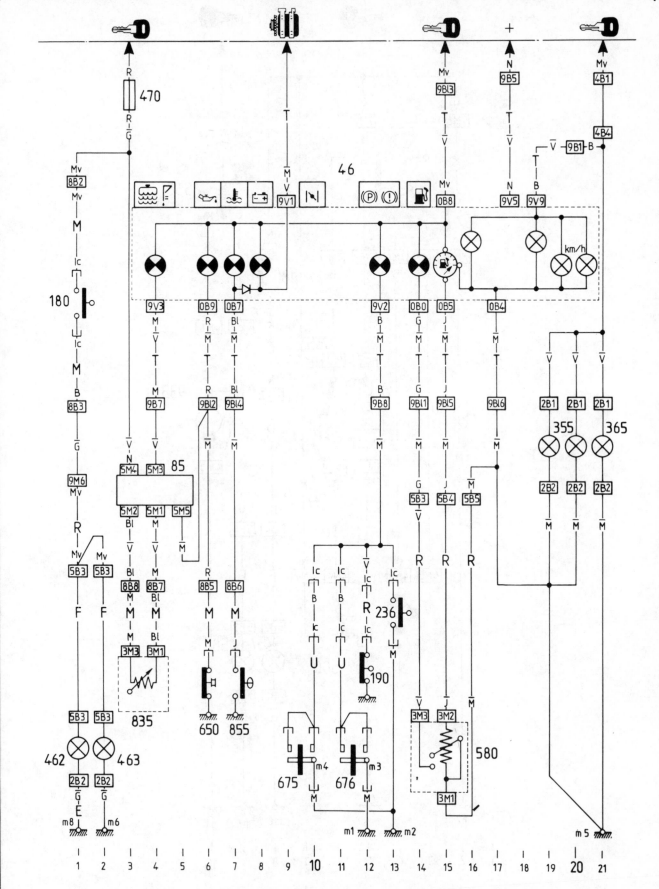

Fig. 7.3 Wiring diagram for Visa Diesel Vans

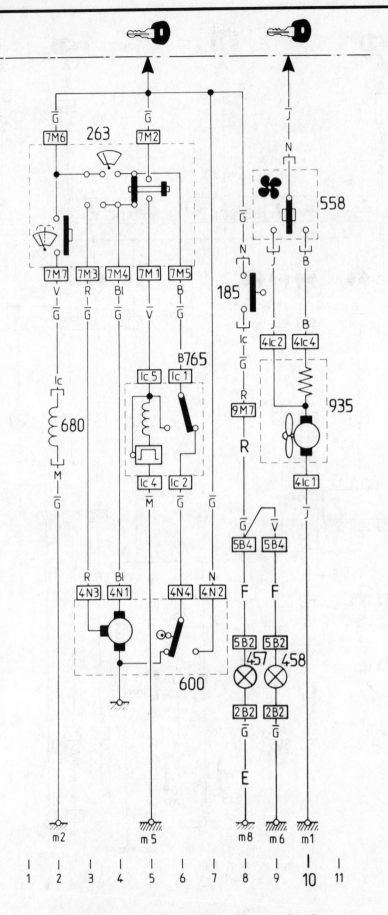

Fig. 7.3 Wiring diagram for Visa Diesel Vans (continued)

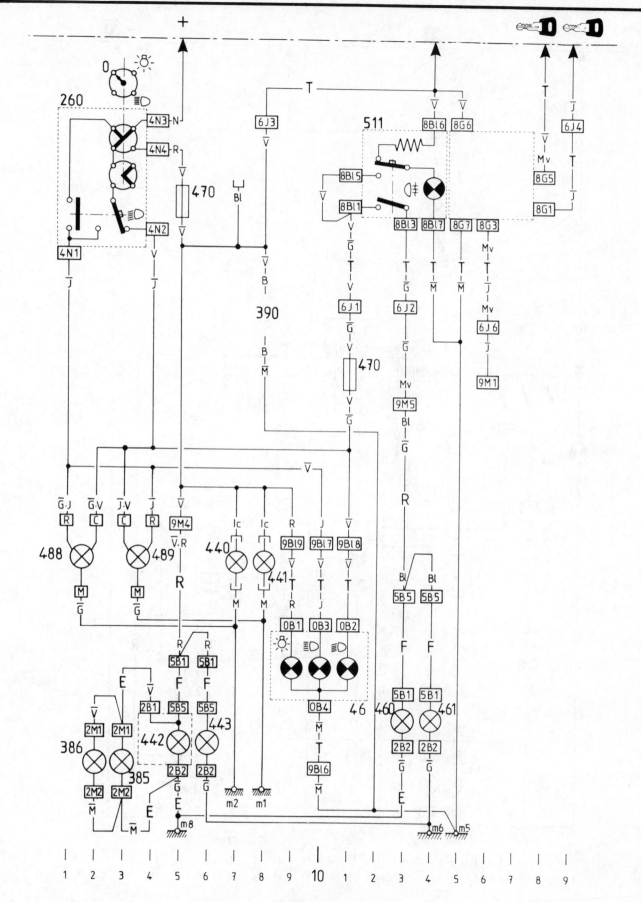

Fig. 7.3 Wiring diagram for Visa Diesel Vans (continued)

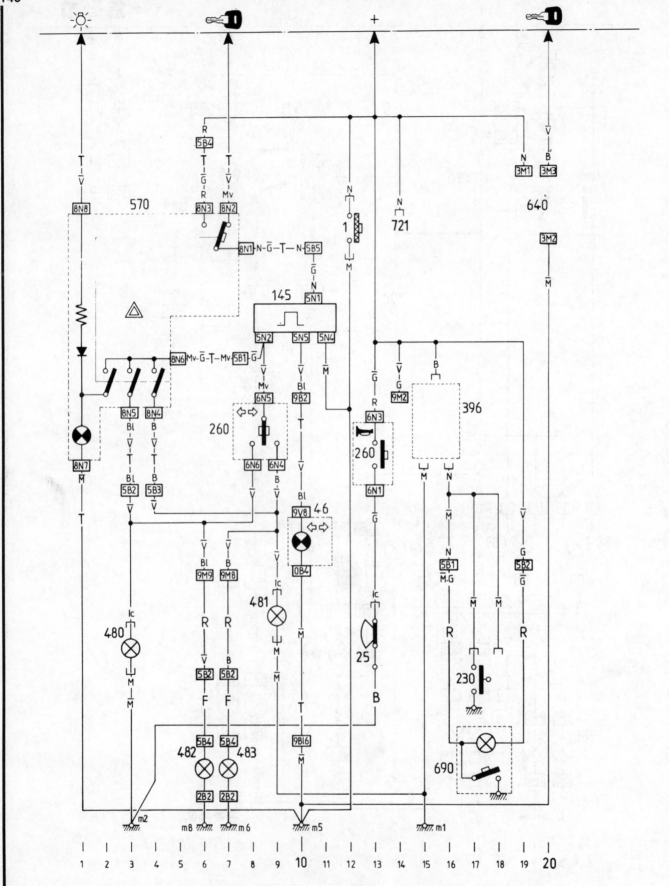

Fig. 7.3 Wiring diagram for Visa Diesel Vans (continued)

Key to wiring diagrams for Visa models

1	Cigar lighter		457	LH stop-lamp
5	Distributor		458	RH stop-lamp
10	Alternator		460	LH rear foglamp
25	Horn		461	RH rear foglamp
45	Battery		462	LH reversing lamp
46	Monitoring unit		463	RH reversing lamp
50	Ignition coil		470	Fuses reversing lamp
75	Ignition unit (module)		476	LH dipped beams
85	Electronic unit for oil level		477	RH dipped beams
110	Preheater control unit		478	LH main beams
114	Sparking plugs		479	RH main beams
115	Heater plugs		480	LH front direction indicator
130	TDC sensor		481	RH front direction indicator
131	Ignition pick up No 1		482	LH rear direction indicator
132	Ignition pick up No 2		483	RH rear direction indicator
136	Ignition vacuum sensor		488	LH main and dipped beams
140	Speed sensor		489	RH main and dipped beams
142	Computer		502	LH rear loudspeaker
145	Flasher unit		503	RH rear loudspeaker
158	Tailgate switches on keyboard		511	Rear foglamp switch
170	Tailgate contact switch		520	Switch for LH front window winder
175	Contact switch for door locking device		521	Switch for RH front window winder
180	Contact switch for reversing lamps		532	Switch for heated rear window
185	Stop-lamp contact switch		547	Check button for brake fluid level warning lamp
190	Handbrake contact switch		550	Switch for rear window wipe/wash
192	Contact switch on throttle spindle		551	Switch for rear screen intermittent wiper
225	Choke contact switch		558	Switch for air cooling fan
229	Anti-theft device contact switch		570	Switch for hazard warning signal
230	Door pillar contact switch (LH front door)		576	Injectors
231	Door pillar contact switch (RH front door)		580	Fuel gauge
236	Contact switch for brake fluid level		590	Map reading lamp
237	Contact switch for min water level		600	Windscreen wiper motor
258	Lighting switch		601	Rear window wiper motor
259	Selector switch for window wiper, flasher, horn		615	LH front window winder motor
260	Selector switch for lighting, flasher, horn		616	RH front window winder motor
262	Switch for lighting, windscreen wiper, flasher, horn		626	Motor for RH front door locking device
263	Selector switch for screen wipe/wash		627	Motor for LH rear door locking device
280	Auxiliary-air regulator		628	Motor for RH rear door locking device
285	Condenser coil "+" terminal		634	Engine electric cooling fan, RH
290	Tachometer		635	Engine electric cooling fan, LH
295	Horn compressor		640	Clock
300	Starter motor		650	Oil pressure switch
302	Flowmeter		670	LH headlamp
340	Electric cut-out control on pump		671	RH headlamp
355	Lighting for heater control		675	LH front brake pads
365	Ashtray lighting		676	RH front brake pads
370	Boot lighting		680	Windscreen washer pump
385	Lighting for LH number plate		681	Rear screen washer pump
386	Lighting for RH number plate		683	Petrol pump
390	Lighting for anti-theft switch		690	Centre interior lamp
396	Floor lighting, passenger side		720	Diagnostic socket
420	Idle cut-off		721	Radio terminals
440	LH sidelamp		731	Injection relay
441	RH sidelamp		733	Electric fan relay
442	LH tail lamp		737	Dipped beams relay
443	RH tail lamp		743	Horn compressor relay
445	LH rear lamp (cluster)		761	Front window winder relay
446	RH rear lamp (cluster)		765	Windscreen wiper relay

Key to wiring diagrams for Visa models (continued)

766	Rear screen wiper relay	840	Water temperature sensor
770	Relays for accesories	841	Water temperature sensor (injection)
772	Relay for electric fan 2nd speed	842	Oil pressure sensor
773	Relay reversing the electric fan speeds	843	Oil temperature sensor
788	Electric fan 2nd speed resistance	850	Electric fan thermal switch on coolant circuit
795	Rheostat for illumination	855	Water temperature switch
810	LH side repeater	935	Air conditioning cooling fan
811	RH side repeater	945	Heated rear window
835	Probe for oil level	958	Preheating warning lamp

Not all items fitted to all models

Harness code

A	Front (no mark on feed and function diagrams)	M	Engine
B	Electric fan	N	Rear door
C	LH front door	P	Interior lamp, gauge
D	Diagnostic	R	Rear
E	Boot lighting	S	Tailgate, LH
F	From LH rear lamp to RH rear lamp	T	Instrument panel
G	Rear screen washer time-delay	U	Brake wear
H	Tailgate, RH	V	Rear window wiper
J	Gauge	W	Rear window wiper switch
K	Passenger's door	Y	Injection
L	Window winder locking device	Z	Ignition

Colour code

B	White	Mv	Mauve
BL	Blue	N	Black
G	Grey	Or	Orange
Ic	Transparent	R	Red
J	Yellow	V	Green
M	Brown		

Key to wiring diagram for BX models

No	Description	Position	No	Description	Position
1	Front direction indicator, RH side	40		Direction indicator warning lamp	38
2	RH headlamp: sidelamp	98		Rear foglamp warning lamp	92
	Main and dipped beams	101, 102		Door locking device warning lamp	32 to 35
3	Water level switch	29		Handbrake warning lamp	39
4	Electric fan double thermal switch	15, 16		Clock	90
5	Electric cooling fan	15		Engine oil level indicator	24, 25
6	Electric fan resistor	15		Fuel gauge indicator	17
7	LH headlamp: sidelamp	97		Tachometer	18, 20
	Main and dipped beams	99, 100		Battery charge warning lamp	11
8	Connector for LH side repeater	42		Fuel min level warning lamp	16
9	LH front direction indicator	41		Water temperature warning lamp	22
10	Connector for RH side repeater	39		Front brake wear warning lamp	31
11	Starter motor	2 to 4		Emergency stop warning lamp and "STOP"	
12	Horn	50		test-button	22, 25, 27, 30
13	Alternator with integrated regulator	7 to 11		Hydraulic fluid level warning lamp (pressure	
14	Hydraulic fluid level switch	28		and level)	28
15	Stop electrovalve on injection pump	8		Engine oil pressure warning lamp	26
16	Heater plugs	4 to 6		Coolant level warning lamp	29
17	Engine oil pressure switch	26		Preheating warning lamp	20
18	Water temperature warning switch	22	54	Anti-theft switch	3, 6, 36, 55
19	Water temperature switch (flasher)	21	55	Lighting rheostat (via anti-theft switch)	78
20	Reversing lamp switch	12	56	Stop-lamp switch (braking)	74
21	Battery	1	57	LH loudspeaker	89
22	Stop electrovalve relay on Roto-Diesel pump	7, 8	58	LH control unit: lighting	92 to 99
23	Preheating box	4 to 6		Direction indicators	40, 41
24	LH front brake unit (wear)	30	59	Electronic unit for engine oil level	23 to 25
25	RH front brake unit (wear)	31	60	LH front door switch	81
26	Diagnostic socket	9, 18 to 21	61	LH front window winder motor	62 to 64
27	TDC sensor (diagnostic)	18, 19	62	LH front door locking device unit	103, 104
28	Plug for tachometer	9	63	LH interior lamp	81
29	Rear window washer pump	61	64	LH front door locking device switch	32
30	Engine oil level sensor	23, 24	65	RH interior lamp	83
31	Windscreen washer pump	56	66	RH rear window winder motor	71 to 73
32	Hydraulic fluid pressure switch	27	67	RH rear door locking device motor	107
33	Windscreen wiper motor	51 to 55	68	RH rear door locking device switch	34
34	Connection box (see detail)		69	RH rear door switch	81
35	Double channel "Boomer"	87, 88	70	Handbrake switch	39
36	RH front door switch	82	71	Accessory plug	79
37	RH loudspeaker	86	72	RH rear window winder switch	71 to 73
38	RH front window winder motor	65 to 67	73	LH front window winder switch	62 to 64
39	RH front door locking device unit	107, 108	74	RH front window winder switch	65 to 68
40	Rear window wiper timer unit	58, 59	75	LH front window winder switch	68 to 70
41	RH front door locking device switch	35	76	Fuel gauge rheostat	16 to 17
42	Glove compartment lighting	83	77	Map reading lamp	81
43	Electronic unit for door locking device	103, 109	78	LH rear window winder motor	68, 70
44	Ashtray lighting	78	79	LH rear door locking device motor	104
45	Cigar lighter and lighting	79, 80	80	LH rear door switch	82
46	Air blower resistors	36, 37	81	LH rear door locking device switch	33
47	Air blower	36	82	RH rear lamp cluster: tail lamp	97
48	Ashtray lighting	79		Stop-lamp, Foglamp	75, 92
49	Air blower control and lighting	36, 37, 75 to 77		Reversing lamp, Direction indicator	13, 44
50	Radio connections	86 to 89	83	Number plate lighting, RH	95
51	RH control unit: horn	50	84	Heated rear window	49
	Windscreen wiper and washer	53 to 56	85	Tailgate locking device motor	105
	Heated rear window	46 to 48	86	Rear window wiper motor	57 to 59
	Hazard warning device	42 to 45	87	Number plate lighting, LH	94
52	Water temperature flasher	20, 21	88	Boot lighting switch	85
53	Dashboard: lighting	77, 78	89	Boot lighting	85
	Main beam warning lamp	95	90	LH rear lamp cluster: tail lamp	96
	Dipped beam warning lamp	94		Stop-lamp, Fog lamp	74, 91
	Sidelamp warning lamp	93		Reversing lamp, Direction indicator	12, 43

Earthing points

m1	Earthing point for RH front brake pad wear		m6	Earthing point on windscreen frame upper part
m2	Earthing point for battery on bodyshell		m7	RH rear earthing point (rear window wiper)
m3	Earthing point for LH front brake pad wear		m8	LH rear earthing point (heated rear window, boot LH
m4	Earthing point for connection box and dashboard			and RH rear lamps)
m5	Earthing point an console			

Colour code

B	White	J	Yellow	Or	Orange		
BL	Blue	M	Brown	R	Red		
G	Grey	Mv	Mauve	V	Green		
Ic	Transparent	N	Black				

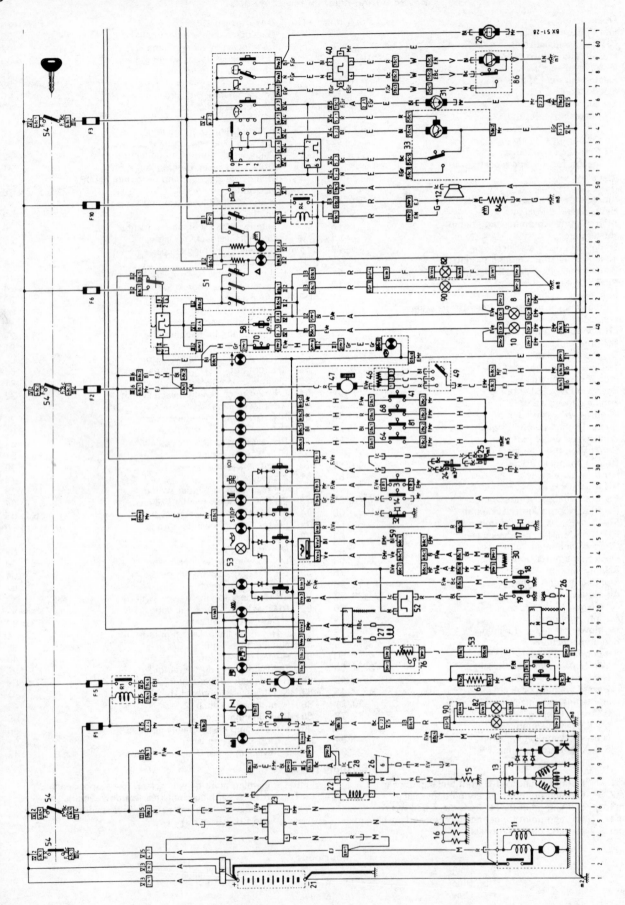

Fig. 7.4 Wiring diagram for all BX Diesel models

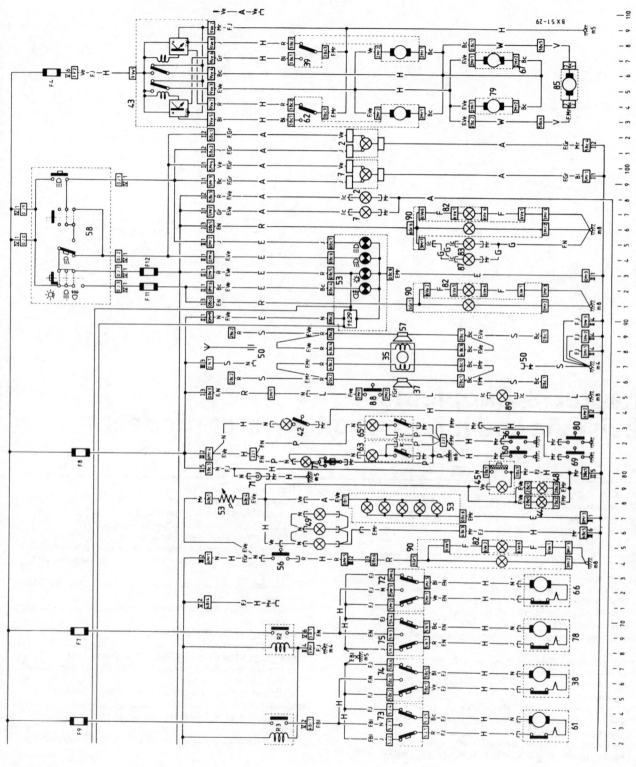

Fig. 7.4 Wiring diagram for all BX Diesel models (continued)

BX 51-29

Chapter 8 Supplement:
Revisions and information on later models

Contents

1 Introduction

This Supplement contains information which is additional to, or a revision of, material in the preceding Chapters. Most of it relates to the A8A engine fitted to BX Turbo models, and associated equipment, but some items apply to all models.

The Sections in the Supplement follow the same order as the Chapters to which they relate. The Specifications are all grouped together for convenience, but they too follow Chapter order.

It is recommended that before any particular operation is undertaken, reference be made to the appropriate Section(s) of the Supplement. In this way any changes to procedures or components can be noted before referring to the main Chapters.

Under-bonnet view of a BX Turbo Diesel – intercooler removed

1   LHM fluid reservoir
2   Fuel filter
3   Suspension units
4   Air cleaner-to-turbo
    trunking
5   Turbo-to-intercooler
    trunking

6   Inlet manifold
7   Brake pipe unions
8   Battery
9   ABS control block
10 Air cleaner

11 Air intake
12 Intercooler air inlet duct
13 Engine oil filler/dipstick
14 Cold start accelerator
15 Richness limiter

16 Fuel injectors
17 Crankcase ventilation oil
    trap
18 Thermostat housing
19 Expansion tank cap
20 Hydraulic pump drive
    pulley

2   Specifications

These specifications are revisions of, or supplementary to, those which appear at the beginning of the preceding Chapters.

Engine – all models
Valves
Stem diameter:
    Inlet, engines 161A and 162 .... 7.995 mm (0.315 in)
    Inlet, engines 162B, D9B and A8A .... 8.005 mm (0.3154 in)
    Exhaust, all engines .... 7.985 mm (0.3146 in)
Valve guide bore (fitted) .... 8.020 mm (0.316 in)

Torque wrench settings

	Nm	lbf ft
Cylinder head bolts (September 1986 on – see text):		
Stage 1	30	22
Stage 2	70	52
Stage 3	angle-tighten 120°	angle-tighten 120°

Engine type XUD 9A – D9B
General
Application .... BX 19 models from April 1987
Compression ratio .... 23.0 : 1
Maximum torque .... 120 Nm (89 lbf ft) @ 2000 rpm
Maximum power .... 51 kW @ 4600 rpm (68.5 bhp)

Valves
Valve timing (at 0.8 mm clearance):
    Inlet opens .... 4° BTDC
    Inlet closes .... 35° ABDC
    Exhaust opens .... 43° BBDC
    Exhaust closes .... 0° (TDC)

Engine type A8A
General
Application .... BX Turbo models
Compression ratio .... 22.0 : 1
Cubic capacity .... 1796 cc (107.9 cu in)
Maximum torque .... 180 Nm @ 2100 rpm (133 lbf ft)
Maximum power .... 66 kW @ 4300 rpm (88.5 BHP)
Maximum speed:
    No load .... 4800 rpm
    Loaded .... 4300 rpm

Pistons
Gudgeon pin bore .... 28.003 to 28.008 mm (1.1033 to 1.1035 in)
Gudgeon pin diameter .... 28 ± 0.006 mm (1.1032 ± 1.1032 ± 0.002 in)
Small-end bush inner diameter .... 28.007 to 28.020 mm (1.1034 to 1.1039 in)

Crankshaft
Thrustwasher thickness:
    Standard .... 1.85 mm (0.073 in)
    Oversizes .... 1.95, 2.00 and 2.05 mm (0.077, 0.079 and 0.081 in)

Valves
Seat angle – inlet and exhaust .... 90°
Valve timing (at 0.8 mm clearance):
    Inlet opens .... 4° 30′ BTDC
    Inlet closes .... 20° ABDC
    Exhaust opens .... 39° BBDC
    Exhaust closes .... 4° ATDC

Lubrication system
Oil pressure (at 80°C/170°F) .... 3.4 bar (49 lbf/in^2) @ 2000 rpm

Cooling system – later models
General
Coolant capacity – BX Turbo .... 6.5 litres (11.4 pints)
Thermostat opening temperature:
    BX Turbo .... 83°C (181°F)
    All other BX models from April 1987 .... 88°C (190°F)

Cooling fans – BX Turbo:
    1st speed cuts in at .... 93°C (199°F)
    2nd speed cuts in at .... 97°C (207°F)

Fuel and exhaust systems
Injection pump (Bosch) – later models
Timing values at TDC (see text):

Engine code	Date		Pump code	Timing value
161A	From October 1987		VER 171-1	0.90 mm (0.035 in)
D9B	April 1987 to April 1988		VER 272-1	0.83 mm (0.033 in)
D9B	From April 1988		VER 272-2	0.90 mm (0.035 in)
A8A	From start		–	0.80 mm (0.032 in)

Turbocharger
Make .... KKK or Garrett
Type:
    KKK K14
    Garrett T2
Boost pressure .... 0.8 to 0.9 bar (11.6 to 13.1 lbf/in²) at full load

Torque wrench settings

	Nm	lbf ft
Turbocharger mounting bolts	45	33
Turbocharger oil feed pipe unions	20	15

Clutch and transmission
Clutch (BX Turbo)
Driven plate diameter .... 215 mm (8.5 in)

Manual gearbox type BE3
Application .... Superseding BE1 from 1989
Code:
    4-speed BE3/4
    5-speed BE3/5
Oil capacity .... 1.8 litres (3.2 pints)

Dimensions, weights and capacities – BX Turbo
Dimensions
Overall length:
    Saloon .... 4.237 m (166.8 in)
    Estate .... 4.399 m (173.2 in)
Overall width .... 1.682 m (66.2 in)

Weights
Kerb weight:
    Saloon .... 1025 Kg (2260 lb)
    Estate .... 1077 Kg (2375 lb)
Gross train weight:
    Saloon .... 2600 Kg (5733 lb)
    Estate .... 2710 Kg (5976 lb)
Roof rack maximum load:
    Saloon .... 75 Kg (165 lb)
    Estate .... 100 Kg (220 lb)

Capacities
Coolant .... 6.5 litres (11.4 pints)
Fuel tank .... 66 litres (14.5 gallons)

---

3 Routine maintenance

Maintenance intervals (1989 on)
1 From 1989 model year, maintenance intervals are extended from 5000 miles (7500 km nominal) to 6000 miles (10 000 km nominal) and multiples thereof. The time interval (six months, one year etc) is unchanged.

Fuel filter renewal (all models)
2 The fuel filter should be renewed at the beginning of every winter, even if the mileage specified for renewal has not been covered.

4 Engine

General
1 Few changes have been made to the XUD engine. The most significant development has been the introduction of a turbocharged engine (A8A). The design of the turbo engine is the same as the normally aspirated version, but components such as the crankshaft, pistons and connecting rods are uprated.

Oil level and temperature sensors – general
2 An oil level sensor is not fitted to all models. When it is fitted, it is

4.12 Cylinder head bolt with spiral grooving on its shank

4.15 Angle-tightening a cylinder head bolt

4.19A Home-made tool for unscrewing the engine mounting rubber

4.19B Engine mounting rubber showing slots

located on the rear face of the engine, at the flywheel end – see Chapter 1, photo 23.18A.

3   An oil temperature sensor is fitted to some models. When fitted, it is next to the oil pressure sensor, itself located just above the oil filter.

Engine A8A – access to top of engine
4   For almost any job involving work on the top of the engine (for example valve clearance adjustment) the intercooler must be removed. This is described in Section 6.

Cylinder head (A8A) – removal and refitting
5   The intercooler must be removed at an early stage (Section 6).

6   The procedure is then as described in Chapter 1, Section 9, but additionally the turbo oil feed and return pipes must be disconnected – see Section 6.

7   The turbocharger itself may be removed with the manifolds.

8   After refitting and before initial start-up, prime the turbo lubrication circuit by disconnecting the stop solenoid lead at the fuel pump and cranking the engine on the starter for three ten-second bursts.

Cylinder head gasket identification – A8A
9   The head gasket for the A8A engine is identified by having two notches on the centre line – Fig. 1.7 in Chapter 1.

10   Thickness identification is the same as for other gasket types, ie by the number of holes or notches near the right-hand corner.

Cylinder head bolt tightening (all models)
11   Early type cylinder head bolts (up to September 1986), which are tightened as described in Chapter 1, have a plain shank.

12   Bolts fitted since September 1986 have coarse spiral grooving on the upper shank (photo). The tightening procedure for these bolts is as follows.

13   Refer to the Specifications at the beginning of this Chapter, and to Fig. 1.8 in Chapter 1. Following the sequence in Fig. 1.8, tighten the bolts to the Stage 1 specified torque.

14   In the same sequence, tighten the bolts to the Stage 2 specified torque.

15   Again in the same sequence, tighten each bolt through the angle specified for Stage 3. To determine angular movement, either make up a template, paint marks on the bolt heads, or use a proprietary angle-tightening indicator (photo).

16   On models from 1989, Torx head bolts may be found instead of hexagon head bolts. The bolts are interchangeable, singly or in sets, and the tightening procedure remains unchanged.

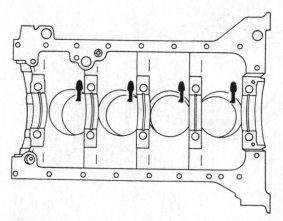

Fig 8.1 Piston cooling oil jets in crankcase – A8A engine (Sec 4)

17   Bolts subject to the angle-tightening method do not need retightening after warm-up.

Engine right-hand mounting rubber (all models) – removal and refitting

18   Gain access to the mounting rubber as described in Chapter 1, Section 17.

19   Make up a tool similar to that shown to engage with the slots in the rim of the rubber (photos). Assuming that the rubber is being renewed, the new component can be used as a guide when making the tool.

20   Unscrew the old rubber from the body using the tool.

21   Refit by reversing the removal operations, tightening the rubber firmly to the body using the tool.

Oil pump (later models) – removal and refitting

22   From July 1987, the oil pump spacer and location dowel are no longer fitted. The height of the pump is increased to compensate.

23   A new pump may be fitted in place of an old one provided that the spacer and dowel are discarded. Thicker washers must be fitted under the heads of the oil pump bolts.

24   On A8A engines a thin spacer is still fitted between the oil pump and the block.

Engine type A8A – dismantling for overhaul

25   The procedure is basically as described in Chapter 1, Section 23, with the addition that the turbocharger must be removed at the same time as the manifolds.

26   If complete dismantling is being undertaken, remove the piston cooling oil jets from the crankcase and clean or renew them (Fig. 8.1).

27   Note that many other components are specific to the turbocharged engine and are not interchangeable with those from

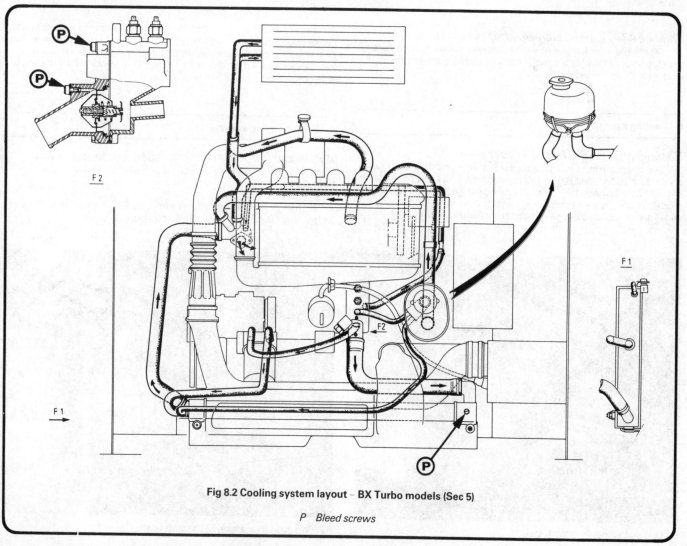

Fig 8.2 Cooling system layout – BX Turbo models (Sec 5)

P   Bleed screws

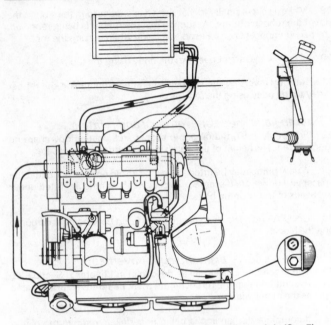

Fig 8.3 Cooling system layout – later Visa/C15 models (Sec 5)

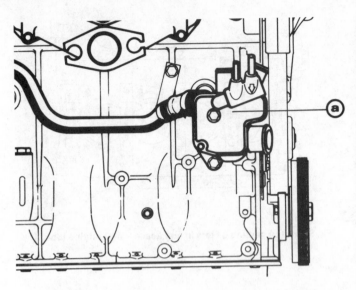

Fig 8.4 Fuel heater (a) on the rear face of the block (Sec 5)

normally-aspirated engines, even though they may appear to be the same.

Engine (A8A) – initial start-up after overhaul
28   Prime the turbo lubrication circuit before start-up by disconnecting the stop solenoid lead at the fuel pump and cranking the engine on the starter for three ten-second bursts.

Cooling system (later Visa/C15 models) – description
2   From 1989 model year, a remote expansion tank is no longer fitted. The cooling system filler/pressure cap is now on the radiator, at the right-hand end. The radiator, hoses and surrounding components are modified.

3   At the same time the electric fuel heater fitted to some models was discontinued. A coolant-fed fuel heater is fitted instead. This is mounted on the rear face of the engine block, at the timing belt end (Fig. 8.4). If it has to be removed or disconnected for any reason, note the arrow showing the direction of fuel flow.

---

5   Cooling system

Cooling system (BX Turbo) – description
1   The basic cooling system on BX turbocharged models is similar to that described for other BX models in Chapter 2, except for the addition of a remote expansion tank. The radiator is specific to the turbocharged model, as are the water pump and radiator cooling fans. Maintenance and repair procedures however, remain unchanged.

---

6   Fuel and exhaust systems

Air cleaner (turbocharged models) – element renewal
1   Unclip the rigid air intake tube on the right-hand side of the engine bay (photo).

2   At the air cleaner end of the intake tube, remove the stub hose which joins the tube to the air cleaner (photo).

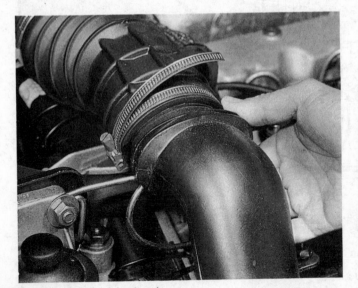

6.1 Unclipping the air intake tube

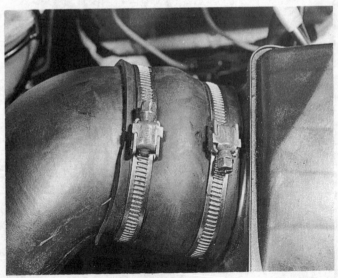

6.2 Two hose clips securing the stub hose

6.3 Disconnecting the crankcase ventilation hose

6.6 Removing the air cleaner lid

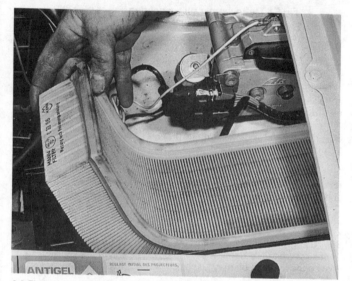

6.8 Fitting the air cleaner element

6.14 View of the compressor wheel end of the turbocharger (KKK type)

3   Disconnect the crankcase ventilation hose (photo).

4   Release the spring clips which secure the air cleaner body to its mounting.

5   Release the spring clips which secure the air cleaner lid.

6   Remove the air cleaner lid (photo). It is a tight fit, but by manipulating the lid and the air cleaner body at the same time, the lid can be removed.

7   Remove the element and clean out the housing.

8   Fit the new element. It can only be fitted one way up (photo).

9   Refit and secure the other disturbed components.

Air cleaner (turbocharged models) – removal and refitting
10   Remove the air cleaner element as just described.

11   Remove the air cleaner body by pulling it off its rubber mountings.

12   Refit by reversing the removal operations.

Turbocharger – description
13   A turbocharger is fitted to the A8A engine. It increases engine

efficiency by raising the pressure in the inlet manifold above atmospheric pressure. Instead of the air simply being sucked into the cylinders, it is forced in.

14   Energy for the operation of the turbocharger comes from the exhaust gas. The gas flows through a specially-shaped housing (the turbine housing) and in so doing, spins the turbine wheel. The turbine wheel is attached to a shaft, at the end of which is another vaned wheel known as the compressor wheel. The compressor wheel spins in its own housing and compresses the inducted air on the way to the inlet manifold (photo).

15   Between the turbocharger and the inlet manifold, the compressed air passes through an intercooler. This is an air-to-air heat exchanger, mounted over the engine and supplied with air ducted through the bonnet insulation. The purpose of the intercooler is to remove from the inducted air some of the heat it gained in being compressed. Removal of this heat further increases engine efficiency.

16   Boost pressure (the pressure in the inlet manifold) is limited by a wastegate, which diverts the exhaust gas away from the turbine wheel in response to a pressure-sensitive actuator. A pressure-operated switch operates a dashboard warning light in the event of excessive boost pressure developing.

17   The turbo shaft is pressure-lubricated by an oil feed pipe from the

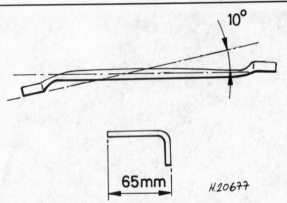

Fig 8.5 Tool modifications for turbocharger removal (Sec 6)

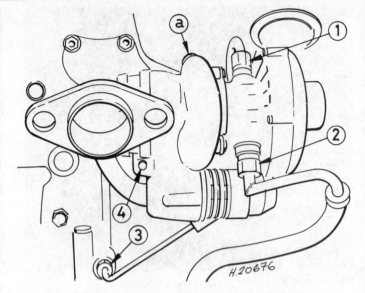

Fig 8.6 Turbocharger disconnection points (Sec 6)

a	Turbocharger	3	Oil feed on block
1	Oil feed on turbo	4	Turbo mounting bolt
2	Oil return on turbo		

main oil gallery. The shaft 'floats' on a cushion of oil. A drain pipe returns the oil to the sump.

Turbocharger – precautions

18   The turbocharger operates at extremely high speeds and temperatures. Certain precautions must be observed to avoid premature failure of the turbo or injury to the operator.

19   Do not operate the turbo with any parts exposed. Foreign objects falling onto the rotating vanes could cause excessive damage and (if ejected) personal injury.

20   Do not race the engine immediately after start-up, especially if it is cold. Give the oil a few seconds to circulate.

21   Always allow the engine to return to idle speed before switching it off – do not blip the throttle and switch off, as this will leave the turbo spinning without lubrication.

22   Allow the engine to idle for several minutes before switching off after a high-speed run.

23   Observe the recommended intervals for oil and filter changing, and use a reputable oil of the specified quality. Neglect of oil changing, or use of inferior oil, can cause carbon formation on the turbo shaft and subsequent failure.

Turbocharger – removal and refitting

24   Because the manifolds and turbocharger are on the back of the engine, access to the fastenings is difficult. The work will be made easier if two standard tools, a 6 mm Allen key and a 16 mm ring spanner, are modified as shown in Fig. 8.5.

25   Disconnect the battery earth lead.

26   Raise and support the vehicle. Remove the exhaust system; recover the two dowels which locate the exhaust downpipe on the turbo outlet flange.

27   Prepare for some oil spillage. Disconnect the turbo oil feed and return pipes from the block. Undo the return pipe union and remove the return pipe completely. Also remove the feed pipe bracket.

28   Unbolt and remove the engine bottom mounting torque link. The engine will move forwards slightly when this is done.

29   Using the modified 16 mm spanner, remove the turbo mounting bolts which are accessible from below.

30   Lower the vehicle. Remove the intercooler and its hoses as described in this Section.

31   Remove the radiator hose support bracket on the right-hand side of the radiator.

32   Support the engine, either with a hoist from above or with a jack

and wooden blocks from below. Whichever method is used must allow for movement of the engine in subsequent operations.

33   Protect the radiator with a piece of hardboard, or for greater security remove it altogether.

34   Remove the engine right-hand mounting bracket. Move the engine forwards as far as possible, making sure that it is still securely supported and that the radiator is not damaged.

35   Remove the air hoses from the turbocharger.

36   Using the modified Allen key, remove the inlet manifold bolts. These may be very tight. The middle bolt hole is in fact slotted, so if wished the middle bolt may just be slackened.

37   Remove the inlet manifold. The gasket is shared with the exhaust manifold, so it will stay in place for the time being.

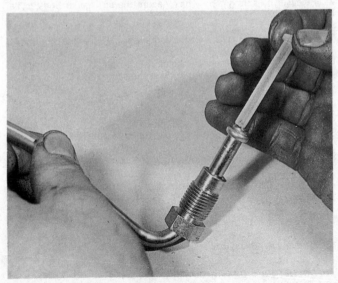

6.38 Oil strainer in the turbo oil feed pipe

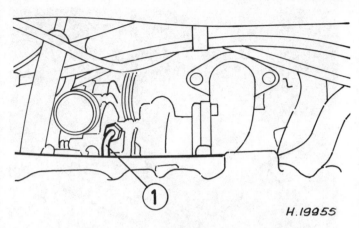

Fig 8.7 Turbo oil feed (1) seen from above (Sec 6)

H.19955

38   Disconnect the oil feed pipe from the top of the turbo. Remove the pipe. Note the strainer in the pipe (photo).

39   Slacken the remaining turbo mounting bolt. This fixing bolt is also slotted.

40   Manipulate the turbocharger and lift it out.

41   Refit by reversing the removal operations, noting the following points:

    (a)   If a new turbocharger is being fitted, change the engine oil and filter. Also renew the strainer in the oil feed pipe

    (b)   Do not fully tighten the oil feed pipe unions until both ends of the pipe are in place. When tightening the oil return pipe union, position it so that the return hose is not strained

    (c)   Before starting the engine, prime the turbo lubrication circuit by disconnecting the stop solenoid lead at the fuel pump and cranking the engine on the starter for three ten-second bursts

42   After initial start-up, do not race the engine. Inspect the turbo and its lubrication pipes for oil leaks. Stop the engine and check the oil level.

43   A new turbo should be run in like any other major mechanical component.

Turbocharger – examination and renovation

44   With the turbocharger removed, inspect the housings for cracks or other visible damage.

45   Spin the turbine or the compressor wheel to verify that the shaft is intact and to feel for excessive shake or roughness. Some play is normal since in use the shaft is 'floating' on a film of oil. Check that the wheel vanes are undamaged.

46   On the KKK turbo the wastegate and actuator are integral and cannot be checked or renewed separately. On the Garrett turbo the wastegate actuator is a separate unit. Consult a Citroën dealer or other specialist if it is thought that testing or renewal is necessary.

47   If the exhaust or induction passages are oil-contaminated, the turbo shaft oil seals have probably failed (On the induction side, this will also have contaminated the intercooler, which if necessary should be flushed with a suitable solvent.)

48   No DIY repair of the turbo is possible. A new unit may be available on an exchange basis.

Intercooler – removal and refitting

49   Slacken the intercooler inlet trunking clip (photo).

50   Remove the three screws which secure the front edge of the intercooler (photo).

51   Remove the three Allen screws which secure the rear edge of the intercooler. These screws are concealed by the intercooler rubber seal (photo).

52   Disconnect the intercooler-to-injection pump hose (photo).

53   Unclip the crankcase ventilation system oil trap (photo).

54   Lift off the intercooler. Note the seal between the intercooler outlet and the inlet manifold.

55   Before refitting, clean the intercooler matrix with a soft brush or by blowing air through it. Flush the intercooler internally with a suitable solvent if contaminated with oil. Make sure that the inlet manifold seal is in good condition, and renew it if necessary.

56   Refit by reversing the removal operations.

Fuel injection pump (turbocharged models) – description

57   The injection pump fitted to turbocharged models is similar to that fitted to normally-aspirated models, but incorporates the following additional features.

6.49 Slackening the intercooler inlet trunking clip

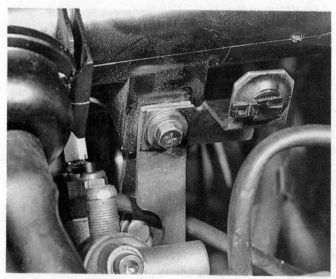

6.50 One of the three screws securing the front of the intercooler. This one secures a hose guide as well

6.51 Pulling back the rubber seal to reveal the rear securing screws

6.52 Disconnecting the hose which runs to the injection pump (arrowed)

6.53 Unclipping the oil trap

6.58 The overfuelling device – Lucas CAV/Roto-Diesel pump

Lucas CAV/Roto-Diesel

58   On overfuelling device varies the quantity of fuel injected in response to turbo boost pressure. Pressure is sensed via a host connected to the inlet manifold (photo).

59   An electromagnetic timing system advances injection timing when the engine is cold. The system is switched off by a contact activated by movement of the fast idle control lever (photos).

60   These additional devices cannot be checked or adjusted by the home mechanic.

Bosch

61   A richness limiter takes the place of the overfuelling device just described, and a cold start accelerator takes the place of the electromagnetic timing system (photos).

62   The cold start accelerator received its own coolant feed. Because it is a mechanical device, it must be disconnected when timing the pump.

Fuel injection pump (turbocharged models) – removal and refitting

63   Proceed as in Chapter 3, Section 4, but additionally disconnect the

boost pressure hose from the overfuelling device or richness limiter.

64   On the Bosch pump, the coolant hoses must be disconnected from the cold start accelerator. If the cooling system is first depressurised by removing the expansion tank cap (system cold), and preparations made to plug the disconnected hoses, coolant loss can be kept to a minimum.

65   Refit by reversing the removal operations. Check the pump timing if necessary as described in this Section. Top up the coolant level if necessary.

Fuel injection pump (later Lucas CAV/Roto-Diesel) – checking and adjusting the static timing

66   From mid-1987 a modified pump is fitted. The pump can be recognised by the presence of a white or blue plastic disc on its front face. A timing value is engraved on the disc (photo).

67   The pump timing is now carried out at TDC. Only one dial test indicator is needed, but it will be necessary to make up a bent rod or similar tool to enter the TDC setting hole. The tool made up in the workshop consisted of an M8 bolt with the threads filed away, attached to a piece of welding rod (photo). Alternatively the starter motor can be removed and a twist drill or straight rod can be used – see Chapter 1, photo 23.26.

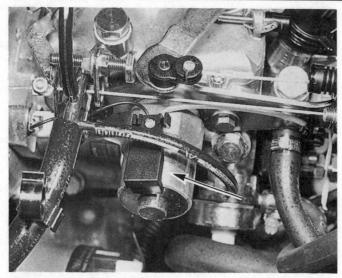

6.59A Electromagnetic timing device (arrowed) – Lucas CAV/Roto-Diesel pump

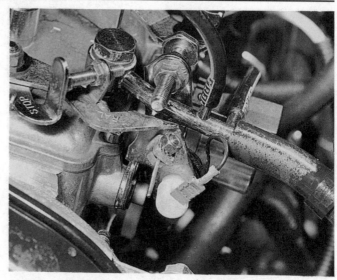

6.59B Electromagnetic timing contact on the fast idle lever

6.61A Richness limiter – Bosch pump

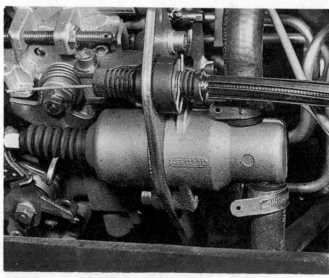

6.61B Cold start accelerator – Bosch pump

6.66 Plastic disc on later Lucas CAV/Roto-Diesel pump

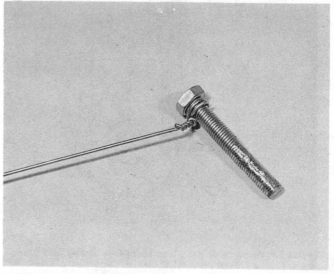

6.67 Home-made TDC setting tool

6.70 TDC setting tool (arrowed) in position

6.71 Removing the inspection plug from the pump

68   Prepare the engine as described in Chapter 3, Section 5, paragraphs 1 to 4.

69   Turn the engine to bring No 4 cylinder (timing belt end) to TDC on compression. To establish which cylinder is on compression, either remove No 4 cylinder heater plug and feel for pressure, or remove the valve cover and observe when No 1 cylinder valves are 'rocking' (inlet opening and exhaust closing).

70   Insert the TDC setting tool into the hole, and turn the engine back and forth slightly until the tool enters the hole in the flywheel. Leave the tool in position (photo).

71   Remove the inspection plug from the top of the pump (photo). Position a dial test indicator so that it can read the movement of a probe inserted into the hole. If a magnetic stand is to be used, the absence of ferrous metal in the vicinity poses a problem; a piece of steel plate can

be bolted to the engine mounting or valve cover to carry the stand.

72   Insert a probe into the inspection hole so that the tip of the probe rests on the rotor timing piece (Fig. 8.8). Position the dial test indicator so that it reads the movement of the probe.

73   Remove the TDC setting tool. Turn the engine approximately a quarter-turn backwards. Zero the dial test indicator.

74   Turn the engine forwards slowly until the TDC setting tool can be re-inserted. Read the dial test indicator: the reading should correspond to the value engraved on the pump disc (± 0.04 mm).

75   If the reading is not as specified, proceed as follows.

76   Disconnect the injector pipes from the pump. Slacken the pump mounting nuts and bolts and swing the pump away from the engine. Zero the dial test indicator.

77   With the engine still at TDC, slowly swing the pump back towards the engine until the dial test indicator displays the value engraved on the pump disc. In this position, tighten the pump mountings, then remove the TDC setting tool and recheck the timing as just described.

78   When the timing is correct, reconnect the injector pipes, remove the dial test indicator and TDC setting tool and refit the inspection plug.

79   Refit any other disturbed components, remove the plastic bag from the alternator and lower the vehicle to the ground.

Fuel injection pump (later Bosch) – checking and adjusting the static timing

80   Later Bosch pumps are timed at TDC. Refer to the Specifications for pump identification and timing values. Only one dial test indicator is needed, but it will be necessary to make up a TDC setting tool as just described for the Lucas CAV/Roto-Diesel pump.

81   Prepare the engine as described in Chapter 3, Section 6, paragraphs 1 to 4. On turbocharged models disconnect the cold start accelerator.

82   Bring the engine to TDC, No 4 cylinder on compression, and insert the TDC setting tool, as just described (paragraphs 69 and 70).

83   Fit a dial test indicator to the rear of the pump as described in Chapter 3, Section 6, paragraphs 11 to 13.

84   Remove the TDC setting tool. Turn the engine approximately a quarter-turn backwards. Zero the dial test indicator.

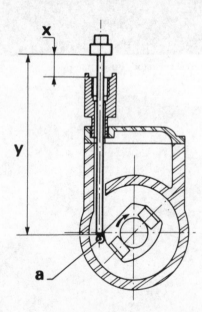

Fig 8.8 Timing probe details – later Lucas CAV/Roto-Diesel pump (Sec 6)

a	Timing piece	*y*	95.5 ± 0.01 mm
x	Timing value (engraved on disc)		(3.7600 ± 0.0004 in)

6.91 Auxiliary fuel tank – BX Turbo model

7.1 Manual gearbox filler/level plug (arrowed) in end cover

85   Turn the engine forwards slowly until the TDC setting tool can be re-inserted. Read the dial test indicator: the value should correspond to that given in the Specifications.

86   If the reading is not as specified, proceed as follows.

87   Disconnect the remaining injector pipes from the pump. Slacken the pump mounting nuts and bolts and swing the pump away from the engine. Zero the dial test indicator.

88   With the engine still at TDC, slowly swing the pump back towards the engine until the dial test indicator displays the desired value. In this position, tighten the pump mountings, then remove the TDC setting tool and recheck the timing as just described.

89   When the timing is correct, remove the dial test indicator and TDC setting tool. Reconnect the injector pipes.

90   Refit any other disturbed components, remove the plastic bag from the alternator and lower the vehicle to the ground.

Auxiliary fuel tank (BX Turbo) – general
91   An auxiliary fuel tank is fitted to BX Turbo models. It is located in the rear right-hand corner of the vehicle, immediately below the fuel filler (photo).

92   The auxiliary tank is removed in the same way as the main tank: the fuel must be drained, the hoses and pipes disconnected and the tank mountings released. Appropriate safety precautions must be observed.

---

7   Clutch and transmission

Manual gearbox (later models) – oil level checking
1   Commencing in 1987 model year, an oil level plug is fitted in the gearbox end cover. Access is easiest through the left-hand wheel arch (photo).

2   Having gained access to the oil level plug, check the oil level, but clean around the plug before removing it. With the vehicle level, the oil level must be up to the bottom of the plug hole.

3   Top up if necessary with the specified oil (photo), then refit and tighten the filler/level plug. Check for leaks if regular topping-up is required.

7.3 Topping-up the gearbox oil

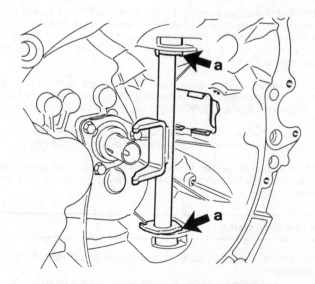

Fig 8.9 Clutch release pivot shaft – BE3 gearbox (Sec 7)

a Bearings

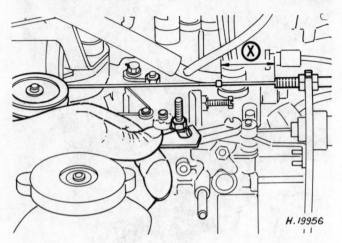

Fig 8.10 Kickdown cable adjustment. For X see text (Sec 7)

Clutch release mechanism (with BE3 gearbox) – description

4   Instead of the clutch release fork pivoting on a ball stud as in the BE1 gearbox, in the BE3 gearbox a pivot shaft is used.

5   Clutch adjustment procedure is unchanged. Overhaul procedures will be found in the relevant manual for petrol-engined models.

BE3 gearbox – description

6   The BE3/4 and BE3/5 gearboxes progressively replaced the BE1/4 and BE1/5 gearboxes from the beginning of 1989. The main difference being in the gearshift components. The driver will notice that reverse gear is now in the same plane as 2nd and 4th gears – opposite 5th, when applicable – and that the lifting collar below the gear knob is now obsolete for reverse selection.

7   Overhaul procedures will be found in the relevant manual for petrol-engined models.

8   The oil filler/level plug for the BE3 gearbox is in the end cover (as on later BE1 gearboxes).

Kickdown cable adjustment (automatic transmission)

9   Before attempting to adjust the kickdown cable, make sure that the fuel injection pump is correctly timed and adjusted, and that the throttle cable is functioning correctly.

10   Check that, with the throttle pedal released, the kickdown cable inner at the pump is free of tension without being slack. There should be a small clearance 0.5 to 1.0 mm (0.02 to 0.04 in) between the lug on the cable and the tip of the adjuster. Slacken the adjuster locknuts and turn the adjuster if necessary until the setting is correct.

11   Have an assistant depress the throttle pedal as far as, but not beyond, the kickdown point. In this position, measure the distance from the lug to the adjuster tip ('X' in Fig. 8.10). It should be 39 mm (1.54 in).

12   Have the assistant depress the pedal to the floor and remeasure the lug-to-adjuster distance. Now it should be 47 mm (1.85 in).

13   If either of the last two values were incorrect, reposition the kickdown cable end within the limits of the adjustment slot on the pump lever.

---

8   Electrical system

Alternator drivebelt (later models with air conditioning) – general

1   During 1988 the 'three' pulley system previously used was replaced by a pulley system. The new system is shown in Fig. 8.11.

2   With the new system, drivebelt tension is adjusted by movement of

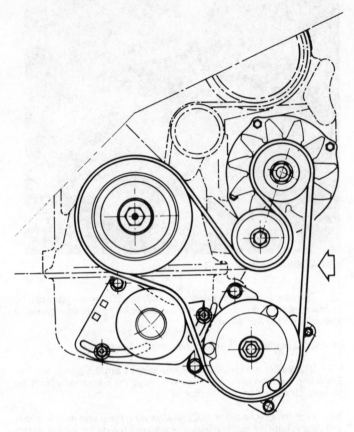

Fig 8.11 Drivebelt run – later models with air conditioning. Arrow shows tension checking point (Sec 8)

the bottom idler wheel. Tension is checked at the longest belt run, that is, between the alternator and compressor pulleys.

Turbo overpressure warning switch – removal and refitting

3   Unbolt the switch from the battery carrier.

4   Disconnect the hose and the wiring from the switch and remove it (photo).

5   Refit by reversing the removal operations.

8.4 Removing the turbo overpressure warning switch

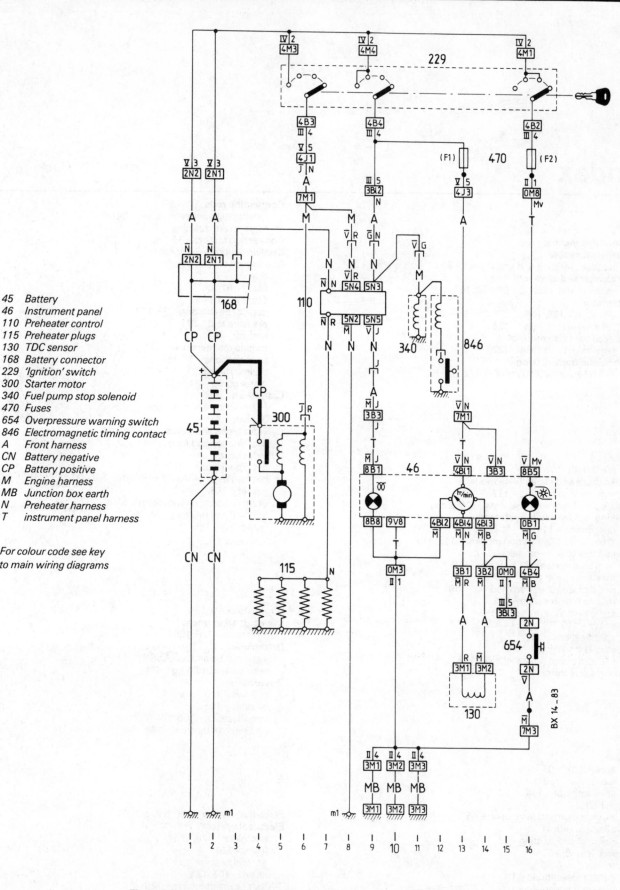

45   Battery
46   Instrument panel
110   Preheater control
115   Preheater plugs
130   TDC sensor
168   Battery connector
229   'Ignition' switch
300   Starter motor
340   Fuel pump stop solenoid
470   Fuses
654   Overpressure warning switch
846   Electromagnetic timing contact
A   Front harness
CN   Battery negative
CP   Battery positive
M   Engine harness
MB   Junction box earth
N   Preheater harness
T   instrument panel harness

For colour code see key
to main wiring diagrams

Fig 8.12 Supplementary wiring diagram – BX Turbo Diesel models (Sec 8)

Index